# THE
# Early Tudor
# Country House
## Architecture and Politics 1490-1550

# THE
# Early Tudor
# Country House

## Architecture and Politics 1490-1550

## Maurice Howard

GEORGE PHILIP

British Library Cataloguing in Publication Data
Howard, Maurice
    The early Tudor country house.
    1. Country homes — England — History
    I. Title
    942.05'2     DA660
ISBN 0-540-01119-3

© Maurice Howard 1987


First published by George Philip,
27A Floral Street, London
WC2E 9DP


Filmset and printed in Hong Kong
through Bookbuilders Ltd.

*Illustration Sources and Acknowledgements*

Ashmolean Museum, Oxford 15;
The British Library 57;
Country Life 47;
Redrawn from the researches of R. Fawcett 38;
Reproduced by gracious permission of Her Majesty the Queen. Copyright reserved 24;
Hertford Museum 29;
A.F. Kersting 2, 20, 73, 97, 125;
Layland Ross Photography/Nottingham Castle Museum 99;
The National Trust 86;
Nonsuch Excavation Committee 35;
Public Record Office, document reference MPF 272 (ex SP 12/75, No. 47), colour plate 3;
Royal Commission on the Historical Monuments of England 1, 6, 33, 54, 65, 66, 89, 91, 102;
Edwin Smith 79;
Topham Picture Library 74;
By courtesy of the Trustees of Sir John Soane's Museum 124;
J. Turquet 110;
Victoria History of the Counties of England 31.

All other illustrations are by the author.

HALF-TITLE PAGE   *Detail of the bay window over the inner gate at Hengrave Hall, Suffolk (1538), with the royal arms placed over those of the builder, Sir Thomas Kytson.*

TITLE PAGE   *Tillemans' eighteenth-century painting of Newstead Abbey, Nottinghamshire, one of the most significant monastic conversions of the 1540s.*

PAGE 6   *Layer Marney, Essex. Detail of the brick gatehouse, early 1520s.*

ENDPAPERS   *Compton Wynyates, Warwickshire. The courtyard house of Sir William Compton, one of Henry VIII's closest associates in the 1520s.*

# Contents

*For my parents, H.G. and E.M. Howard*

# Preface and Acknowledgements

THIS BOOK is one result of studies for my doctoral thesis on the buildings of Henry VIII's courtiers and I should like to thank the Universities of London, St Andrews and especially Sussex for financial help and other support during the eleven years that work has been progressing. There are five groups of people without whom this book and the work leading to it could not have been completed, but which collectively include so many individuals that I cannot thank them all personally. The owners of many sixteenth-century houses have allowed their privacy to be invaded and given me hospitality and assistance. National Trust administrators have similarly been kind and helpful. The staffs of many libraries and record offices have met a series of extraordinary requests; my special thanks to those of the Universities of London and Sussex, the Public Record Office and the Society of Antiquaries. The members of the Media Services Unit of the University of Sussex have unfailingly and promptly met my requests for photographs, some of which made considerable demands on their time and busy work schedule. Finally, the footnotes are by way of acknowledgement to the many scholars of Tudor history and the visual arts whose work I have tried to build on and discussions with whom have proved so stimulating. The opinions expressed in this book are the result of their example, but any errors are entirely my own.

There are special debts to individuals. Dr Nigel Llewellyn has given generously of his time and considerable skills as teacher, friend and colleague. John Newman supervised my thesis and was instrumental in securing many opportunities for me to publish and give conference papers on this material whilst it was in progress. Dr David Starkey allowed me to draw on his unrivalled knowledge of the upper servants of Henry VIII's Privy Chamber at a crucial stage when I needed a firmer grip on the limits of my material and later read this text. Dr Rosalys Coope has been a great support through her enthusiasm for the period and its architectural problems, and her advice on this book. Pauline Cherry drew the plans and, in doing so, helped me see more clearly what I wanted. Lydia Greeves has been the most supportive and conscientious of editors. I must also thank, for support and help in various ways, Dr Mark Brown, Maxine Partridge Copeland, Paul Drury, Dr Mary Eminson, Professor Jean Guillaume, Professor Erika Langmuir, Dr Helen Rendell, Alan Robinson, Dorothy Scruton, Betty Thorp and Dr Josephine Turquet. Finally, I should like to thank my parents for help of every kind in getting this book to press.

*Maurice Howard*

# Introduction

OST PEOPLE have a mental picture of what they think of as the typical early Tudor country house; many will also have a sense of the early Tudor period itself, seeing it as a time of change in England with the coming of the Reformation and a time of cultural dynamism in Europe, which has come to be called the Renaissance. The popular image of a building of the early Tudor period is a house like Compton Wynyates in Warwickshire (Fig. 1), low-lying, brick-built, unpretentious in its appearance. When compared with the highly individualistic houses of the Elizabethan and Jacobean periods, such as Hardwick Hall, the pleasing overall character of a house such as this is often put down to an accident of construction, rather than to any carefully planned design. Writers have tried to describe its qualities and their efforts are perhaps typified by a comment from the earlier part of this century: 'In form the house is square, low in height, and varied in outline, of some complexity of plan, and thrown up at the far corner into a rich skyline of tower and gable, fused in one harmonious group. Elaborate detail there is none nor any suggestion of a sought-after effect; it seems the creation of some necessity and utility.'[1]

These houses have always been seen as having some indefinable quality of Englishness. This was explicitly recognized in the 1830s by the Commission charged with giving guidance to competitors for a design for the new Houses of Parliament in London, which stressed that the style should be 'Gothic Elizabethan'.[2] The very term indicates that they were seeking something that did not really exist. Their intention was that the successful design should be something not quite medieval, not quite modern, but represent a visual embodiment of the nationalism born of the Reformation and the foundation of the English Church. In fact, the builder

of Compton Wynyates would be surprised to see his house today, without its moat and its rambling and fragile outbuildings of timber. Our image of these houses is shaped by the accidents of survival and by a rather false picture of what they were like originally.

When the country house is considered in the context of the Renaissance, the issue here might seem to be the way in which England was open to Continental influences, and particularly the art of Italy. It might seem appropriate perhaps to look for evidence that these buildings shared the concern for symmetry, order and proportion that Continental buildings are said to have been developing at this period. In fact links with the Continent had long helped to shape the visual arts of England. Those who practised them might be indebted to European art and architecture for particular features of design or solutions to problems, but always ultimately shaped and adapted what they took to native traditions. The resulting buildings are interestingly hybrid in style. Moreover, since England was not alone in responding to external influences on the arts, there are clear parallels between the English experience and what happened in other European countries, particularly France. These parallels are not confined to what the houses looked like, but also extend to the circumstances of their construction, who built them and the image their builders wanted to project.

Many other influences were at work on English architecture of this period. First, houses were primarily the products of the great and powerful and they demonstrate clearly the workings of the power structure of this time; they tell us how and why the initiative for great building projects passed from Church to Crown and then to the aristocracy, gentry and merchant classes. The Court was a highly competitive place and we might suppose

1 *Compton Wynyates, Warwickshire, completed by c. 1520. The picturesque asymmetry is deceptive since the house was originally moated and had timber service buildings in front of it.*

this would have engendered a common style of architecture, but surviving houses show how vigorously local traditions were maintained despite the pressure on great courtiers to build in the manner of their rivals at Court. In their individuality, these houses shed an interesting light on the relationship between London and the regions.

Second, although these buildings demonstrate a curiosity about the new and ingenious in ornament and about techniques of construction, paradoxically they also provide evidence for a tenacious clinging to the past, and to older forms of custom and behaviour. As so often when a nation state appears to take a new direction, as England did in the Reformation, a new past had to be invented to give

those in power credibility. In early Tudor England this desire for a sense of history emerged in the persistence of the cult of chivalry, displayed in heraldry on the buildings themselves and on their original contents, as brought back to life for us in inventories.

Third, this is the only period in English history when political and religious events had a particularly direct and sudden impact on domestic architecture because a substantial amount of property of a particular kind, the former monasteries, came on to the market for conversion into private residences. These prompted some ingenious solutions to the planning and arrangement of houses that took Tudor architecture in new directions. Moreover, because conversions were often carried out at great speed and strove to imitate pre-existing houses, they provide important illustrations of contemporary expectations of domestic comfort.

Early Tudor architecture is usually judged on

the basis of a few prominent and very famous houses, such as Sutton Place. These feature in this book, but a mass of other, lesser-known buildings are also included, many of which have not been fully researched before and which in many ways contradict the conclusions to be drawn from the well-known material. Many of these buildings have disappeared, but are recorded for us in drawings, descriptions and other information. Moreover, the evidence of wills and inventories, and references in the State Papers, have been used to reconstruct the way in which these buildings were lived in and their importance in the lives of the great figures of the period.

The themes which are followed in this book could not have been explored without the ground-work laid in recent years. First, the vast amount of material gathered in *The History of the King's Works* is now available, showing the importance of the Crown in providing the impetus for domestic building.[3] As a result of the documentation in the *King's Works*, it is now possible to set royal activity in the context of the general pattern of large-scale domestic building. Second, we have the important and pioneering books of Mark Girouard and Malcolm Airs.[4] Through the influence of these and other works, the outward appearance of houses is now seen as very much the result of all the practical circumstances (the costs of materials and workmen, the restrictions imposed by building on pre-existing sites) that went into their making and of the lifestyle they were designed to contain. As the embodiment of a continuous, yet constantly changing upper-class culture and the vehicle through which their owners demonstrated their pre-eminent place in society, they were indeed the power houses that Girouard has called them. This book presents the early Tudor country house as a key to what was happening in the violent changes of this period.

# 'Simple and Plain to Sight':
# Building in Early Tudor England

A REPORT OF a Venetian traveller in England from the closing years of the fifteenth century, known as *A Relation . . . of the Island of England*, has frequently been used by historians as evidence of the state of the country at this time. The report is biased and selective but it is useful nevertheless because it takes the evidence of material goods, including houses and furnishings, as an index of the state of the economy. The Venetian notes that the country is very sparsely populated (research in modern times has suggested that England's population probably did not exceed two and a half million) and seemingly not fulfilling its economic potential. He observes that there is no surplus food production and hence that there are no agricultural goods for export. This economic observation is part of the foreigner's more general point about the English as a parochial, insular people who see the world only in their own terms and, though he is not without praise for certain English customs and institutions, his main conclusion suggests an economically backward country.[1]

It is often asserted that England was not as technologically advanced at this time as mainland Europe, a situation that improved marginally during the course of the sixteenth century.[2] The lack of technical expertise in working with raw materials and creating compound materials from them (such as bronze from copper and tin) had a direct impact on the visual arts. In Italy at this time, new technical skills prompted new ideas, and inventiveness of design went hand-in-hand with pushing forward the boundaries of technique in artistic production. The ability to handle the difficult and challenging medium of true fresco, for example, was clearly as important as the painter's ability to realize the kind of large-scale narrative composition for which fresco was used. Florentine sculptors attempted to outshine each other in the production of life-size figures in cast bronze, the technical hazards and risks of which are immortally captured for us in the autobiography of Benvenuto Cellini. However, the fame of the arts in Italy was supported and publicized by written commentaries on their qualities and these have had much to do with the central place accorded to Italian art in all subsequent histories of this period. Brunelleschi's dome for the cathedral of Florence, for example, completed in the 1440s, was thereafter praised continually in the literature, which used such great achievements as evidence of the power and wealth of the city itself. In England, no such literature existed and the inception of some of the greatest building projects of the period is recorded only in fragmentary documentary remains. In 1512–13, for example, an agreement was drawn up between King's College, Cambridge, and the mason of the building works and his warden for the construction of the vault of the college chapel . . . 'the said John Wastell and Herry Semerk shall make and sett upp or cawse to be made and sett upp at ther costes and charges a good suer (sure) and sufficient vawte for the grete churche ther to be workmanly wrought made and sett upp after the best handlyng and fourme of good workmanship accordyng to the platt therof made'.[3] This legal document tells us nothing about the debate that must have preceded and followed this important stage in the construction of the chapel, or the expertise that must have been summoned to create what is seen today as one of the greatest technical achievements of the period. What we do have, lacking the platts (plans) and models that are sometimes referred to in documents, is the evidence of surviving buildings themselves. These tell us how architecture changed and what particular buildings were influential and therefore famous in their day, but above all they testify to a prodigious amount of building activity in late medieval England.

Although England no longer had any territorial interest in Europe save for a token presence at Calais, the country's place in the community of Christian nations had never been questioned. It still saw itself as part of the Christian civilization that had in past centuries responded as one, if at times with patchy consistency, to the call for a crusade against the infidel occupying the Holy Land and that had overcome political crises and interdicts to continue to respect the spiritual leadership of the Pope in Rome. Indeed Luther's threat to papal supremacy of the Church, a challenge which began in 1517, was at first taken most seriously in England where it was most actively counterargued. To add to this moral support, England remained one of the most reliable sources of papal revenue in the years immediately preceding the English Reformation, at a time when the Pope's income from France and Germany was being curtailed.[4] Contemporaries noted how the English appeared particularly devout, both in the observance of their faith and in acts of charity. The Venetian traveller noted: 'Although they attend Mass every day, and say many Paternosters in public (the women carrying rosaries in their hands, and any who can read taking the office of our Lady with them, and with some companion reciting it in the church verse by verse, in a low voice, in the manner of churchmen), they always hear Mass on Sunday in their parish church, and give liberal alms ...'.[5] The background to these devotions was the increasing involvement of lay people in the running of the Church's day-to-day business, in the building of new churches and their maintenance, in the custody of plate and other valuables, and in the management of the Church's dependent estates.

This period is often justly described as the take-off point for the age of the country house, but the reconstruction and re-embellishment of parish churches was as actively pursued during this period as at any other during the Middle Ages. This was so until, and indeed a little beyond, the Reformation of the 1530s, a decade when it has often been assumed that church-building suddenly ceased altogether. But the patronage of ecclesiastical and domestic building were not mutually exclusive; in fact, the continued enthusiasm for putting time and resources into church architecture is of direct relevance to contemporary country houses in a number of ways. To begin with, the rebuilding

of a house and perhaps part or even the whole of the local church was undertaken simultaneously and often at the behest of the same patron. The same building materials might be used and even the same building workshop. There is especially abundant evidence for this in East Anglia, where brick was the common material for late medieval houses and churches alike. At Castle Hedingham, in Essex, John de Vere, 13th Earl of Oxford, constructed new brick ranges and towers around the twelfth-century keep of the castle at the same time as he paid for a new brick upper storey to the nave, porch and tower at the local church, all emblazoned with his personal arms and insignia. The church was thus suitably prepared for the burial of the 15th Earl here in 1540, after the nearby church of Earl's Colne Priory, the traditional site of family burial, had been dissolved. The unfinished courtier house at Layer Marney in Essex (Fig. 2), begun in the years before 1525 for the first and second Lords Marney, is likewise contemporaneous with a complete rebuilding of the nearby church; both were constructed from the same building materials, underlined by the use of terracotta to form the mullions and transoms of the windows and the cresting to the tops of the towers at the house, and as a substitute for stone on the tombs of the two patrons.

Expenditure on both the building fabric and the furnishings of churches was in some ways prompted as much by the need to be seen in competition with one's peer group on earth as by a desire to honour God. Late medieval building contracts frequently cite other nearby churches as models for new work to be carried out, clearly indicating that individuals and communities were keen to equal, and if possible excel, their neighbours. The contract for the new tower of the church at Helmingham, Suffolk, drawn up in 1487/8, specified a structure 60 feet high in knapped flint, with features copied from recently-improved churches nearby. The four worthies who undertook to pay the mason for this work thus ensured that their church was the equal of neighbouring parishes.[6]

Similarly, new houses were also used as visual references for later building in the same region. The building accounts of 1506 and 1509 for the now-vanished house of Little Saxham in Suffolk refer to payments to skilled workmen, the prin-

cipal carpenter and glazier, to enable them to travel to Horham Hall in Essex (a distance of some 30 miles), in order that they might see work already completed in their respective fields of competence. The builders of both houses held important administrative jobs in the last years of Henry VII's reign, Thomas Lucas of Little Saxham that of Solicitor-General, Sir John Cutte of Horham that of Under-Treasurer of England. The power and wealth of private individuals in late medieval England raised both churches and houses alike, a fact that is emphatically underlined by the prominent display of personal heraldry on these buildings.

On churches, this heraldry might record a communal purse, as at Cirencester, Gloucestershire, where the interior of the nave, rebuilt in the years

1516–22, bears the personal arms or merchants' marks of all who paid for it. Sometimes two or three dominant interests might be involved, as at Lavenham in Suffolk (Fig. 3), where the church exterior is replete with the heraldry of two families, the De Veres, Earls of Oxford (Lords of the Manor), and the Springs (the wealthiest of the clothing families in the town). Sometimes just an inscription makes the point, telling us that it was the patron, rather than the architect, who took the credit and who, in a sense, 'signed' the building.[7] Walking from the present Claydon House in Buckinghamshire across to the church of All Saints nearby, the chancel of the church is entered from the north. The overdoor there (Fig. 4) tells us that Roger Gyfford and his wife Mary paid for building the new chancel in the year 1519, and their tomb lies just inside the church. This growth in personalized heraldry and inscriptions celebrating secular benefactors was to prove a problem for the authorities in later, post Reformation times. It was often difficult to draw the line between the destruction of religious imagery and the defacing of carved and painted references to the most powerful local family, often still resident in the manor house nearby.

LEFT 3  *Lavenham Church, Suffolk, rebuilt in the late fifteenth century. A subtle aspect of the decoration is the continuous variation in the form of the tripartite leaf motif.*

BELOW 4  *Middle Claydon Church, Buckinghamshire. 'Roger Gyfford and Mary his wife [built?] this chancel 1519'. The patron, rather than the mason, was more likely to 'sign' new building work in late medieval England.*

The question is whether this widespread renewal of the fabric of the church in the early sixteenth century was accompanied by an increased momentum in country house building and whether this is in turn indicative of a more general replenishment of the country's domestic building stock. There has long been debate about when this process of replenishment actually took off. Since the early 1950s, when W. G. Hoskins' article on the rebuilding of rural England was first published, the age of the 'great rebuilding' of England's villages and outlying farmsteads has usually been placed in Elizabethan and early Stuart times, rather than the early Tudor period.[8] As for the towns, these are often portrayed as the victims of sharp economic decline in the early sixteenth century. Their visible decay prompted a series of government statutes between 1536 and 1542 which sought to encourage an urban rebuilding programme. It has tended to be assumed that the country house building boom also had to wait until the later sixteenth century. This is partly because an appreciable number of prominent houses have survived from this period; as one historian has eloquently described the Elizabethan and Jacobean prodigy houses, they 'still lie heavily about the English countryside like the fossilized bones of the giant reptiles of the Carboniferous age'.[9] Although survivals are fewer and less imposing, documentary and archaeological evidence suggests that early Tudor country houses were built in equally great numbers (Fig. 5). And there is also the evidence of contemporaries.

The peculiar circumstances of London are an important factor in the consideration of contemporary evidence, particularly that of foreign visitors, whose business in England, whether diplomatic or mercantile, and hence their experience, was likely to be largely confined to the capital. London, of course, was something of an exception to the picture of urban decay, growing wealthier at the expense of other English towns, so that by the time of the assessment for the tax subsidy of 1534–5 the capital was judged to be able to contribute as much to the national purse as all other towns put together.[10] The Venetian visitor mentioned earlier noted the wealth of goldsmiths plying their

*5 Stansted Park, West Sussex. Kip's view of the late fifteenth- or early sixteenth-century house built for the Earls of Arundel. This is one of the many houses of this period of great building activity which has largely disappeared. Only a fragment incorporated into an eighteenth-century chapel remains.*

trade in the Strand and wrote of London: 'Although this city has no buildings in the Italian style (*all'usanza italiana*), but of timber or brick like the French, the Londoners live comfortably, and, it appears to me, that there are not fewer inhabitants than at Florence or Rome.'[11] But the scholar Erasmus, who lived in the houses of the English nobility and travelled more widely around the country, castigated living conditions in England, which he thought were filthy in comparison with other countries.

Some English sources give a clearer sense of change over a longer time-span. William Harrison, whose *Description of England* was first published in 1577 but first written by the early 1560s, speaks of the way that higher standards of living, originally confined to the upper classes, had percolated down to the middle and entrepreneurial ranks in his lifetime, so that 'the basest house of a baron doth often match in our days with some honours of princes in old time'.[12] He makes it clear that comforts within are not necessarily reflected in a building's outward appearance, for 'many of our greatest houses have outwardly been very simple and plain to sight, which inwardly have been able to receive a duke with his whole train and lodge them at their ease'. Changes have been the result of various amendments and improvements, but Harrison points specifically to three innovations; the new multitude of chimneys (indicating the use of fireplaces as opposed to open hearths); better provision of lodging with more comfortable beds and improvements in the quality and quantity of other furniture; everyday utensils for eating and cooking made from pewter, tin or even silver rather than wood.[13]

Harrison's general comments have been corroborated to some extent by archaeological evidence, obtained from beneath the floors of standing sixteenth-, or part sixteenth-century houses and also by investigating behind present wall surfaces (which has revealed changes in wall-openings and points of access). There is evidence from all over the country that older buildings were improved in the late fifteenth and early sixteenth century. Fireplaces were inserted and medieval halls that rose through two storeys were divided into two floors to give greater domestic privacy. At the half-timbered Rufford Old Hall, in Lancashire (Fig. 6), for example, the south front of the hall appears to have been reconstructed in the sixteenth century in order to insert a stone fireplace.[14] Also, if particular regions are examined in detail, there is an increasing amount of information to suggest that the age of

the great rebuilding should be pushed back in certain parts of the country. In areas such as the Weald of Kent and Devon, where new patterns of land use were yielding greater agricultural profits, house improvement or even new building was relatively widespread across the whole social range from the wealthiest farmers to small landowners.

However, the great majority of new early Tudor country houses were built on pre-existing sites and involved the renewal of older buildings rather than an original construction. New houses were in some instances built on a site adjacent to the old house. At Sissinghurst, in Kent, for example, the Baker family of Cranbrook began to build a new house west of the site of the earlier moated settlement, probably in the years immediately following the purchase of the site from the de Berham family in about 1490. At Kenninghall, in Norfolk, John Leland's description of the early 1540s confirms that the Howard Dukes of Norfolk had recently raised a large new house. Like Sissinghurst, this was outside the moat of the old: 'There apperith at Keninghaule not far from the Duke of Northfolk's new place a grete mote, withyn the cumpace wherof there was sumtyme a fair place.' At Sutton Place, in Surrey, Sir Richard Weston took the unusual step in the 1520s of building his new house some quarter of a mile away from the old manor. But it was more customary to use the old house as the basis of the new; indeed it was usually a question of piecemeal renewal, pulling down the old range by range, for the old house could still serve until the new was finished. At Layer Marney, for example, the present imposing entrance range with its huge gatehouse was all that was ever completed of the ambitious building programme. Other, older buildings must have continued to be used for John Marney's will of 1525 makes it clear that the house was already being occupied. It is likely that the plan was to effect a gradual replacement of an old house, which may have been of wood, with a much larger house of brick.[15]

Whilst the spirit of competition is self-evident in all this building activity, it is also necessary to ask to what extent those involved were also affected by the growing critical debate in late fifteenth- and early sixteenth-century Europe about the purpose of architecture, a debate advanced and fostered by the advent of the printed book. Italian treatises categorized buildings into types according to function for which certain materials and certain kinds of ornament were variously appropriate. They looked to the example of the ancient world and particularly to the *Ten Books on Architecture* by

Vitruvius (active in the first century BC) for guidance. The built environment was seen as the expression of the order of a civilized world with the buildings echoing the moral, political and religious codes of the people who used them. The corollary of this viewpoint was that an interest in architecture was the natural concern of the educated.[16] In early sixteenth-century England there was no body of writing in the native language that matched the theoretical treatises of Renaissance Italy. Moreover, architecture was outside the usual programme of education for a gentleman, and there was not even an assumption that the members of the ruling, literate classes shared an interest in it. This situation was to change as the century progressed, at least in the degree of enthusiasm for discussing buildings shown in private correspondence of the courtier class.

In the early sixteenth century, there was no sophisticated language to describe architecture in an aesthetic sense; people did not verbalize very profoundly or discursively about whether the appearance of a particular building was appropriate to its function as a castle, a house in town or country, or a church.[17] Building contracts, which by their very nature were quite specific and legalistic, made recourse to precedent in order to state what a commissioned piece of architecture should look like, as in the aforementioned case of Helmingham church. A contract might use a word like 'semely' (seemly) to evoke the intended finished appearance; a building looked 'right' according to expectations based on similar structures elsewhere. Standards of workmanship and value for money were of chief importance and details of work to be carried out would be itemized to show exactly how the materials allowed for were to be used. When James Nedeham, Master Carpenter to the King, undertook to construct wooden galleries around the garden of the Marquess of Exeter's London house in 1530 he was charged to 'wele clenly substancially and workemanly new make of good and substancial oken tymber'. The contract goes on to list particular features such as bay windows and wooden cornices (called 'Jowe peces') for hangings of cloth or tapestry on the inside walls of the galleries. This contract clearly includes unwritten expectations; the standard of craftsmanship would have been assumed to be

6 *Rufford Old Hall, Lancashire. A nineteenth-century lantern tower replaces the original louvre for the open fire, redundant when the fireplace was inserted in the sixteenth century.*

quite high, given the rank of the patron, the price agreed (£110, plus all the materials from the older galleries that Nedeham had to remove) and the carpenter's experience and standing at Court.[18]

Vitruvius' treatise was preserved in several manuscript sources in medieval England, but it is his practical advice on where to site buildings and what materials to use that is likely to have been understood and respected if his book was read at all.[19] Practical information on architecture was not perceived as a separate issue but formed part of the more general, instructional literature printed at this time. Architecture forms part of the scheme of advice in several late medieval and early Tudor handbooks on health and everyday behaviour. William Horman, Headmaster of Eton College from 1485 and subsequently bursar and vice-provost there in the early sixteenth century, published his *Vulgaria* in 1519, a book of observations on all manner of English customs and practice. His comments on the basic necessities of the commodious house are a mixture of practical common sense and the wisdom of pre-planning and supervising construction to ensure the right materials are used. He betrays the belief universally held at this time that the key to healthy living lay in attention to siting, drainage and consideration of climate: 'A mannys dwellynge shulde be chosen out: if it maye be where is an holsome soyle bothe wynter and sommer. It is not good dwellynge on the see costis ... The hylley countrey rounde about us kepeth awey parellous wyndis and pestylent infections.'[20]

Much of this advice is repeated some twenty years later in the more famous (and much reprinted) book of Dr Andrew Boorde, the *Compendyous Regyment or Dyetary of Health*. The first securely dated edition is of 1542, though interestingly the three chapters that deal with building were also printed separately and possibly before the composite text, as if for a particular patron of Boorde's about to engage in house building. Boorde was a cleric-turned-physician and well travelled in Europe, but his book is directed very specifically to an English audience. His advice will be looked at again more particularly in relation to the layout and planning of the courtyard house in Chapter 4. Through his service to the Duke of Norfolk and his contacts at Court, Boorde is likely to have had particular knowledge of the building plans of leading political figures. It is interesting, therefore, that in addition to strictures like those of Horman about the practical aspects of the house, he also warns about over-ambition, about the need to make adequate provision beforehand lest the

PRIVATE
NO THROUGH
ROAD

NO LORRIES OR HEAVY
TRAFFIC ALLOWED

builder be mocked for failing to complete: 'This man dyd begyn to buylde, but he can not fynysshe or make an end of his purpose.'[21]

An awareness of change in the building fabric of the country and a sense that the profundity of this change has resulted in a good many unfinished buildings emerges from a contemporary account that is without doubt the most valuable single source for the early Tudor house, the *Itinerary* of John Leland. Whilst Leland is full of particular observations about local traditions, the country-wide nature of his notes gives the impression of a view of building which transcends regional differences and places it within the context of England's wealth and resources as a whole. On first sight, Leland's *Itinerary* reads as an annotated travelogue. One might well suppose that the literature of travel would be full of the sharpest insights into attitudes to building, for it is the traveller who will have valuable first impressions and will make direct comparisons between the things he or she sees. But the compass and intentions of travel writing in the medieval period were quite different from those of today. Travel for pleasure, as we know it, was unheard of. Long-distance travel was traditionally associated with religion, with pilgrimage to important shrines such as Canterbury or Walsingham, or as far as the Holy Land. Medieval travel literature is most useful to the historian when the writer has been entrusted with recording things seen and customs observed for someone else, usually the traveller's patron. Even so, such descriptions demanded relatively little of the writer, since the object was to list what was seen rather than to be selective or critical. By the early sixteenth century travel writing was beginning to be used in a new way, to celebrate or eulogize one's native country. One of the reasons Leland's work is so valuable is that he uses both the new and the old forms of recording.[22]

Born in 1503, Leland studied at both Cambridge and Oxford, travelled to Paris and gained his first experience of service to an influential patron as tutor to the Duke of Norfolk's son in the early 1520s. He later became chaplain at Court, where he was part of a circle of writers of prose and verse lauding Henry VIII and the ancient past of England. Their output was in a sense an assertion of national identity that was vital as a confidence-building

exercise during the religious changes of the 1530s and the war with France in the 1540s. Leland himself never used the word *Itinerary* to describe what is in effect a series of rather random notes gathered when travelling in England during the early 1540s. One of his appointed tasks at this time and the initial reason for his countrywide journeys was to seek out the nation's literary heritage, its manuscripts and libraries. Like certain others at Henry VIII's court, Leland undoubtedly felt that the dispersal of monastic libraries was to be regretted, however welcome the overthrow of those 'super-stycyouse mansyons'. It is not clear how he might eventually have organized his notes (his mind was deranged from about 1547 and he died in 1552), but they have proved of great value to historians of building.

Leland is highly informative about buildings which are otherwise unrecorded and, equally, he can make us rethink our view of what we have come to see as significant houses simply because they are the ones that have survived. Occasionally his comment on a building is the only surviving contemporary record that actually points to a particular patron at work on a particular house at a specific time. For example, he notes that Bromham, in Wiltshire (Fig. 7), now gone but for a much-altered and displaced gateway, was built by Sir Edward Baynton 'yn Quene Annes dayes' (i.e. during the brief period when Anne Boleyn was Queen and Baynton Vice-Chamberlain of her household from 1533–6). At the same time there are some notable gaps in his account. It so happens that he does not visit now famous houses like Sutton Place (or he chooses not to mention them if he does) and he does not cover East Anglia at all, so omitting houses such as Layer Marney and Hengrave Hall.[23]

Leland's ideas about what is important differ from those of present-day architectural historians; he does not judge the houses he sees in terms of the sort of detail by which we now conventionally chart architectural history, such as how the heads of window lights are shaped. He betrays no sense of what is 'new' in terms of the latest fashion other than what is 'newly built', and this will not necessarily be better than the old if it is practically unsound. Leland's sense of what is 'new' is not confined to what was built in the most recent past but includes buildings from a much broader time-span. He describes the house at Collyweston, Northamptonshire, as 'new', though it was built for Lady Margaret Beaufort, grandmother to Henry VIII, who died in 1509, at least thirty years

7   *The gate from Bromham House, Wiltshire, a surviving fragment of an important lost house. Only the oriel window and the overdoor date from the 1530s.*

before Leland saw it. He is never systematic; he mentions interiors only occasionally and then usually only when new work has recently been carried out, as in Bishop Tunstall's 'goodly new galery and a stately stair to it' in the castle of Durham. He is especially drawn to the curious in construction or appearance, and it is characteristic of him that he gives a detailed description of the tower study called 'Paradise' at Wressle, Yorkshire, a house of the Percy Earls of Northumberland, with its ingenious apparatus for raising and lowering desks on which to read.[24]

His descriptive language is of equal importance to the factual information that he gives us. Leland perceives quite a clear distinction between a castle and what he calls a 'maner-place', the former being strong and well-built of stone, the latter by definition constructed of a more temporary material. He says that the house at Rotherfield Greys, Oxfordshire (transformed into a comfortable house by Robert Knollys, who was usher of the chamber to Henry VII and Henry VIII) was once a castle because towers survive, but it is now clearly a manor house. Castles are strong, 'well-waullid'; manor houses are 'praty' (pretty), 'fayre' or (presumably because they are richly decorated) 'sumptuus'. Some buildings which Leland clearly categorizes as houses have pretensions to the castle; Croft, in Herefordshire, is 'rokky, dychid and waullyd castle-like'. Stone can give a house the strength and appearance of a castle, which is presumably why he comments on the fifteenth-century house of South Wingfield, Derbyshire, as 'but a

*8   Hanwell Castle, Oxfordshire, from the west, showing the surviving corner tower of the Cope family's early sixteenth-century house.*

maner place, but it far passes Sheffield Castle'. Something of his perception of the blend of the spirit of the past with modern domesticity emerges from his description of Hanwell, in Oxfordshire (Fig. 8), as 'a pleasaunt and gallaunt house'.[25] He seems to suggest that signs of castellation are statements of the prestige and antiquity of the families who lived in such buildings. Leland's comments are especially interesting because many of the country's older castles were in decay at this time. As Henry VIII preferred to lavish money on new palaces, this was also true of many royal castles.[26] As Chapter 3 will show, some castles were being turned into more open buildings, their strongholds and keeps being put to pleasurable uses.

At the time Leland was writing, some monastic properties were being converted to private houses; other monastic sites were being robbed of their building stone by their new owners, by speculators, or simply by local people. He mentions several new houses constructed with 'abbay stone' like Fulke Greville's new house of Beauchamp's Hall (from the materials of Alcester Priory). But he also mentions the fact that materials from houses being demolished or altered were transported to where they could be used again, a demonstration of the fact that new building work went on not only in place of, but also at the expense of, the old. This re-use of material did not only apply to the basic building stone, but also to complete fittings such as bay windows and wooden roofs. It has to be remembered that the well-made, however old, may in some cases have been preferable to the completely new when the chance to acquire material from other houses presented itself. The clever informality of a house like Compton Wynyates is perhaps more aptly discussed as the architecture of compromise in view of Leland's comment that 'Sir William Compton, Keeper of Fulbrooke Park and castle, seeing it go to ruine helped it forward, takinge part of it for the buyldinges of his house at Compton by Brayles in Warwickshire'. The hall bay window and the roof of the hall in the present house may well have come from that source.[27] This sort of practice would have been unthinkable in the new houses of the architecturally and fashionably conscious courtier of similar standing to Compton by the end of the century. As we shall see, early Tudor houses were so constantly changed, and were often put up with such speed and with such makeshift construction, it is something of a miracle that any of them have survived at all. The courtier's hold on his property was not always secure and houses were not always the obvious way to spend one's income at the faction-ridden Court of Henry VIII.

# Power and the Courtier House

SHORTLY AFTER his appointment as Lord Chancellor in 1533, Thomas Audley wrote to the King's chief minister, Thomas Cromwell, to ask for the site of the Augustinian monastery of Holy Trinity, Aldgate, in London. This had been dissolved the previous year, ahead of the more general suppression of the monasteries, because of its impoverished state. Audley wanted to use the former monastery as a residence for himself, while the site was large enough for him to rent parts of it at a profit. In his letter, he claims that he has had to sell his house at Hoxon, in Essex, to settle debts and that he needed a new property urgently for 'if a Chancellor of England, when he dieth, have not 200 marks [£133] of land, it is to be noted, when a merchant and one of the law will not be so satisfied'. This stress upon what was expected of someone of his high office shows Audley's keen awareness of the importance of visible signs of status and his indignation that others he considered less exalted than himself should be perceived to be better off. Land and great houses were very much to the fore in upholding the dignity of the powerful. Audley won his suit for Holy Trinity and by the end of his life in 1544 had half a dozen other houses scattered across his 'home county' of Essex, led by his 'chief and capitall mansion house' of Audley End, another monastic spoil.[1]

Audley represented just one of several interest groups striving to impress their newly-achieved social position on their contemporaries. Those who perceived themselves of the old guard, whether wealthy or not, also had standards to keep up. Henry Howard, the young Earl of Surrey, got himself into debt doing so and was anxious to make sure that his fellow courtiers knew exactly how great the lineage of his family was. In 1544 he crossed swords with Sir Christopher Barker, the Garter King-at-Arms, at his house in London

because, when discussing his plans for the decoration of his houses, he insisted on quartering the arms of Edward the Confessor with his own, a privilege granted only to royalty. The incident was a key weapon in the prosecution case at Surrey's attainder for treason two years later, revealing the importance attached to these visible marks of status and the sensitivity about the expression of rank by such outward signs.[2]

Looking at Europe as a whole, the period of the Renaissance has often been described as a time of assertive individuality in patronage of the arts. But the impetus toward patronage was usually born of the spirit of competition with social rivals, so that individuality was often subsumed in the desire to match what those of the same rank had newly commissioned. This was particularly true of the patron who was a newcomer to his or her social or political class, as was true of so many of the country house builders of early Tudor England. Building a country house that equalled that of an already well-established family was one way of signalling arrival at a certain degree of status and income. This concern might operate at a purely local level in just the same way that the aggrandizement of churches discussed in the last chapter expressed competition between communities in a given locality. But the most interesting examples of houses of this kind are connected with the group at the very centre of power, the courtiers, those one hundred or so figures who held high positions in England in the first half of the sixteenth century in the offices of government and in the privileged world of the King's Privy Chamber.

All these figures were of course men, a consequence of the patriarchal society of the time which determined that all offices of state were automatically a male preserve. In addition, because all English sovereigns were male until the accession of

Queen Mary in 1553, those positions of power which stemmed from personal service to the King, whether in the royal palace or on the field of battle, were also necessarily filled by men, since only they could be intimates of the monarch. Therefore, notwithstanding the significance of the building patronage of a handful of leading royal women (like Lady Margaret Beaufort, the mother of Henry VII, who founded Cambridge colleges and rebuilt the house of Collyweston in Northamptonshire, and Margaret, Countess of Salisbury, cousin of Henry VII, who built a house at Warblington in Hampshire), the discussion of power in relation to architecture is essentially about the role of building in the lives of leading male political figures.

There is considerable disagreement among historians about the relative importance of the Court in the government machinery of early Tudor England, but none have denied its new significance as an unrivalled centre of political and therefore cultural activity. Its leading figures were expected to dance continual attendance on the King and to express loyalty in various ways. A splendid house in the fashionable style of the day might be as much part of the 'uniform' of the favoured courtier as the white and green of the King's colours that he wore at Court as the sign of his allegiance.[3]

The competition in building was set in motion by the enterprise of leading churchmen. By the fifteenth century, all the higher ranks of the clergy expected to live in greater domestic comfort. Among the several ecclesiastical posts held by the Archdeacon William Pykenham was that of Rector of Hadleigh in Suffolk, where he built a splendid new house in about 1490 (Fig. 9), the remains of which are now attached to the deanery. In doing so he was merely following his superiors, since the powerful bishops of the Church were setting the pace at the top end of the power structure. The scale of the Church's expenditure on domestic building was to be matched, and subsequently overtaken, by the Crown after 1500 and the pace was then taken up by leading courtiers and by those of the merchant class wealthy enough to spend liberally on building.

The early Tudor period was the last time in English history when it seemed part of the natural order of things that leading churchmen should hold high office in government. The social position and responsibilities of the bishops were such that they might hardly ever be present in their episcopal seats, but spent all their time moving to or from their London residences via their many palaces and manor houses. By the late 1520s the Archbishop of

9  Hadleigh, Suffolk. The brick gatehouse of c. 1490 was the entrance to Archdeacon Pykenham's residence and shows the fashionable quality of domestic building for leading ecclesiastics at this period.

Canterbury, for example, had some 21 houses. Over 30, or approximately one sixth of the total number of known episcopal residences were undergoing radical improvements between the years 1470 and 1535.[4] Many of these improvements involved the construction of splendid new gatehouses and ranges of lodgings in brick, and it seems that it was these ecclesiastics who were chiefly responsible for promoting brick as a fashionable building material.

Two of the last churchmen to hold high office, William Warham, Archbishop of Canterbury, and Cardinal Thomas Wolsey, Archbishop of York and Lord Chancellor, were the most extravagant of all. Wolsey's three principal new houses demonstrate the plurality of his office-holding and the amount of his private wealth. Whitehall was his as the London residence of the Archbishops of York, The More in Hertfordshire through his position as the titular abbot of St Albans, whilst Hampton Court was essentially a private venture following the lease of the old manor house there from the Knights Hospitaller in 1514.[5] It has always been known that Warham was an equally active builder, but only in recent years, after much archaeological excavation of the site, have we come to appreciate the extent and magnificence of his great palace of Otford in Kent (Fig. 10), one of the chain of residences that the Archbishop enjoyed between London and his see of Canterbury. Here Warham not only rebuilt the earlier manor house standing within the moat, but also added a new court whose dimensions (270 by 238 feet) were probably unparalleled by any domestic building of the day, though they were shortly to be exceeded by those of the great quadrangle of Wolsey's new Cardinal College (now Christ Church) at Oxford.[6]

*10   Otford, Kent. This corner tower is the most substantial of the remains of Archbishop Warham's vast outer court of 1514–18.*

By the time Leland was travelling around England in the early 1540s, bishops' residences were still plentiful enough to invite his constant comment, but the Crown had already begun to appropriate the finest of them as part of its wider assault on Church property during these years. By the end of the sixteenth century about one third (between 60 and 70) of former bishops' houses had been through the hands of the Crown in a series of forced exchanges and inequitable deals. These were passed on by sale, or similar forced exchange, to leading courtiers and servants of the King.[7] Several of the largest and choicest properties, among them Wolsey's houses, remained in the possession of the Crown and became royal palaces. It is interesting and perhaps historically fitting that the history of royal and episcopal palace building in England should overlap so fundamentally at a time when Church and State took on a new, common political identity.

The Crown's own contribution to the explosion of domestic building activity began at the very

dawn of the sixteenth century, for it was at that time that Henry VII began rebuilding his palace of Sheen, later renamed Richmond. This palace set the tone for subsequent royal buildings for it was built at great speed and with a clear sense of audience in mind. It was hurried through in order to be ready for a specific occasion (the marriage of Henry's son Arthur to Katherine of Aragon in 1501), and was designed to impress visiting foreign ambassadors who would report back on the King's magnificence. Its skyline of turrets and weather vanes, as well as its internal decoration, emphasized an attitude to the English past that celebrated well-established ideals of chivalry, recharged and re-awakened by the advent of the Tudor dynasty.[8]

By the end of Henry VIII's reign in 1547 the Crown possessed about 60 houses of varying size scattered all over the southeast and, to a lesser extent, the Midlands and southwest of England. Some of these were no more than hunting lodges for the King's favourite sport; others were designed to house the whole Court or retinue of the sovereign. Few in fact (and the palace of Nonsuch, begun in 1538, is the chief exception in this respect) were built as entirely new structures. To say that Henry VIII 'built' almost 60 royal palaces would therefore not be true. Many of these houses were only modestly transformed or temporarily fitted out to meet the demands of a brief royal visit; the accounts of the Royal Works show that they soon fell into disrepair between spells of royal occupation (although, as we shall see, the absence of the sovereign did not always mean that a particular building was unoccupied). Yet at no time before or since in the history of England has the Crown been so active in domestic building. This level of activity and the expenditure devoted to it was subsequently to be matched in the architectural enterprise of the King's courtiers.[9]

To gauge the impact of royal building on courtier houses much reconstructive work has to be done. Direct visual comparison between royal and other domestic buildings is difficult to do today since the temporary structures erected for Court festivities were just as influential as the permanent palaces and many of the latter were left ruinous and destroyed by later sovereigns. Today little remains to demonstrate the character and splendour of Henry VII's and Henry VIII's works. Of the sixty or so houses for which the early Tudor kings had some degree of responsibility, only two survive with any substantial evidence of Tudor work both outside and inside the building, namely the palaces of Hampton Court and St James's. In addition, part

of a range survives of the converted priory of Dartford in Kent, but only small fragments can now be seen of other houses, in some cases incorporated into later buildings on the same site, in others removed to later buildings elsewhere. Contemporary or later descriptions, building accounts, prints and archaeological evidence are therefore vital in reconstructing these royal buildings and judging their influence.

In the past thirty years archaeological excavation of the lost Tudor palaces has yielded much information about their size, building materials and the provision of water supply. Unfortunately, the recovery of cellars and footings cannot tell us very much about the arrangement and use of the upper floor (where the important rooms of state usually were), and whilst fragments of materials recovered from the earth can perhaps hint at the range of decorative or other features that existed, they cannot tell us their exact disposition. However, it is evident from documentary sources in particular that as far as style was concerned the royal palaces were a significant channel for the introduction of Continental fashions in decoration and luxury furnishings, since it is clear that many foreign craftsmen worked at the Court (see Chapter 6). It is clear also that, along with bishops' houses, the royal palaces established certain norms for the basic shape of large courtyard buildings. In particular, there was an emphasis on splendid, 'multi-storey' gateways and new internal arrangements were introduced which changed the relationship between important rooms (or rooms of 'state') and servants' quarters (or rooms of 'service').

However, we should not be misled into thinking that this is simply a question of the royal palaces setting a dominant stylistic mode. The houses of kings and bishops served particular needs and it is perhaps mistaken to assume that courtiers automatically copied them. For one thing, they were built on a huge scale, and it proved both unnecessary and impolitic for courtiers to do likewise. Royal and episcopal palaces were the setting for the entertainment of great numbers of people; bishops in particular were expected to be hospitable, both in terms of the general charity they were expected to bestow on the poor at the outer gate and in their role as hosts to important foreign visitors, both religious and secular, in the inner court. These great buildings were also places of ceremonial and of other functions of a kind that would take place in the private residences of only the very highest-ranking courtiers. Like courtier houses, bishops' palaces sometimes had military functions and supported armed troops, as Bishop Rowland Lee of

Durham was forced to do in his capacity as President of the Council of the Marches, protecting the border with Scotland. On the other hand, they might also be the setting for the ordination of priests and thus temporarily assume a sacred role.[10]

The arrangement of the royal palaces was beginning to reflect the use of individual rooms for very specific purposes, with a division between the king's state and private life. The royal apartments developed at this time into a complex sequence of rooms. The king's guard chamber, followed by his presence chamber, where official receiving was carried out, were the essentially 'public' rooms of the suite. Then followed the privy chamber, which had often served as a bedchamber in medieval times, but was now increasingly a room for private dining and reception. Beyond this were the king's bedroom and withdrawing chamber, with closets and a 'stool chamber' in which the king could relieve himself. Admittance to this suite of rooms was very carefully regulated and only those close to the king would have the privilege of entry to the

*11   The tomb of Sir John Tregonwell in the north aisle of Milton Abbey, Dorset. He appropriated an earlier tomb and only the brass is original to him.*

private as opposed to the public rooms; those admitted to the privy chamber and beyond were especially high in the royal favour and were members of the king's personal suite, his 'Privy Chamber' in the collective sense of a body of men around the royal person. (The Privy Chamber as a term denoting a body of courtiers close to the king appears to have come into existence in about 1495.) Power at Court, and indeed power to exercise the king's will beyond it, was determined by how far one was admitted in the royal apartments; those who were allowed the closest physical proximity to the king were in the best position to argue for their own or others' interests.[11]

It is true that sixteenth-century accounts of the houses of some leading peers, like Edward Stafford, Duke of Buckingham, and Thomas Howard, Duke of Norfolk, mention suites of apartments for the lord of the house and his lady, echoing something of the arrangement of state rooms in royal palaces. At Thornbury Castle, the Duke of Buckingham had a great chamber, leading to a dining chamber and the Duke's bedroom.[12] But this was exceptional; the 'Master's Lodging' often referred to in the contemporary inventories of important courtiers usually consisted of one large room and perhaps a closet off it. In early Tudor England, leading peers were the most vulnerable of all courtiers to the suspicion that they were exceeding their power under the King and a mighty house could incriminate them. In the case of both the Duke of Buckingham in 1521 and, as we have seen, of the Earl of Surrey at the end of 1546, splendid houses were key points of accusation in the process of attainder. The newcomers to the power game were careful to dissociate themselves from such blatant self-aggrandizement.

Many of the newcomers to the courtier group were establishing themselves as landed proprietors for the first time; they were constantly on the move between their lodgings (or, if they were fortunate enough, their town houses) in London or at Court and their country properties. This mobile lifestyle reflected a desire to pursue the consolidation of their landholdings through influence at Court rather than a need to fulfil the ceremonial and official functions that the King and his bishops observed. These courtiers certainly built in more than one place, but usually one house became identified as their main 'seat' and its nearby church as the place of family burial. Those whose wealth and position were newly acquired often sought power in the region of their humble origins. Sir John Tregonwell, commissioner for the suppression of the monasteries in the West Country, secured the cloister buildings of the dissolved abbey of Milton, in Dorset, in 1540 to use as his house. The monastic church became the local parish church and Sir John Tregonwell was eventually buried here in 1565 (Fig. 11), rather ironically in view of the fact that this was the church whose religious community he had been instrumental in expelling. Even the tomb chest was appropriated from someone else; he simply fixed in his kneeling figure and heraldry in brass.[13]

The houses and tombs of these 'new' men had significant points of comparison with royal and episcopal houses. Like them, they were overt signs of their builders' stake in the power structure of the day, with emphatic display of heraldry and castellation laying claim to a respectable pedigree and suggesting a social position that was already enshrined in time and established by the honour of serving the king. This achievement of social respectability was the foundation of generations of power and wealth in some cases, from the Russells of Chenies and later of Woburn at the highest courtier level, to the Brudenells of Deene at the highest county level. In both cases, the church local to the great house preserves a family chapel with an unbroken line of family tombs. For other men, social respectability proved illusory and short-lived.

If the powerful men at the Tudor Court were a mixture of the old nobility and a new professional class, everyone was dependent on the king's favour. As the source of office, honours and titles, the king acted as the arbiter in determining the courtier's position in society, a system that was tightly controlled by the early Tudors. The fifteenth century had seen a marked decline in the numbers of the nobility, due more to the failure of many peerages in the male line than to the bloodshed of civil war. This decline continued into the sixteenth century; of 55 noble families recorded between 1485 and 1542 (of which 12 were new Tudor creations), 30 died out in the male line.[14]

Whilst many key members of the old nobility continued to play a significant role at Court and no one could have doubted, especially on any military or ceremonial occasion, that they held the highest place under the King, the overall number of the nobility did not grow significantly under Henry VII and Henry VIII and the defunct ranks of the peerage were augmented with only a handful of new creations. Courtiers came to realize that elevation to the nobility was not the automatic reward for loyal political service. Even the conferment of a knighthood remained primarily a reward for military and ceremonial service, rather than for excel-

lence in the administrative and political sphere. The great majority of knighthoods were conferred on important royal occasions, such as the marriage of Henry VIII to Anne Boleyn or (in considerably greater numbers) following military victories, in England against pretenders to the throne during Henry VII's reign, abroad in France and Scotland during that of Henry VIII.[15] Only in the last years of Henry VIII, when the various factions at Court scrambled for control in the face of the King's decline, was elevation to the nobility directly equated with the highest political office, namely membership of the King's Council. Even so, only the machinations that surrounded the making of the King's will ensured that some of the leading figures of the 1540s were elevated to the nobility in the early days of Edward VI.[16]

The system of rewards was largely based on the granting of land or other privileges, such as the right to certain trading concessions, rather than on the award of honours. The Crown could control such grants and privileges by short-term leases and patents, without encouraging the inflated sense of status that nobility might bring. Conversely, grants of land were not the automatic result of the conferral of a peerage or high office, and where land was given it seems that the King played a game of cat and mouse, using the opportunity to keep courtiers in permanent debt to the Crown and hedging such grants about with conditions that preserved a dimension of royal control, such as the obligation to render outdated feudal dues.[17] This control extended to the houses that courtiers might choose to build on their newly-acquired estates. Royal policy here may have been influenced by Wolsey's building works, for after his downfall in 1529–30 there was an increase in the King's manipulation of courtier building activity, as if it was recognized that the visible sign of the Cardinal's pride in his power had been his expenditure on building on a grand and luxurious scale, and that this should never be allowed to happen again. After about 1530 the building initiated by courtiers is only explicable with reference to the fact that royal interests dominated the land market. By its actions, the Crown could both encourage and discourage the construction of houses.

To begin with, two aspects of the Crown's policy towards its own buildings must have played some part in deterring courtiers from undertaking work of their own. The holding of high office in the realm sometimes carried the right to use buildings maintained at Crown, or 'public', expense. Offices such as the Mastership of the Rolls, for example, carried an official residence, sometimes attached to the working premises of the government department the official headed. After the Court of Augmentations was established in 1536 to supervise and maintain suppressed monastic properties and then to sell them profitably, a house was built for its officers within the Palace of Westminster.[18] But the most useful kind of accommodation that came, as it were, with the job was that attached to an appointment to the position of Keeper, Steward or Constable of great buildings and the lands around them. Such positions as these were in the gift of all members of the élite who had buildings to maintain and were clearly lucrative in many ways; noblemen might, for example, take on the stewardship of a royal or a bishop's palace simply in order to enjoy the hunting rights that went with it, whilst the same nobles might in their turn allow rights of hunting or fishing to local gentry on their own estates. The duties of those who held the position of Keeper or Steward often involved nominal responsibility for the upkeep of the buildings, or such liabilities could be deputized. It has usually been assumed that such posts were therefore purely honorific and rights of occupation were never exercised. Yet it is evident that some courtiers granted such positions at the royal palaces used the building concerned as a residence during the king's absence and the royal accounts sometimes specified sums for constructing lodgings for the Keeper or Constable. Moreover, the marked lack of evidence for expenditure on their own houses in the case of a number of prominent men during the period of their tenure of such posts suggests that these courtiers inhabited their 'official' residence on a semi-permanent basis.

Sir Francis Bryan, one of Henry VIII's leading courtiers and one of the most vivid personalities at Court, is a case in point. He was resident ambassador in France for a time in the early 1530s and became Chief Gentleman of the King's Privy Chamber in 1536. Yet he is not known to have built any kind of new, lavish residence. During much of the 1520s and 1530s he lived at the house of his wife, Philippa Fortescue, at Faulkbourne, in Essex, and later, though he probably did not do very much to adapt the property, he certainly lived briefly at the abbey of Woburn, which he leased from 1539. What he did use extensively were his lodgings at the royal house of Ampthill (where he was Steward), created for him in 1536, and the lodge in the park there.[19] Sir John Gates, created Gentleman of the Privy Chamber in Henry VIII's last years, clearly lived in some splendour at the royal house of Pyrgo Park, in Essex, where he was Keeper; an

inventory of his goods there in 1553 includes a tapestry in the hall bearing his arms, and a bed with his arms in the silver bed chamber.[20]

One of the clearest examples of a beneficiary of the practice of living in royal houses was Sir Henry Guildford, Master of the Horse and subsequently Comptroller of the Household to Henry VIII. He was Constable of Leeds Castle, a royal property in Kent, from 1512 and so was officiating at the very time when royal building works were being carried out there between 1518 and 1522.

At his death in 1532 his goods at Leeds were inventoried separately from those of his house in London and provision made for their removal to the capital. Leeds Castle, therefore, which Henry VIII visited only occasionally during these years, effectively served as Guildford's own house, and he was very much a man of Kent when away from Court, since this was the centre of his landed interests.[21]

How widespread this practice of enjoying the privileges of residence was is difficult to determine; it is perhaps indicative, however, that the expansion of courtier building activity in the second half of the sixteenth century came just at the time when Queen Elizabeth was rapidly shedding many of her father's palaces. In other words, increased building activity may have been the result of the fact that there were fewer privileges of accommodation for courtiers to enjoy.

The second royal 'deterrent' to courtiers' own building schemes was the system of impressment. This was the means whereby the Crown could call on building expertise from all over the country for its own projects. For example, bricklayers and freemasons were summoned from all over the south of England to contribute to the King's work at Hampton Court and Whitehall in the 1530s. This could mean that courtiers and others seeking to employ sufficient numbers of skilled craftsmen to work on their own country houses would at best have a difficult time. In the early 1540s this problem escalated. The royal domestic building programme was as vigorous as ever with the royal palaces of Oatlands and Nonsuch nearing completion. At the same time, a massive programme of defensive works had also been initiated to protect the country against the threat of foreign invasion. Although this spate of royal activity coincided with a period when fewer completely new houses, at least on the largest, courtier scale, were in progress anyway because many former monastic properties were currently being adapted, the tide of courtier building was nevertheless stemmed quite a lot. For a few years such new houses as were initiated were marked by a new modesty in some of their dimensions and external decoration.[22]

Apart from these two 'deterrents' associated with the Crown, the King might in other ways impoverish or positively paralyse courtiers who wanted to build. The most direct and brutal intervention the King could make in the property of his servants accompanied a dramatic fall from his favour, which often led to attainder and subsequent execution for treason, real or imagined, against the State. This process has left us much precious information about lost houses of the period because, at the time of attainder, each offender's properties were forfeit to the Crown and were therefore visited and inventoried. Many of these documents survive among the State Papers, such as those concerning the fall of Edward Stafford, Duke of Buckingham, in 1521, of Thomas Howard, Duke of Norfolk, and his son Henry, Earl of Surrey, at the end of 1546 and of John Dudley, Duke of Northumberland, and his circle at the opening of Queen Mary's reign.[23]

Amongst Northumberland's circle, we would know nothing, for example, of the domestic life of such important courtiers as Sir John Gates and Sir Thomas Palmer, both of whom originally rose to prominence under Henry VIII, if they had not fallen in the decimation of the Protestant faction in 1553. From the State Papers we know that Palmer had a house at Backenho (or Backnoe) in Bedfordshire and the fairly lavish extent of Gates' lodgings under the royal roof has already been described. Sometimes this kind of evidence is very useful for specific information about the process of building itself. The papers seized at the fall of Thomas Cromwell in 1540, for example, include letters from his Steward concerning the state of building at several of his houses in the course of 1535. These documents are of great importance for what they tell us about the speed and organization of construction and about the expectations of the patron and his need to delegate work when he was busy with affairs of State. In Cromwell's case the irony is that it was only because of his public office that these essentially private business papers became State property and thus were preserved. Without them, we would know little of the building work he initiated.[24]

Confiscated houses and lands became the property of the King for him to dispose of to favoured courtiers as he wished. The fall of the Duke of Buckingham proved a great bonus to rising courtiers in the early 1520s, as many of them secured a slice of the vast Stafford estates. Sir Richard Weston, for example, received the land on which he built Sutton Place in subsequent years, whilst Sir Richard

Wingfield obtained the castle of Kimbolton, where he constructed new lodgings in the years before his death in 1525.[25] In these two cases the courtiers concerned gained markedly in status and were given the opportunity to increase their standard of living considerably, but this was the exception rather than the rule. Outright generosity was rare, and the King was more likely to sell or exchange holdings for other things he wanted. Often Henry VIII used confiscated properties in ruthless forced exchanges which were invariably to the courtier's disadvantage. This process of exchange was accelerated after the dissolution of the monasteries began in 1536, because the Crown thereafter had many former monastic buildings and large land holdings available to bargain with. The King might appear to be giving in exchange for what he received in these transactions, but in reality he used them to influence where his leading subjects lived and how they invested their money in building projects. Every new country house was built in the knowledge that what the King gave, he could also take away.

The Crown did not always act purely out of envy, malice or the suspicion that luxurious building reflected the overweening power of a particular figure. On the other hand, there are plenty of signs that the King kicked his servants when they were down by forced exchanges of property, particularly if an acquisition would help meet the royal need for hunting land. In 1538 the King's 'honour' or manor of Hampton Court was being expanded for the needs of the chase and the royal eye fell on the house and adjacent land at Molesley in Surrey. The owner-occupier could hardly stand in the way for he was Richard Page, formerly a favoured Gentleman of the Privy Chamber but disgraced two years previously as a member of the circle around the ill-fated Anne Boleyn. In recompense he was given the small and undistinguished house of a recently-dissolved Benedictine nunnery known as St Giles in the Wood at Flamstead in Hertfordshire. The previous lessee of this nunnery, John Tregonwell, was in turn moved on, despite writing a letter of complaint to Thomas Cromwell in which he said that he had spent £120 in converting the site into a working farm. Tregonwell's true recompense, as we saw earlier in this chapter, was to come in the following year when he secured Milton for £1000.[26]

Another courtier who lost favour and found himself forced to exchange property to his disadvantage was Thomas West, Lord de la Warr. He had been a successful soldier in the French wars early in Henry VIII's reign, but by the 1530s had become a kind of *persona non grata* at Court, securing only minor offices, continually excusing his absence and being identified as an opponent, albeit a passive one, of the King's religious policy. In 1536, despite his obsequious protests, the priory of Boxgrove in West Sussex (Fig. 12), which housed his family's most important religious benefaction, a splendid chantry chapel, was suppressed. Three years later, West suffered a further rebuff when the King drove him from his house of Halnaker, which stood within walking distance of the former priory, and forced him to accept the dissolved nunnery of Wherwell in Hampshire in exchange.[27] In this way, by removing someone from his house and thus from a position where he could exercise local patronage, the Crown could effectively destroy the basis of that individual's control of a particular locality. However, this did sometimes work in reverse and new power bases were created for the more favoured of Henry VIII's intimates if this suited government policy.

*12  Boxgrove Priory Church, West Sussex. The de la Warr chantry chapel of c. 1530, a church within the church for prayers for the dead.*

Exchanging houses and their adjacent lands could be a sign of royal favour, though one which carried with it a degree of responsibility that the courtier dare not fail to meet. Henry VIII learned from the policies of his grandfather, Edward IV, that loyal courtiers could be 'planted' in those parts of the country where the royal control was at its weakest, or where insurrection had recently taken place. One of the King's closest associates was Charles Brandon, Duke of Suffolk, a man whom historians have always noted not only for his physical resemblance to the King himself (on the evidence of portraits), but also as a match for that bluff, military character that Henry himself aspired to. Brandon survived incurring the royal disfavour on account of his secret marriage to the King's sister Mary in 1515, after the death of her first husband, the aged Louis XII of France. Thenceforth, until Mary's death in 1533, the couple made their principal country home at Westhorpe in Suffolk. It suited the King at this time that Brandon should be a powerful figure in East Anglia as his presence made it less likely that the Howard Dukes of Norfolk would become too dominant in the region.

But following the Pilgrimage of Grace in 1536, when the county of Lincolnshire rose in armed rebellion for redress of grievances against the King, Brandon was encouraged to abandon one regional power base for another. It was recognized that this rather remote part of the country, off the beaten track of the main north-south lines of communication, needed the leading resident and royalist nobleman that it had hitherto lacked. Conveniently, in 1534 Brandon had remarried, this time to the young Lincolnshire heiress, Katherine Willoughby, so he now had the firm foundation of his new wife's inheritance as a basis for building up landed interests in Lincolnshire. He exchanged Westhorpe with the King for further Lincolnshire lands and, as a sign of new responsibilities, Brandon and Katherine Willoughby began rebuilding her house at Grimsthorpe (see colour plates). It was doubtless necessary to underline Brandon's new position by building a house at least equal to the one recently built just a few miles away at Irnham by the Thimelbys, who were among the leading gentry of the region. The basic outline of Brandon's Grimsthorpe can still be seen today in the outer faces of the three great ranges of the present building, the inner facades of which were given a new architectural skin by Vanbrugh in the early eighteenth century.[28]

A similar concern for security and the need to encourage a courtier into establishing himself in a new area lay behind the granting of extensive estates in Devon to John Russell, a holding which was taken largely from the appropriated lands of the dissolved abbey of Tavistock. The King and Cromwell perceived something of a power vacuum in the west of England following the threat posed by a plot hatched there in 1537–8; Henry VIII's cousin, Henry Courtenay, Earl of Devon, had been accused of being involved and had been executed. Russell was originally from the West Country and was now expected to promote the King's interest there. In fact the policy rather misfired, for Russell's attention to his West Country estates proved only fitful during the next few years. Only the rebellion of 1549 in the reign of Edward VI convinced him that he should intervene there more often. Russell was of a different breed from Brandon, whom the King relied on mainly for his military prowess and experience. He knew that his future lay in his willingness to serve the King in a wide range of duties and he gambled on staying close to the Court, at least for much of the year. He was therefore chiefly interested in his extensive landholdings in the southeast of England, centred on his newly-built house at Chenies in Buckinghamshire.[29]

Presence at Court and proximity to the person of the King were essential if favour were to be constant and replenished by new grants and Court appointments. Others counted the cost of absence. Sir Thomas Wharton, for example, was firmly established on inherited estates in Cumbria, centred on his house at Wharton Hall, which he enlarged in the 1540s and 1550s. He was very much the King's man in the far north, looking after the royal castles and acting as Warden of the Western Marches. He quarrelled with other great northern lords in pursuit of protecting the King's interests. Rewards came, including a peerage in 1544, and he was able to build up estates near his wife's home at Healaugh in Yorkshire, where he secured the grant of the dissolved priory. Yet he never gained the great income from land that others of his rank and status achieved by continual Court attendance. This he noted in a letter to the Lord Chancellor in 1544, blaming his 'servys of the Kinges Majestie in ane

13 *Shurland House, Isle of Sheppey. The remains of the entrance range photographed in 1983.*

outwarde and extreme part of the realme far from his highnes presence'.[30]

The security of the realm of course presented external as well as internal problems and these too could push courtiers out of their houses. The danger of foreign invasion was felt to be particularly acute in the 1540s and no chances were taken with national security; as well as the Crown's massive programme for the construction of coastal forts, it also sequestrated useful properties, especially defensible places, where necessary. One of these was the castle of Westenhanger, in Kent, for which the owner, Thomas Poynings, was granted lands in Dorset and Wiltshire in exchange.[31] This was something of an innovation in policy since the Crown had traditionally deputized responsibilities for defence to local landowners. A sign that defence was increasingly perceived as the responsibility of central government is shown in the fate of an important early Tudor house during Queen Elizabeth's reign. While Henry VIII was still on the throne, Sir Thomas Cheyney, Lord Warden of

the Cinque Ports and Treasurer of the Household, built the large brick house of Shurland, on the Isle of Sheppey in the Thames Estuary (Fig. 13). When, some forty years later, his son moved his household elsewhere, local people complained to the Queen about the neglect of the house and estate, given the island's important position in the seaborne approaches to London. The Crown responded by sequestrating the property and repairing it; the bird's-eye view now in the Public Record Office (see colour plates) was part of the initial Crown survey of the site.[32]

The royal will that shadowed a courtier's ability to meet his aspirations in terms of his country property was even more interventionist in the London housing market, though here it was the courtiers who generally gained from the Crown's appropriation of the houses of leading ecclesiastics — bishops and the abbots of the larger monasteries who often had properties in the capital. As churchmen were removed from positions of power in the capital, so the places which housed their retinues passed to the new class of Tudor politicians. A glance at the names of these houses reveals their origins, as they were called after the bishopric that once held them. William Fitzwilliam's Bath Inn,

15 *Suffolk Place, Southwark, built in the years after 1515. The Tudor house, with its turrets and ogee domes, stood off the road to London Bridge. A detail from Wyngaerde's panorama of London.*

John Russell's Carlisle Inn, Edward Seymour's Chester Inn (which he demolished to make way for Somerset House), William Paget's Exeter Inn and William Parr's Winchester House all betray the fact that they were once bishops' houses.[33] Since the Court was increasingly centred on London, having a base in or near the capital proved essential. In Henry VIII's last years, some courtiers who were building up the landed estates of their family for the first time chose to build what were effectively their 'country' houses in a sort of Tudor commuter belt within twenty miles or so of London. Such men included Secretaries of State William Petre at Ingatestone in Essex, William Paget at West Drayton (then in Middlesex) (Fig. 14) and Ralph Sadler at Standon in Hertfordshire.

In the early sixteenth century there is some evidence that those powerful enough at Court to need permanent lodgings in or near London were beginning to expect higher standards of accommodation. When Sir Robert Southwell took up his post as Solicitor to the Court of Augmentations in 1537 he wrote to Sir Ralph Sadler, a close associate of Cromwell and later to be Secretary of State, to ask for better lodgings. His Chamber at the Temple was 'a good mile from my Lord Chancellor's, so

that in going thither and returning, I spend a great part of the day'. He wished to obtain a house from the King at Elsingspytle in London for himself and his wife.[34] This was the sort of modest start that many figures associated with the Court must have made; Southwell doubtless lived more splendidly in London in later years, when he rose to become Chancellor of the Court of Augmentations and Master of the Rolls.

In the later sixteenth century, living expensively in London was to bring many Elizabethan and Jacobean courtiers seriously into debt. Whilst this seems to have been less of a problem in the early Tudor period, town houses seem to have taken on a new splendour as the years passed and in rare cases even approached the standards expected in a country house in their size and layout, as in the case of Charles Brandon's Suffolk Place at Southwark (Fig. 15), built contemporaneously with Westhorpe. From the papers confiscated at his fall we know that Thomas Cromwell had two houses in the City of London under major repair and embellishment in 1535, as well as a third just outside the City walls, at Hackney.

So it would seem that the Crown acted as a sort of clearing house for courtier property in the early sixteenth century. This was an important means of control which the King could exercise according to the dependence of the individual and use to advance the Crown's own particular regional interests. A rough survey of the one hundred or so most important courtier houses of this time would show that only something like one third of these were gained by inheritance; considerably more, over two fifths, were obtained through gift or grant-purchase from the Crown. Some of these were to become great family seats and still remain the property of the twentieth-century descendants of their Tudor grantees, but just as many were reclaimed by the State in the violent changes of political fortune characteristic of the age.[35]

It is hard to elucidate the reactions and intentions of the players in this snakes and ladders drama concerned with powerful, landed interests, for there is a lack of surviving personal correspondence that specifically discusses buildings on a descriptive or comparative level. However, official papers, accounts, and the sense of where people spent their time that can be obtained through State documents, give us some clues as to how important houses were in the lives of their builders. These sources suggest to what extent courtiers perceived expensive building projects to be the natural result of high social position, what proportion of income they were prepared to spend on them, how strongly they felt about committing money and time to houses, and their views about where they stood in relation to their peers.

Those holding certain offices of State were increasingly obliged to entertain and therefore to maintain a large household for this purpose. The bishops' residences had had an important role as places of lodging for important State visitors and it seems that this function continued after these houses became the property of lay owners. Sometimes there was no clear dividing line between public and private responsibility for this kind of expenditure. There were particular responsibilities, for example, attached to holding high office at Calais, since all manner of visitors (English and foreign alike) passed to and from the mainland through this English outpost in Continental Europe. In 1536, Arthur Plantagenet, Lord Lisle, the King's Deputy at Calais, pleaded from there in some distress about the state of his finances: '...

for as much as no man in this town was ordinarily charged with keeping of households whereunto any daily haunt and resort was made but only I, as well as in banqueting and feasting of strange ambassadors and other foreign potestes (potentates) and great personages as otherwise.'[36]

The prospect of a royal visit might also have involved much expense on building work and certainly on the equipping of a great house. There is no evidence that Henry VIII made progress between the houses of his leading servants quite the annual affair that Queen Elizabeth was later to do, but the Court tended to keep on the move between the royal palaces since its large numbers drained local food supplies in a short space of time (especially when the Court moved away from the navigable River Thames) and courtier houses might enjoy the King's presence. Sometimes, there were informal and impromptu visits to courtier houses; when fear of sickness in the Royal Household caused the King to move, royal buildings nearby were sometimes unprepared to receive him. This was so, for example, when the King made an unplanned visit to Sutton Place in 1533.[37] Since the majority of royal houses were concentrated in the southeast of England, the King's longer journeys, such as the extended progress to the north in 1541, were partly organized around accommodation at the houses of his servants. In some cases, a royal visit has helped to suggest a date for the completion of building work, when other, documentary evidence is unavailable. Shurland can be dated stylistically to the 1520s, or possibly earlier, but it can be safely assumed that the house was finished, or nearly so, for the King's visit in 1532.

Planned royal visits called for special arrangements. As is so emphatically evident in Queen Elizabeth's later well-documented visits to houses, a very clear hierarchy of status was established on these occasions. The sovereign became the temporary 'lord' of the house and the royal retinue likewise took precedence over the resident community. When Henry VIII visited the Seymour family home of Wolfhall in 1539, Edward Seymour moved his own servants and staff out into his barn, hastily fitted up for the purpose.[38] The domestic quarters of the family took on the role of apartments of state with the full provision of the necessary sequence of rooms. This also appears to have happened, for example, at The Vyne, the home of William, Lord Sandys, the King's Lord Chamberlain, on the occasion of the royal visit in 1535; six years later, in the inventory of the house taken after Sandys' death, rooms are still given their royal names, such as the Queen's Great Chamber and her Lying (bed) Chamber.[39] Later records such as this inventory testify to the lasting sense of honour that such occasions lent the house, and furnishing installed at that time might remain for generations to come. At Appuldurcombe, on the Isle of Wight, a carpet woven with Henry VIII's arms, recorded in the inventory of Sir James Worsley at his death in 1566, undoubtedly recalls the King's visit more than thirty years earlier, when Worsley was Captain of the island. At Chenies, John Russell's house in Buckinghamshire, a bed of gold and silver with Henry VIII's arms embroidered on the tester is still recorded there in an inventory drawn up nearly fifty years after the King's stay.[40]

Henry VIII's visits might be costly, but there is no evidence that they ever proved as financially ruinous as those of Queen Elizabeth. We know from plentiful documentary evidence that problems for the Elizabethans began with the high cost of building itself. In the early sixteenth century, before inflation hit hard, there was a greater degree of control over expenses. Sometimes costs were noted as one of the reasons for impoverishment, but in no case can an expensive house be said to have been the sole cause of impecunity. The Earl of Surrey appears to have been living beyond his means in the years up to the time of his attainder and execution in 1546. His father's treasurer had expressed concern about Surrey's finances the year before and only months before his imprisonment the Earl was hoping for the gift of the buildings of the suppressed monastery of Christ Church, Norwich, from the King 'to discharge me out of the misery of debt'. The building and furnishing of his new house of Mount Surrey, on the property of St Leonard's Hill outside Norwich, and also of his London residence must both have made heavy demands on his purse in these years. But the costs of building were only part of the necessary expenses involved in making a show of status. The Italian chronicler Polydore Vergil noted that Charles Brandon spent 'vast sums' in the years after 1515 on establishing his new household at Westhorpe and in London and that this exacerbated his financial problems, but his embassy to France and his marriage to the King's sister Mary had also depleted his resources.[41]

It is difficult to be precise in comparing costs of building with average income. How much annual revenue a man like Charles Brandon could command is impossible to quantify. In a private note of 1535 he assessed his own income at about £2500 but this figure is likely to be an under-estimate and it cannot take account of the revenues he subsequently gained from the dissolution of the monasteries. In

fact, the more the revenues of these men are looked at in detail, and the further all possible sources of perquisite and privilege are probed, the more it seems that the figure for average income needs to be revised upward. Salaries from duties at Court are usually documented and there is some evidence that there was some general rise in the level of these during Henry VIII's reign, but the sums which accrued to office yielded more and income from land can only be estimated in many instances since holdings were often widely scattered. The wealthier courtiers could generally count on an income of between £2000 and £3000 during the latter part of Henry VIII's reign; Sir Ralph Sadler, Secretary of State in the 1540s, enjoyed a revenue of about £2600 during these years and his fellow Secretary, Sir William Petre, seems to have commanded over £3300 by the following decade.[42]

Matching sums like these against the cost of houses seems to show that spending on building was well within the income of these people. However, only for a few privately-built (as opposed to royal) houses of the early sixteenth century do we have anything like adequate building accounts. Three well-known East Anglian examples, Little Saxham, Redgrave and Hengrave, all newly-built at this time, are quite revealing. The fact that they are close to each other in a single region of the country gives us information on local building materials and also on the degree of local competition about house-building. Though the building of these houses spans the entire first half of the sixteenth century, their relative costs are comparable because the cost of building materials only caught up with the more general inflation after mid century. Thomas Lucas, Solicitor General to Henry VII, built the house of Little Saxham in Suffolk between 1505 and 1514 at a total cost of £1425. Thirty years later, Sir Nicholas Bacon, Solicitor to the Court of Augmentations, spent less than this on his new house of Redgrave in Suffolk, completed by 1554 for only £1253. However, Bacon's greatest days were yet to come and he was to go on, during Queen Elizabeth's reign, to build more extensively and expensively at his Hertfordshire house of Gorhambury.[43]

Little Saxham and Redgrave were both fairly modest, red brick houses, with small projecting wings. Little Saxham was in fact relatively costly for its day and unusual in East Anglia in that it was constructed with expensive stone dressings. By contrast, Hengrave (Fig. 16), the third East Anglian house of these years for which accounts survive, is perhaps representative of the upper end of the market. Interestingly, it was built not for a courtier

16 *Hengrave Hall, Suffolk. The courtyard house was finished in 1538, when the oriel over the gate was paid for. The projecting bay to the left of the gate is the chapel.*

figure in the literal, occupational sense, but for a wealthy businessman, Sir Thomas Kytson. His house, just outside Bury St Edmunds in Suffolk, was a larger, more ambitious building than Little Saxham or Redgrave, arranged around a principal courtyard with a service court attached. It was constructed in specially manufactured yellow brick with stone dressings and was given expensive and specially commissioned architectural features, notably the extraordinary oriel window over the entrance gateway to the main court. This house was built between 1525 and 1538 and cost somewhere in the region of £3500, suggesting that a courtier would have to think in terms of a sum somewhere near the upper limit of his annual income should he wish to build on this scale and with this pretension.[44]

A second index of expenditure on houses is the price paid for former monastic properties, although these sums can never be taken at face value. In the first years after the suppression of the monasteries, the realistic market price was sometimes reduced if a favoured courtier was the recipient; as time went by, however, higher charges were made as the government sought to make as much money as

possible from these sales. Also, buildings varied widely in their state of repair according to the degree of attention paid to them by the last members of the monastic community and to the extent of defacement by the royal commissioners at the time of suppression. Transactions were also complicated by whether lands and other chattels were attached. The sum of money handed over by the recipient of a monastic site was therefore never a pure and simple reflection of the value attached to the monastic buildings, so any comparison with other domestic buildings has to be made with caution. Nevertheless, it is interesting that a great many leading men purchased these properties for less than £1000 and that they made substantial residences out of them, in many cases their chief property. The amounts they subsequently spent also varied widely, partly depending on whether the monastery contained any accommodation which met the latest standards in domestic comfort. A new owner who was lucky enough to find that the last abbot had already built new and luxurious lodgings need have spent very little in the first instance. But Sir William Sharington claimed to have spent 2000 marks (£1333), more than one and a half times as much again as the purchase price of £783, on new buildings at Lacock Abbey (Fig. 17) within nine years of his taking up residence there in 1539.[45]

*17 Lacock Abbey, Wiltshire. Sharington's tower, with its high prospect room, part of his adaptation of the nunnery in the 1540s, is shown at the centre of the Bucks' eighteenth-century print of the house.*

Given the income of the greatest in the land, it appears that spending on individual buildings was relatively modest in comparison with later periods, and in comparison with the King, who might spend up to £20,000 or more on a single house.[46] Evidence suggests that courtiers preferred to spread the amount of income they were prepared to spend on building over several houses. During his years as Lord Chancellor, Thomas Audley converted two former monasteries to domestic use, Holy Trinity in London and Walden (later known as Audley End) in Essex. He had other houses in Essex at Berechurch, Colchester, Terling and Barking (called Brittons). It is unlikely that he spent very much on any of these individually and there is no evidence that any of them presented anything extraordinary or stylistically new to the eye in their external features. What is revealed by his auditor's account book of 1541–2 is that Audley was paying out a constant stream of small sums for patching up the fabric, mending chimneys and replacing broken glass.[47] Thomas Audley clearly needed several residences and spent fairly modestly on each of them and he was not untypical of many courtiers in this respect. However, this did not mean that he was unaware of the status that houses could bring and courtiers often saw building as a competitive activity.

A rare documentary instance of an attempt to goad a courtier into taking a more active interest in his new house by an appeal to his competitive instincts took place early in 1538 in the course of the conversion of Titchfield Abbey, Hampshire, into a residence for Thomas Wriothesley. At this time he was rising rapidly in the King's service and within two years was Secretary of State. Later he was to become Lord Chancellor. Though he corresponded regularly with those on site charged with the day-to-day business of building, Wriothesley clearly was not inclined to find time from his duties in London to visit Titchfield; so little did he know of the place that he even had to be told that the cloister was to the north, rather than the south, of the abbey church. The commissioners on site urged him to see the works in progress and make decisions about the practical details of transformation for 'Mr Treasurer is now at Netlee and lately my Lord Admiral was at his own, and you may not be spared to see that you never saw and correct all'.[48] The commissioners are appealing to Wriothesley's desire to have a house which would be the equal of fellow courtiers by referring to other works being

LEFT 18 *Cowdray House, West Sussex, completed in the 1540s. View from the top of the kitchen tower towards the gatehouse. The house was destroyed by fire in 1793.*

BELOW 19 *East Barsham Manor, Norfolk, c. 1520–30, with royal heraldry cut into the brickwork over the gate. Most of the finials and chimneys in cut brick and terracotta are renewed.*

undertaken in the vicinity — the conversion of Netley Abbey, only a few miles from Titchfield, by William Paulet, then Treasurer of the Household, and the completion of the great house of Cowdray (Fig. 18), about 25 miles away and en route to London by William Fitzwilliam, Lord Admiral and Earl of Southampton.

The conversion of Titchfield is unusual for the survival of evidence about the relatively small degree of the patron's involvement, but this is likely to have been true of most leading courtiers. Their busy lives meant that they invariably worked through stewards and bailiffs who made decisions for them, paid the wages of building labourers and worried about the provision of materials. The wives of these great men, who often acted as the effective head of the household for much of the time, probably had as much to do with the final appearance of these houses as their husbands whose political position was the inspiration for the building in the first place. In certain instances, as we have seen in the case of Charles Brandon, courtiers' wives were the initial source of the land and income that made building possible. This fact might not be directly alluded to, but the family lineage of women, especially if it was more respectable than that of their upstart husbands, was exactly what was needed to underline social and political arrival. Thus, though women were excluded from any position in political life, their social importance was stressed through the heraldry so prominent in country houses.

In this period, when most courtiers did not appreciate architecture on an intellectual level, or even indulge in the sort of conversation where consistency of style would have been noticed and commented on, power was expressed in outward show; the message, if it was going to succeed, had to be evident and striking on first appearance. It is often stressed what a significant part the display of heraldry played in the status of the powerful in Tudor England. Heraldry often engaged in a double allusion, to the owner, his family ties and his chief local connections on the one hand, and to his allegiance to the King on the other. Examples from interior decoration include the many different coats of arms in the panelling of the Oak Gallery at The Vyne (undoubtedly from the Tudor house but not in its original arrangement) and the panelling formerly at the house of Sir Edward Wotton, Boughton Malherbe in Kent.[49] In both cases the juxtaposition of personal, local and familial heraldry with royal shows the importance placed on the social and political circle with which the owner in each case identified.

The interplay of personal and royal heraldry can be seen on the exterior of such houses as East Barsham in Norfolk (Fig. 19) and Madingley in Cambridgeshire and in both cases the royal arms help to date the house. At East Barsham, built for the wealthy Sir Henry Fermor (Sheriff of Norfolk in 1532–3), the arms are supported by a greyhound on the hall porch, but by a lion on the detached gatehouse; since we know that the supportive heraldic animals in the royal arms were changed in 1527, this puts the building of porch and gatehouse either side of that date. Here the heraldry is large and emphatic, cut into the brickwork of the gatehouse in the boldest sculptural manner. At Madingley, heraldry is more discreet; the royal insignia appear on the broad band of stone on the great bay window to the hall with the owner's initials tucked into the string course at its very top. Again, dating is possible because the initials 'JH' and 'VH', for the builders John and Ursula Hynde, are counterpoised by 'H' and 'K' for Henry VIII and Katherine Parr and 'PE' for Prince Edward, indicating a building period between 1543, when Hynde assumed the estate, and 1547, when the King died.[50] This kind of allusion may have been mere deference, politic in a dangerous age. However, it serves well to emphasize the direct link between social position (very newly acquired in the case of both the Fermors of East Barsham and the Hyndes of Madingley) and the means to express that status. In every case heraldry of this kind refers to the magnanimity of the King whose control of offices and honours and their consequent revenues ultimately made these great houses possible. Heraldry was also the symbolical representation of values rooted in the past which those new to the ranks of the powerful were anxious to adopt and those there by tradition and lineage were keen to preserve and uphold.

# 3

# 'Tournid to Pleasure':
# Architecture and the Sense of the Past

IN THE CONTINUOUS DEBATE about the character of the early Tudor period, concerning government policy, literary output or visual artefacts, two schools of thought have emerged. One interprets the age as conditioned by new, humanist ideas, the other emphasizes the essentially backward-looking and chivalric nature of its culture. The debate seems to have begun in the Tudor period, and historians often regard the discussion about education which took place at the time as indicating a ruling class on the horns of a dilemma. The question was whether they should become a learned élite following the advice of Continental writing on the role and lifestyle of the aristocracy, or remain the unlettered, military caste of the past, bound by the values of chivalry. In fact, it is probably wrong to believe that the early Tudor élite saw the alternatives in such a cut and dried way. Although Richard Pace is reported to have said that he would rather have a son hang than study letters, and the Duke of Norfolk to have remarked that 'England was merry England before all this New Learning came in', these comments misrepresent men of scholarship who had travelled widely and had a considerable appreciation of the value of education. Essentially the dilemma poses two alternative routes to the same goal, for the end in view was to revitalize a sense of social responsibility among those in power, who were felt to have increasingly neglected this obligation of their position.[1]

It is clear, however, that the chivalric tradition remained vigorous and for a time provided the ruling class with a cloak of self-confidence. The introduction of the new learning at Court was received with considerable hostility in some respects and there was something of a new conservatism evident in the careful orchestration of attitudes to the past.[2] The Crown sponsored a new definition of English history. The Italian Polydore Vergil was commissioned by Henry VII to write his *Historiae Anglicae,* in which the author attempted, firstly, to be critical of the ancient and medieval chroniclers of English history whilst remaining deferential to the Tudor dynasty and, secondly, to summarize something of the character of particular periods and historical situations. It is a form of history that sees the past as a mosaic of empirical solutions to particular situations. By contrast, the chronicle of Edward Hall, probably first published in 1548, is an unashamed celebration of the triumph of the Tudor house, seeing the present age as a summation of the best values of the past, embodied in the life and actions of Henry VIII himself. Hall's view was to form the basis of the chronicles of Holinshed and subsequently of the interpretation of historical events in Shakespeare's history plays.[3] At a time when loyalties were becoming increasingly focused on king and commonwealth rather than local lords, the King himself led a revival of certain feudal obligations, using outdated feudal dues as a way of commanding and retaining loyalty.[4] Behind the mask of this revived chivalric ideal, however, changes were taking place, politically, economically and in the art of war itself, which were transforming the old loyalties and behaviour. Developments in architecture display this paradox very eloquently, bearing witness to an apparent respect for selected past values whilst also incorporating the increased comforts and practical arrangements of the contemporary world.

Some traditional features of domestic architecture were disappearing; the history of moats in particular shows the victory of practical sense over conservatism and the retention of a convention from the past for its own sake. Chapter 1 showed how some of the few early Tudor houses on completely new sites involved abandoning the old moated enclosure where the previous house had been built. This practice raises a crucial issue about the extent to which defence was still a primary consideration in domestic architecture. It used to be commonly assumed that the coming of the undefended house marked the essential transition from medieval building conventions to those of the early modern period, the first phase of which was presided over by the Tudors. Increasingly, however, archaeological and other evidence has shown that it is the pretension to defence that is slowly abandoned, rather than the reality, for medieval battlements and moats were not always what they appeared to be. To modern eyes, the moat might appear to be a very obvious and un-equivocal sign of a defensible house; but many moats had been abandoned or allowed to become silted up by the sixteenth century, while even those that were preserved and the few new ones that were created appear not to have been prin-cipally meant as a means of protecting the house.

The moat had been used in early medieval times as a 'curtain' of security for the multivarious activi-ties of an inhabited site, perhaps including more than one house or farm. It certainly gave some protection from marauders but it also acted as an effective means of preventing livestock from get-ting out. There is some evidence that the moat was often resorted to as a means of defence simply because there were restrictions on other defensive measures. Unlike private castle building, which was regulated and controlled by statutory policies that licensed crenellation (topping the building with battlements and other devices which allowed the inhabitants to watch for and ward off intruders), moats were not covered by the law. In the century following 1150 (after the conclusion of a period of civil war), perhaps as many as 800 moats are thought to have appeared in England. The great majority of these had fallen into disuse by the fifteenth century, but even where they survived they were often seen merely as part of the building's outward display. At Oxburgh Hall, in Norfolk (Fig. 20), for example, it appears that the moat was intended to set off an ostensibly fortified facade (for it can be demonstrated how essentially sham these defences are), rather than to act as a protective ditch.[5]

Lack of resources often determined the disappear-ance of moats as long-established moats needed

*20   Oxburgh Hall, Norfolk, the gatehouse range of the 1480s. The gatehouse is very much as it originally appeared, but flanking ranges have nineteenth-century crenellations.*

constant and expensive maintenance; Andrew Boorde's advice was that 'there shulde be some fresshe spring come into it; and dyvers tymes the moote ought to be skowered, and kept clene from mudde and wedes'.[6] It was also becoming increasingly costly to provide new ones. A very late example of a new and only partial moat is at Wolsey's Hampton Court (Fig. 21). Wolsey spent £523 having moats dug in 1517–18 and these by no means surrounded his newly-extended house; to put this figure in context, it was more than one third of the total cost of the complete rebuilding of Little Saxham Hall in the previous decade.[7] The builder of the great house at Rycote in Oxfordshire appears to have followed the example of Hampton Court in only partially moating the house. Rycote was possibly built as early as the 1520s, but was more likely to have been constructed from about 1535 under the ownership of Sir John Williams, Joint-Master (with chief minister Thomas Cromwell) of the King's Jewels and later Treasurer to the Court of Augmentations.[8] Kip's view of the house (Fig. 37), dating from about 1720, shows a moat on just the entrance side, emphasizing how vestigial this feature had become.

It may be that the continued use of a moated site, or the suggestion of a moat by a new, narrow trench in front of the house as at Rycote, were the affectations of a courtier class anxious to suggest the respectability of their lineage through the apparent age of their properties. It may also be that surviving moats were taking on a new role, for the presence of water at or near the site of a house was increasingly seen as desirable for both practical and aesthetic reasons. Boorde recommended 'a poole or two for fysshe' and Leland commended the arrangements at Stowey in Somerset where Lord Audley's house had 'a faire brooke serving al the offices of the maner place', a common feature of monastic establishments but rarely seen in private houses. The pleasurable aspects of water are implied in Leland's description of Sir William Barentine's house of Little Haseley in Oxfordshire as 'a faire mansion place, and marvelus fair walkes topiarii operis (made of topiary), and orcherdes, and pooles . . .'.[9] The important early Tudor house of Beddington in Surrey, the home of Sir Nicholas Carew, Henry VIII's Master of the Horse who was executed for his supposed part in the Exeter conspiracy in 1539, was praised for its

water gardens by Coryate in his *Crudities* of 1600 and later in the seventeenth century by the diarist John Evelyn.[10]

As for the efficacy of the defensive properties of the houses themselves, the still-present threat of assault on these buildings should not be underestimated nor their ability to withstand anything like a serious attack overvalued. It would be simplistic to believe that Tudor England was internally peaceful or that the country was necessarily more settled than in the previous century. In fact, the reverse seems to have been the case. Just as historians have increasingly demonstrated how the civil wars of the fifteenth century were more localized than once was believed and certainly did not result in increased fortification of domestic buildings, so it is also apparent that contemporaries believed the popular rebellions of the first half of the sixteenth century were highly dangerous, threatening internal security in a way unknown since the reign of Richard II 150 years previously. Great households, in varying degrees and according to need, stood prepared for potential conflict. At the beginning of the Tudor period there was still no standing army, so in time of internal and foreign war the Crown depended on the armed manpower that the great households could provide. Here was yet another gap between pretence and reality. The Crown accepted the presence of armed retainers in noble households yet made token efforts to control retaining by statute. Following Henry VII's decree of 1504 which restated the general principle of state control over the practice of keeping armed retainers, George Neville, Lord Abergavenny, was brought before the courts and fined heavily in 1507. Seven years later, however, when Henry VIII was calling on the nobility to muster men for the campaign in France, Lord Abergavenny was able to supply almost a thousand from his own immediate service.[11]

A defended house needed to keep an eye on the outside world. Some private houses near coasts or river estuaries were provided with towers in the Tudor period and this has sometimes led to the suggestion that these were built for monitoring enemy raids. It is likely, for example, that the brick tower Sir William Pelham added to his house at Laughton in East Sussex (Fig. 22) in the 1530s may have been partly intended for this purpose, since he and his successors did play a part in defending the nearby coast from persistent French raids.[12] But these buildings must have been equally important as general outlook towers, especially for those owners with shipping interests, such as Angell Dunne, a grocer and alderman of London. His

*21 Hampton Court Palace, London, begun by Wolsey in 1515. The north corner of the moat in front of the palace was drained in the seventeenth century.*

'high Tower of bricke' attached to his house in the City of London is known to us because John Stow was critical of its pretentiousness in his *Survey* of the end of the sixteenth century, 'the first that ever I heard of in any private mans house to overlooke his neighbours in the Citie'.[13] Occasionally, a particular act of fortification can be explained (or perhaps excused) by anxiety about the possibility of invasion. John Gilbert's extraordinary creation of a dry moat around three sides of Compton Castle, Devon, in the early sixteenth century, by building walls 24 feet high, may have been provoked by the incessant French raids on the Devonshire coast. On the other hand, great care was taken at Compton to create a symmetrical and pleasing approach from the north, or land side, which is not defended by the moat. Moreover, the defensive features were clearly designed partly to improve the internal facilities of the house, since the machicolations on the towers also serve as windows and as seats for latrines. The building's resulting proto-romantic quality belies the apparently simple intention of self-protection.[14]

Although England's north and south borders were vulnerable to raids by foreign powers, defence was generally more necessary against internal troubles. There were parts of the country where the preservation of law and order was difficult and certain sections of society were willing to use disorder as a means of getting what they wanted. The highest in the land were the worst offenders. The possibility of violence was ever present in their lives, land disputes particularly bringing out the innate aggression in a class anxious to withstand affronts to personal prestige.

Houses were sometimes prey to the terrors of casual assault, especially when left unattended for long periods, save perhaps for the presence of a resident porter. There was a lawless and apparently unprovoked attack on Charles Blount, Lord Mountjoy's house of Apethorpe, in Northamptonshire, in 1537, which prompted anxious letters to Thomas Cromwell from William Parr of Horton and Edward Montagu of Boughton, both local landowners and responsible for the King's peace in the county. Local rebellions always made the owners of great houses tremble for their properties. In 1536, the gentry of Lincolnshire, led by John, Baron Hussey from his house at Sleaford (recently, according to the later testimony of John Leland,

newly built by him), were charged with surrendering to the rebels in the Pilgrimage of Grace. They claimed that they feared for their lives and the destruction of their houses had they not done so, but the government was sceptical; Lord Hussey was executed for treason the following year. Kett's Rebellion of 1549 took over and certainly damaged (some sources suggest it actually destroyed) the house of Mount Surrey in Norfolk, still being finished a couple of years earlier when its builder, the Earl of Surrey, was executed.[15]

It was presumably partly to preserve a measure of self-protection that many houses had a supply of arms. Sometimes the room in which these were stored is actually called the 'armoury' in contemporary inventories, as at Sutton Place in 1542 and Kenninghall in 1547. Sometimes, however, arms were simply stored in an upper room, as at Markeaton in Derbyshire in 1545 where they were kept in a 'loft over the new chamber' and at Bingham's Melcombe in Dorset in 1561 where they were found in the chamber over the parlour. The inventory of Hornby Castle in 1523 records arms, gunpowder and 'hagbushes' (hackbuts) in a 'galory over the hall windowe'.[16] Interestingly, the possession of quantities of arms was seen as a sensitive issue; in several cases where the owner of the house had recently been attainted, the inventory of goods specified that the arms were to be entrusted to one of the Sovereign's closest servants responsible for munitions. At the attainder and execution of the Duke of Northumberland in 1553, for example, his store of bows and arrows and javelins at Syon was entrusted to Sir Richard Southwell, a staunch Catholic and recently created Master of the Ordnance by Queen Mary.[17]

There is, however, every indication that armouries were increasingly redundant for practical purposes, and this is particularly evident in the later sixteenth-century and seventeenth-century inventories of houses built in the early Tudor period. These appear to show that the early sixteenth century was perhaps the last time when private individuals took the maintenance and replenishment of their armouries seriously. At Michelgrove, home of the Shelley family in West Sussex, the inventory of 1585 records arms valued in total at under £2 and described as 'old stuff'. At Standon in 1623 the armoury contained only old things, including a suit of gilded armour made for Sir Ralph Sadler, who had built the house in the 1540s. Most telling of all, whilst a 1550 inventory of the old house of Wollaton, in Nottinghamshire, still records a moribund collection of bows and arrows, halberds and broken guns, a later inventory

*22 Laughton Place, East Sussex, during the restoration of 1978–81. The brick tower, built in 1534 but much altered in the eighteenth century, may have been used to watch for French raids, but its primary purpose was to serve as a private tower for Sir William Pelham.*

of 1585 has no record of the armoury whatsoever.[18]

So these houses were not strongholds in any practical sense of the word and casual assault, especially in the case of a revolt by local people who would not have any sophisticated arms, was far short of the organized siege warfare that we often imagine the medieval castle was built to withstand. But the skin-deep quality of defence was no new phenomenon in Tudor times and the effectiveness of the defensive features of late medieval castles should not be over-estimated. Bodiam Castle, in East Sussex, built in the 1380s and licensed to Sir Edward Dalyngrigge '... in defence of the adjacent country against the king's enemies' (that is to say, the French who threatened England's southern coast) has a strength that is more apparent to the eye than real. As long as a century ago doubts were expressed about whether Bodiam would have been truly defensible in late medieval times, given the contemporary advances in the technology of warfare. At the late fifteenth-century Oxburgh Hall (Fig. 23), a gap was still provided between the projecting corbelling and the wall at the top of the gatehouse, ostensibly

23 *Oxburgh Hall, Norfolk, built in the 1480s. The gap between wall and battlements was ostensibly for dropping missiles on intruders but, by this time, the pretension to defence was more important than the reality.*

for pouring hot liquid or throwing missiles on to would-be intruders, but this was purely decorative and seems never to have been used. As well as being cautious about defences contemporary with the original building, it is also important not to be misled by those additions made to late medieval architecture by eighteenth- and nineteenth-century enthusiasts who sought to romanticize the medieval past. Also at Oxburgh, for example, the formidable stretches of wall flanking the gatehouse originally had overhanging eaves; the present crenellated parapets were added in the nineteenth century (see Fig. 20).[19]

The early Tudor period marks the end of the granting of licences to crenellate and fortify by the Crown to private individuals and certain institutions. These licences had clearly long been used to add the trappings of military power rather than to provide genuine strongholds and apparently defensive features were seen principally as a sign of honour and social status. This is shown by the granting of many licences to religious houses.[20] Tudor houses did not, therefore, lose a real capacity for defence, but rather there was an increased emphasis on defensive features as indicators of a pride in tradition. This harking back to the past and to the trappings of chivalry was used as a weapon of personal propaganda by the early Tudor kings, since it emphasized an apparently long-established hierarchical system of which they were clearly at the head.

The chivalric character of the Court of the first two Tudors, particularly as demonstrated by the elaborately organized and staged ceremonial of jousts and tournaments, has been thoroughly analysed and discussed by recent Tudor historians. The English kings were willing to spend large sums on spectacle and pageantry because they fully recognized the propaganda value of such expense, as had been established at the French and Burgundian courts much earlier in the fifteenth century.[21] The supporting literature, which became the early Tudor courtier's recommended reading, stressed emphatic lessons from the chivalric past, illustrating what standards of honour and behaviour the nobility should aspire to. At the same time it was conveniently open to interpretation. In one sense, this literature appeared to support the *status quo* of the established warrior class. The translations of William Caxton, for example, and particularly his prefaces to these works, gave a conservative gloss to the chivalric ideal, confirming the nobility's position as an hereditary and inviolate group at the top of the social structure who would give leadership in time of war. Caxton lamented the loss of integrity and confidence, as he saw it, of a caste born to feats of arms and disparaged the tainting of true noble blood by interlopers. In his preface to the translation of the *Book of the Order of Chivalry* (taken from the French version of Ramon Lull of Majorca's *Libre del ordre de cavayleria*), printed in 1484, he noted that the nobility was unwilling to engage in foreign wars and recommended that its members should read the Chronicles of Froissart and the various accounts of the Arthurian legend. Henry VIII later embodied much of the chivalric ideal; he immediately pursued a highly positive and aggressive foreign policy and renewed the war with France.[22]

In contrast to the view that the nobility was set apart by virtue of birth, another school of thought defined the chivalric ideal as a standard to emulate and attain. War could be depicted as a means to social and financial success, with fortunes to be made by the successful opportunist. Leland commented frequently on the number of great houses built or rebuilt from the profits of the French wars of the fifteenth century, such as Lord Fanhope's castle at Ampthill in Bedfordshire and Lord Sudeley's castle at Sudeley in Gloucestershire.[23] The chivalric literature increasingly emphasized that military leadership was not simply something transmitted by blood; it had to be constantly demonstrated in order to flourish. As one classic fifteenth-century text advocated, 'Knights and esquires should be well mounted, and they and their servants should be well equipped with arms, and bows and arrows, sharply dressed and graciously; and they should spend decently and honourably on the upkeep of their households'.[24] True nobility, therefore, was a way of life and permeated all aspects of social behaviour; involvement in hunting and sport, the unashamed (because it celebrated name and rank) display of wealth, and the maintenance of a large and hospitable household were the true signs of noble bearing and worth. Such a way of life could be pursued by those who had won a recent reputation for valour as well as by those of well-established lineage.

The maintenance of a great household was a key element because the chivalric code of hospitality implied a largesse and beneficence toward society in general and was regarded as the mark of the gentleman. Chivalric romances are full of descriptions of the host meeting his guests as they approach his castle and the area around the castle thus became the setting for the ritual and courtesies of welcome. In entertainments at Court the 'castles' of chivalric romance and legend became a temporary reality, as at the well recorded occasions of the Revels at Greenwich in 1527 and the Field of Cloth of Gold in 1520. For the latter, a temporary palace was constructed near the castle of Guisnes in the Pas-de-Calais, which is well documented in written descriptions and in the celebrated painting by an anonymous artist, now at Hampton Court Palace (Fig. 24). The painting should not be seen as an exact rendition of what the building looked like, but it undoubtedly catches the spirit of part-castle, part-palace that inspired the building's creation. A fountain running with wine is shown in front of the building, demonstrating something of the royal largesse at these occasions. This temporary palace was a very light structure, with low brick foundations supporting upper walls of timber painted to appear as brick. Its construction would have been the logical extension of the activities of the Royal Works, whose craftsmen were experienced in providing prefabricated structures for Court festivities.[25]

Two features of the building seen at the Field of Cloth of Gold were later echoed repeatedly in the houses of early Tudor courtiers; first, both external and internal walls were covered with heraldry, which also broke the rooflines; second, it was notable for its large expanse of glass, such that one French commentator thought '*la moitié de la maison estoit toute de verrine*' (half of the structure must be made up of glass).[26] The courtyard of Sutton Place, for example, was adorned with terracotta decoration and had huge windows, like the palace at Guisnes. Built during the 1520s, it must have expressed something of the reaction to this building. A particularly skilful way of romanticizing the medieval past at this period was by using tall bay windows to break up the expanse of a castellated wall, often built so as to jut out from the main structure. The Royal Works seem to have developed the building technology for features of this kind and produced a whole sequence of variations on the theme at Richmond, Windsor, Henry VII's Chapel at Westminster and the Privy Lodgings at Thornbury, the last two of which still remain. Turning the battlemented stone wall into a transparent surface of glass was a subtle inversion of the original point of such building; other surviving examples include the great gatehouse of the house of the Throckmortons at Coughton in Warwickshire (Fig. 25) and the oriels over the gateways in houses like Hengrave in Suffolk and Kirtling in Cambridgeshire. Inside these great houses, the chivalric illusion was underlined by the coloured heraldic glass, particularly prominent in great halls, parlours and great chambers. Considering how little of the movable furnishings of early Tudor houses sur-

24   The English royal palace built for the Field of Cloth of Gold,
as depicted by an anonymous artist. The King and other patrons of
domestic architecture of this time, including Wolsey, the Marquis of
Dorset and the Duke of Suffolk, appear in procession at the left.
(Hampton Court Palace, London)

vives, quite a lot of heraldic glass from this period still exists, some of it in its original setting, as at Sutton Place, Haddon Hall in Derbyshire and Littlecote House in Wiltshire.[27]

While new building projects ostensibly looked backwards, the early Tudor period also saw the extensive refurbishing of medieval castles by a significant group of royal courtiers. This is especially interesting because it happened at a time when the Crown was largely neglecting the older castles in its possession as places of residence and was concentrating on new buildings.[28] It is also important that the greater number of major castle refurbishments were carried out by the nobility or those well on their way to achieving noble status. Often the people concerned were also involved in large new houses elsewhere, but it is as if the castle and its preservation acted as a demonstration of links with the past. Charles Brandon, Duke of Suffolk, builder of several new and fashionable houses though he was, also maintained the castle of Donnington in Berkshire. In outlining the state of his properties to the King in 1535, he claimed to have spent much on its embellishment, but it is now impossible to judge whether this was so. Though a later, seventeenth-century traveller, Richard Symonds, recorded Brandon's arms in the great hall, Donnington is almost completely lost to us.[29]

In some cases, noblemen restored and internally modernized castles that had long been in the family's possession, such as the refurbishment of Castle Hedingham, in Essex, for John de Vere, 13th Earl of Oxford, with new ranges of buildings and the addition of brick towers to the twelfth-century keep. In other cases, castles were overhauled as part of the trappings of newly-acquired nobility and lordship. Following his acquisition of the title of Lord Mounteagle in 1514, Edward Stanley carried out extensive building works at his castle of Hornby in Lancashire, which he acquired by marriage into the Harrington family, and of which only the chief tower or keep remains today. Similarly, the work of the two Thomas Howards, Dukes of Norfolk, at Framlingham in Suffolk followed their assumption of the castle from the Mowbray Dukes of Norfolk in 1476. And at the end of Henry VIII's reign, John Dudley, soon to become Earl of Warwick and subsequently Duke of Northumberland, transformed the old castle of Dudley in the West Midlands following his quite ruthless machinations to supplant his cousin, the

hereditary Lord Dudley, in the title to the lordship there.[30]

At all these sites, the castle in question was very much a symbolic statement about power, demonstrating outward signs of defence. In truth, these buildings were comfortable places of residence much like any other country house. Sometimes the old parts of the castle were given new functions to suit new, peaceful pursuits. At Framlingham (Fig. 26), the 'prison tower' in the lower court had originally been reached from a raised passage from the postern-gate in the western face of the curtain wall; in the sixteenth century this passage was given new windows with much larger openings and turned into a kind of gallery which served as a leisurely approach to the lower court, now converted into gardens. On the opposite side of the castle, stone battlements were topped with new brick chimneys, some of them

*26 Framlingham Castle, Suffolk. The early sixteenth-century brick chimneys over the east side of the curtain wall were part of the domestication of the castle.*

*LEFT 25 Coughton Court, Warwickshire. Tudor bay windows jutting out from the gatehouse of c. 1518–35.*

*LEFT 27   Skipton Castle, North Yorkshire. The Tudor windows
and doorways in the courtyard set the pattern for the continued
domestication of the medieval castle into the seventeenth century.*

*ABOVE 28   Thornbury Castle, Avon. The privy lodgings range,
with sets of apartments above and below, finished before 1521. The
bay windows are similar to those once found at royal buildings of
this period, suggesting the possibility of their having been designed
by the Royal Works.*

purely decorative in function. At Belvoir Castle in
Leicestershire, held by the Manners family, Earls
of Rutland, the keep itself was put to new use;
Leland recounts how 'the dungeon is a faire rounde
tower tournid to pleasure, as a place to walk yn,
and to se al the countrey aboute, and raylid about
the round (waull and) a garden (plot) in the
middle'.[31]

Whilst there is no certain evidence, it seems
possible that Dudley Castle was transformed in the
same way, as the fourteenth-century 'keep' was
isolated from John Dudley's new hall and
adjoining range across the open court. The castles
of Hornby, Belvoir and Dudley are all situated
on rising ground where the keep had always been
the dominant structure; clearly the terrain was
important in enabling the lord to preserve a sense
of social dominance whilst enjoying the irregular

spread of newer buildings beyond the castle walls
possible in more peaceful times. Those who
owned castles on low-lying, or more gently rising
ground often preserved the strong outer walls of
the old structure (though now perhaps pierced by
larger Tudor windows), but built new, well-lit and
well-appointed ranges around the internal
courtyards. At Allington, in Kent, the Wyatts
bisected the great court of the thirteenth-century
castle by a gallery range which linked sets of
lodgings in two distinct parts of the building. At
Skipton, in North Yorkshire (Fig. 27), the
Cliffords, Earls of Cumberland, undertook extensive alterations in Conduit Court. Begun in about
1535, these changes involved the addition of large
and splendid bay windows to the hall and new
gallery ranges.[32]

Two 'castles' built almost completely anew de-
serve special attention. At Thornbury, now in
Avon (Fig. 28), Edward Stafford, Duke of
Buckingham, constructed a new castle on the site
of a relatively modest manor house in the years
1507/8 to 1521. It was planned on a huge scale and
Stafford's enemies clearly perceived it as reflecting
his pretensions to royal status, as the Duke was
cousin to the King and the premier nobleman of
England at that time. The huge castellated towers
planned for the entry to the base court looked west

across the Stafford lands towards the Avon estuary. Behind them, facing south, was the privy garden, bounded by the private lodgings with their splendid bays and by the wall of the churchyard and galleries on the other three sides. In contrast to the image of the towers, this was a world of gentle sports and of leisurely perambulation.[33]

At Basing, in Hampshire, William Paulet rebuilt the castle he acquired by marriage to Constance, heiress to the de Poynings family, during the 1530s. At the same time he manoeuvred to secure for himself his wife's family title to the barony of St John, which had fallen into abeyance in the fifteenth century. Thus, though his title was new in the personal sense, Paulet probably thought of himself as a member of the established aristocracy. His great circular brick castle, some 300 feet in diameter, was one of the most extraordinary buildings of its time. Though its ruins remain and the site has been extensively excavated more than once, particularly in recent years, we have no accurate visual record of what it looked like when first completed. The gatehouse stood on the north side of the great circular enclosure with two sets of turrets, the outer pair detached from the body of the building. Within the circle of the outer wall, the buildings were irregularly placed around a wedge-shaped courtyard; the cellar to the great hall survives as also do some of the ovens and fireplaces in the kitchens to the west of the hall. Basing is perhaps the only example of a castle where defensive measures appear to have been taken seriously, for royal commissioners came to observe construction work here in 1535 before leaving for Calais to investigate the state of the town's defences. Moreover, the strength of the castle was later to be put to the test, for during the Civil War of the 1640s it withstood a siege of nearly two years before being captured by the Parliamentary forces. It would, however, be wrong to suppose that Basing was simply a grim and fortified place, for Paulet was equally aware of the need to compete with the comfort and splendour of the houses of his contemporaries. In the 1550s or 1560s he added a 'new house' within the great encircling wall of the castle. Excavations have shown that it consisted of a single great range and it was probably intended to rival the great hall range at Dudley and the new range of lodgings recently constructed for Sir Anthony Browne at Battle Abbey.[34]

The taste for chivalric display, and in particular the extensive use of heraldry, influenced everyone in positions of power in Tudor England. Nevertheless, by the last decade of Henry VIII's reign there is a sense that this particular phase in the revival of the chivalric ideal was coming to an end.[35] This could be seen as a breathing-space before the later, Elizabethan cult. In Elizabeth's time the pursuit of chivalry became more literary and artificial and was prompted very directly by the need to encourage a cult of deference and loyalty around the Virgin Queen herself. From a modern standpoint it appears to have been even more self-consciously backward-looking and self-knowingly removed from reality than that of the early Tudor age, even nostalgic in character.[36] This was partly because the practical momentum for the revival of chivalric values had been lost. The age of Henry VIII was the last time when ideals associated with England's medieval and feudal past were played out on the battlefield. His three major engagements against France were the last phase of a spirit of adventurous conquest that originated in the Hundred Years War.

New technology was changing the nature of warfare and, as a result, the role of those who took part was also assuming a different shape. The foreign wars of the 1540s (when England, now isolated from the greatest powers of Catholic Europe, felt itself to be on the defensive) led to what was effectively the first standing army and this began to undermine the last remains of feudal allegiances among the ranks of the military. The signs of personal loyalty, such as the badges identifying soldiers as servants of a particular lord, remained important throughout the Tudor period, but they would eventually be replaced by uniforms which focused men's loyalties on units in the national army. Men-at-arms were now increasingly servants of the sovereign rather than of their immediate overlords.[37]

Similarly, unless sited on vulnerable coasts, most castles no longer served as the military and regional power bases of the local lord, but they might well be used later in the century as a place of delight and nostalgia to entertain Queen Elizabeth. On her third and last visit to the castle of Kenilworth in 1575, an elaborate ceremony was devised to welcome the Queen. The significance of each gate and courtyard of the castle was marked by a contrived incident as she passed through; at the tiltyard gate a porter offered her the keys, at the gate of the inner court a poet extolled her in verse.[38] This was a ceremony devised for a special occasion, but even on an everyday level people in Tudor England would have been used to regarding the parts of a great courtyard in terms of both their practical and their symbolic significance.

# 4

# The Courtyard and the Household

THE APPEARANCE and functions of the courtyard of an early Tudor house would have
had some similarities with the courtyards
of the coaching inns of England in the days before
motor vehicles. This was a place where horses
would be left for stabling, where people would
gather and go their separate ways. The various
activities going on in the courtyard would express
the communal life of those currently in residence
and the enclosure would impart a sense of security;
this was a public space that could be looked down
into for information on what was happening, for
news, or for early warning of a new arrival, or of
external danger. Architecturally, various functions
of the building came together in the courtyard and
were stylistically distinguished; a porch or covered
way in front of the entrance hall would signify the
more public, more important part of the building
in contrast to the kitchen, offices and storerooms
in an adjacent or facing range. The interior facades
might therefore have doors and windows of different sizes and roof levels of varying height. They
could, however, be given a semblance of unity,
despite their different functions, by common
architectural ornament; the sense of visual order
imposed in this way could thus disguise a range of
functions and suggest that all parts of the household
presented a unified face to the outside world.

The majority of large-scale domestic buildings
of the early sixteenth century were formed around
one or more courtyards. These would usually
consist of a main court with hall, family apartments
and principal service rooms and a 'base' court of
further lodgings, perhaps for servants considered
of lower status, as well as stables and storage buildings. This was effectively the last and most sophisticated phase of the use of the courtyard plan,
before it was gradually abandoned in favour of the
outward-looking format of later great houses.[1] The

greater number of the most fashionable courtyard
houses in the southeast and Midlands of England
(usually newly-built, although often on older sites)
were of brick in this period and very much reflected
courtier taste. These are the buildings for which
we tend to have the most information and whose
patrons are most vividly recorded by documentary
evidence (Fig. 29), but their layout and organization
would have been echoed in lesser houses throughout the country, wherever one or more people
waited upon and served someone else. In a fundamental sense, the architecture of the courtyard is a
practical demonstration of life in great households
at this time. Although what follows is largely
based on buildings owned by courtiers, it is true in
some degree for many different kinds of houses in
England as a whole and this is confirmed as the
custom and practice of the period in written, practical advice about the spiritual and physical
well-being of households.

While the courtyard became the key element in
house planning, it had long been used as a way of
organizing ranges of buildings with various functions. Within the irregular walls of some of the
earliest medieval castles the chief domestic rooms
were often informally grouped around a court.
This was so at Sherborne in Dorset, where apartments were built for Roger, Bishop of Salisbury
from 1107 to 1139; at Corfe Castle in the same
county, where King John had domestic apartments
raised at the beginning of the thirteenth century;
and, most emphatically, at Windsor in the mid
fourteenth century when lodgings were built for
Edward III and his wife Philippa of Hainault.[2] But
the origins of many later medieval courtyard houses
can be found in the gradual and rather informal
expansion of a single range. Projecting wings and
then eventually a fourth, enclosing range would be
added to the original hall and basic service rooms.

STANDON-LORDSHIP

To the Right Hono.ble
and truely Noble
WALTER Lord ASTON
Baron of FORFARE in the
Kingdom of SCOTLAND.
This Draught Shewing
the Front and Side Prospect of
STANDON LordSHIP
is most humbly Dedicated by J: Drapentier

*29 Standon, Hertfordshire. A compact brick courtyard house of the 1540s as seen in 1700. Only a fragment of the gatehouse range now survives.*

One of the most important surviving houses showing just this development is Haddon Hall in Derbyshire. Here a new hall range was added to an earlier house in about 1370 and the double courtyard building that remains today took shape during the course of the fifteenth and early sixteenth centuries. The last phase of this development happened during Henry VIII's reign, when the house was lived in by Sir William Coffin, a Gentleman of the Privy Chamber and Master of the Horse to two of Henry's queens, Anne Boleyn and Jane Seymour. He used the house by virtue of his guardianship of his stepson, George Vernon, and it is usually thought that the lodging ranges of the outer court and the great northwest tower were built at this time, completing the enclosed space. (The state rooms were altered and the long gallery created in Elizabethan times, but without basically changing the double-courtyard plan.)[3] Further north, Wharton Hall in Cumbria (Fig. 30) is another example of a single-range house which grew into a courtyard complex in early Tudor times over a period of about twenty years. Here a quite simple hall-house with cross wings was extended after 1540, with the addition of a new great hall and kitchen, a range of domestic apartments and finally a strong gatehouse; though it is generally true that defences were becoming increasingly less necessary, gatehouses were noticeably more defensible the further north a house was situated. Wharton Hall was not only far from London and the control of the King (so that local magnates would be more likely to resort to brute force to settle matters of dispute if all else failed), but was also in a part of the country that was vulnerable to attacks from the Scots.[4]

In houses in the Midlands and south of England, the fourth, enclosing range might not always be a prominent feature like a great gatehouse. It might simply be a high wall facing the hall with a modest gateway at its centre. After Sir Walter Stonor recovered his house of Stonor in Oxfordshire (Fig. 31) in 1535, following a lawsuit against the resident Fortescue family, he modified it by extending the wings to the hall and adding a wall with a central gate; a previously irregular agglomeration of separate buildings was given an enclosed forecourt and a sense of self-containment.[5] Even at some of the largest great houses built at this period the sense of enclosure was created by a forecourt, with three main ranges of buildings and perhaps a low enclosing wall on the fourth side, rather than by building

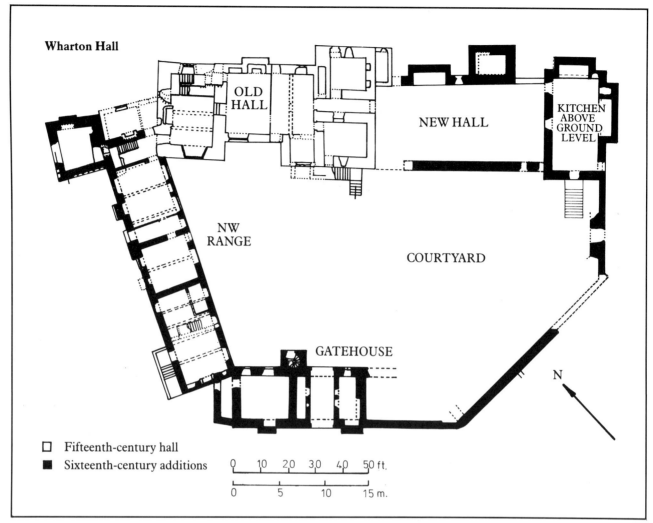

ABOVE 30  Wharton Hall, Cumbria. A fifteenth-century hall with cross wings was extended to create a courtyard house.

RIGHT 31  Stonor House, Oxfordshire. A diagrammatic reconstruction of how the medieval house was successively enlarged.

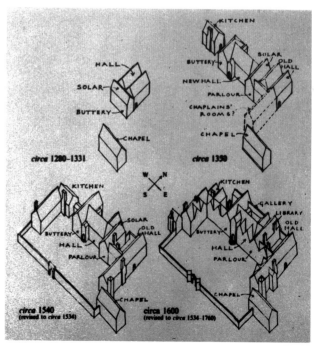

a prominent gatehouse range; notable examples from the reign of Henry VII are the brick houses of Bradgate, near Leicester (now mostly a scant but romantic ruin), built for the Grey family, who were Marquises of Dorset, and Tong in Shropshire, built for Sir Henry Vernon, and described by Leland as 'an olde castel of stone new al of brike' (completely vanished and known to us only from the Bucks' eighteenth-century print).[6]

The addition of great ranges of lodgings to previously modest hall-houses must have similarly given the impression of a large, but informal fore-court rather than a fully-enclosed courtyard. Very similar developments of this kind happened, for example, at two houses in very different parts of the country. At Chenies, in Buckinghamshire (Fig. 32), Sir John Russell added certainly one and probably two ranges of lodgings at right angles to his fifteenth-century house. At Samelsbury, in Lancashire (Fig. 33), the same thing happened. At each house, one range survives, though heavily restored; both examples are essentially of brick, though Samelsbury is fronted on its north side with a nineteenth-century re-creation of the patterned timber-framing familiar to the northwest of England.[7]

So in many cases a courtyard was created in response to a need to expand the building. The result might still be quite an informal grouping of ranges, perhaps irregularly planned, and sometimes having to take account of rising ground, as at Haddon. However, the most characteristic form of early Tudor house, the form which marks the high-water mark of the evolution of the courtyard,

is rather different. A great many completely newly-built examples of early sixteenth-century houses in the south and the Midlands of England show a more single-minded approach and were planned as courtyards from the beginning. Equal importance was given to the hall and the facing gatehouse range and there was a sense of these opposite ranges balancing each other, signified by equality of height and a similar degree of ornament and heraldry. Often the side wings also shared a common roof level with the main ranges. Most of these buildings are low-lying and they sometimes resulted from rebuilding on a moated site.

*BELOW 32  Chenies, Buckinghamshire. The courtyard side of the heavily restored lodgings range of the 1530s. At the back of this range are privies and closets (see Fig. 60).*

*OVERLEAF 33  Samelsbury, Lancashire. The lodgings range built by Sir Thomas Southworth, probably in the 1540s. The patterned timber-framing is a nineteenth-century re-interpretation of the original.*

But houses built all of a piece in this way, the opposite of the varied and irregular patterns just discussed, were not a completely new development; it is more a question of a practice that was once unusual being adopted more generally for prestigious buildings. Much of the compactness of the regular Tudor courtyard plan is heralded in an important sequence of moated medieval domestic buildings. Chief among these are Bodiam Castle in East Sussex (built from 1386 to 1388), Herstmonceux Castle, also in East Sussex (built in the 1440s and 1450s) and Oxburgh Hall, Norfolk (after 1482) (see Fig. 20). Both Herstmonceux and Oxburgh are brick buildings and in both cases only the outer shell of the original house survives. However, unlike Bodiam, the courtyard facades and interiors were rebuilt following fires and other changes and they are still habitable. Bodiam, on the other hand, is now only a ruined shell. Fourthly, there is the lost Shelton Hall, also in Norfolk, built around 1480 and known to us from an eighteenth-century drawing. These four buildings show no consistent development in late medieval architecture, and they are in no sense individually typical of their age or region of the country. Collectively, however, they are examples of houses where the confines of the moated site determined the limit of building from the start and where the extent of the house is defined by high outer walls, in contrast to those houses where the courtyard shape developed from the centre outwards in an unplanned way.[8]

At each of these four houses, the outer walls formed a sort of regular, containing box which encompassed the whole site. The rooms within might or might not be regularly arranged, but in every case they tended to be reflected on the exterior, most notably with window openings, bringing a sense of domesticity to the severity of the outer walls. All four of these buildings were provided with domestic comforts, though they all have great gatehouses and retained the outward appearance of defensibility long after this was practically possible or necessary. They were the perfect recipe for the pretentious house of the early Tudor age; domestic comfort within walls which gave the semblance of age, authority and power. In so far as we can tell from the present ruined structure, the plan of the great moated courtyard of Bodiam was especially single-minded. The entrance hall was situated opposite the gatehouse range and there was a clear division between a 'service' side of the court (kitchens, buttery, rooms for the main servants of the household) and a side of 'state' (rooms for the lord and his family and guest apartments); this prefigured later Tudor practice quite closely.

The collegiate foundations of the fifteenth and early sixteenth centuries were even closer in plan to Tudor courtyard houses. Late medieval building works at the colleges of Oxford and Cambridge paralleled those of country houses in two important ways. First, their endowment was often due to a single great patron, sometimes the King or a member of the immediate royal circle, sometimes a leading statesman-bishop. The guiding presence of these figures meant that they employed the same architects, or master masons, as had worked on their houses. Similarly, the size, architectural decoration and heraldry of the colleges was intended to celebrate the power and magnificence of these individuals much as their great country houses were meant to do.[9] Second, the colleges needed the same range of accommodation as a country house in order to house large communities. They needed to include a large number of small individual rooms for the most dependent ranks (the students), larger and better appointed rooms for those of higher status (the fellows), a set of quite luxurious apartments for the head of the establishment (the Master, or President) and great communal spaces for the whole household to eat and worship together.

In the details of the plan, traditions in Oxford and Cambridge diverged. From the time of the building of New College in the fourteenth century, Oxford colleges took the form of a great cloistered court, with hall and chapel in alignment behind it.[10] This form was followed down to the time of the most ambitious of all Oxford colleges, Wolsey's Cardinal College of the 1520s (Fig. 34). The cloister planned for the entrance court here was matched in size only by the great cloister at the largest Carthusian monastic establishments, notably the Charterhouse in London. The blind arcades to be seen today are a reminder that the cloister walks were never completed before the Cardinal's fall in 1529 or after the college's subsequent re-foundation as Christ Church.

Cloistered courts were not unknown at Cambridge, but tended to be restricted to secondary, inner courts. The outer courts of colleges here, however, took on a shape that was remarkably like those of early Tudor courtyard houses. A turreted gatehouse was built to face the entrance to the hall, with the usual upper end of the hall leading to the

34 *Christ Church, Oxford (known as Cardinal College in the 1520s). A detail of the great court as built by Wolsey's masons John Lubbyns and Henry Redman by 1529. The one-storey cloister that was intended to project into the court was never completed.*

most important 'private' apartments and the lower end leading to buttery and kitchens. Cambridge colleges were also extensively built in brick, which continued to be the dominant material used for fashionable courtier and episcopal domestic building in the early sixteenth century. The use of brick at Cambridge began with the first court at Queens', built in 1448–9, and this was followed most notably by Christ's, re-founded and largely rebuilt after 1505, and St John's, founded in 1511. At Christ's the original brick ranges are almost completely concealed by a later facing in ashlar.[11]

The more tightly planned and compact the shape of the courtyard, the more likely it is to reflect a radical and perhaps total rebuilding in early Tudor times. Houses that were added to tended to be more sprawling, less rationalized. This generalization is borne out by evidence from the bishops' palaces and royal houses of this period. Some of the most ambitious schemes undertaken by bishops involved enlarging an old house by remodelling a cramped and usually moated site and adding a huge outer court to it to meet the need for extensive lodgings. Three of the houses of the Archbishops of Canterbury were altered in this way. At Knole, in Kent, Archbishop Bourchier added an outer court of timber with a stone gatehouse at its entry to a small manor house in the years after 1456; this is the present Stone Court, so called after it was later given a stone facing. An outer brick service court was added to the Archbishop's palace of Croydon, also in the second half of the fifteenth century. The third great house, Otford in Kent (Fig. 10), was extended by Archbishop Warham in the second decade of the sixteenth century. He constructed a new great court with a two-storeyed gallery giving on to it on the west, whilst rooms of lodging behind looked outwards on to a pleasure garden. In each of these three cases the new court was built almost square in plan but the earlier, more private court to which it gave access, though perhaps largely rebuilt, had a rather random arrangement of structures determined by earlier, unplanned growth.[12]

With the building of Wolsey's Hampton Court a sense of an overall rationale becomes more evident and the familiar early Tudor plan begins to emerge. Hampton Court also involved an extension to an older moated site, but the new court of lodgings was directly aligned with the rebuilt inner court. Hall and chapel were also planned in alignment with each other.[13] As we have seen, many of these bishops' houses became royal property; indeed Hampton Court became one of Henry VIII's chief palaces. It seems that the first Tudor royal palaces were very similar in plan to episcopal residences. What we would term the subsidiary parts of the domestic establishment, the service and lodging quarters, were built with some regularity of plan, but the royal apartments of state were an agglomeration of separate buildings. This is particularly true of Richmond, the first of the great new Tudor palaces; the service areas were made up of courtyards but the royal apartments were housed in a structure more like a great medieval keep, built in a different material. Given the lack of English precedents and Henry VII's conscious attempt to rival European monarchs, this design has been compared with the French idea of a *corps-de-logis* (great keep or tower of lodgings).[14]

In the same way that the building of Hampton Court marked a new direction in bishops' houses, so there was a turning-point in the development of royal buildings and it comes, interestingly, with the building of a completely new structure, Henry VIII's palace of Nonsuch (Fig. 35), begun in 1538. This was a highly compact two-courtyard building and its plan echoes the sense of order that is apparent at Hampton Court. These buildings suggest that a designer has been at the drawing board and devised them as an integral whole. At Nonsuch, as we know from excavation, the two main courts were approximately the same width, as were the enclosing ranges with the exception of the chief royal apartments at the rear of the second court.[15]

But the plan of a building like Nonsuch is to some extent deceptive and we should not assume that what was planned rationally was experienced as such from the ground. A seventeenth-century painting shows that the first court was rather conventional and even old-fashioned in appearance, with castellations and turrets like earlier buildings. But the second court, built on a higher level and approached by a flight of steps out of the first court, was quite different. Both the facades facing the court and those looking out on to the gardens and park were covered by the famous and extraordinary scheme of figurative stuccoes illustrating classical stories and by decorative carved slate. These were designed to amaze and impress the visitor and would have given a completely different visual and intellectual challenge from the appearance of the first court (see Fig. 72). Nonsuch is a unique building in the history of English architecture for many reasons, not least because of its internal plan. In particular, both excavation and the chief sixteenth- and seventeenth-century accounts of it suggest that there was no conventional great hall. Visually, it suggests that there was no contradiction in juxtaposing the ordinary and serviceable with the curious and splendid, a characteristic that it shares with other buildings of this time.[16]

The loss of the unique decorative splendour of the second court at Nonsuch leaves one kind of gap in our knowledge of great Tudor houses, but, more typically, it is the loss of buildings at the opposite end of the spectrum, the working service areas, that can mislead us just as much. Most surviving Tudor houses originally also had outer courts of timber and these impermanent service buildings have now almost entirely disappeared. What survives at houses like Compton Wynyates is simply the brick inner court; a visitor approaching such a house in the early sixteenth century would not have seen a building entirely constructed in the same material. The survival of the service buildings at Hampton Court is exceptional and is entirely due to the fact that Wolsey and Henry VIII could afford to construct them in the relatively permanent material of brick. The palace is the best example of a house where we can see main courts with important lodgings and rooms of state and also multiple service courts (in this instance to the north), which housed particular functions of the great household. Another extraordinary survival of a service court is that at the great Carthusian monastery of Charterhouse in London (Fig. 36), which became the post-dissolution house of Sir Edward North after 1545. Here again, the use of permanent materials, in this case brick and stone, ensured survival.[17] Visual records can give us some idea of the outbuildings which have disappeared at other houses.

The artist and topographer Kip's views of great English houses, published in the early eighteenth century, include a number of Tudor buildings which were then still in existence but which have been demolished since. One of these, still largely intact 250 years ago (only a fragment of the stable range remains today), was the house of Rycote in Oxfordshire (Fig. 37), whose moat was mentioned in the previous chapter. Kip's view shows clearly that some of the windows of the main part of the house were altered during the course of the seventeenth century and the gardens and terraces around also speak of later changes. However, there are telling details which betray the Tudor origins of the house; stepped gable ends, round-headed doorways, small windows and familiar sixteenth-century fireplace projections with huge chimney-stacks. All these features figure prominently in the substantial Tudor outbuildings to the west of the principal courtyards. Kip's view also points the contrast between the formal and integrally

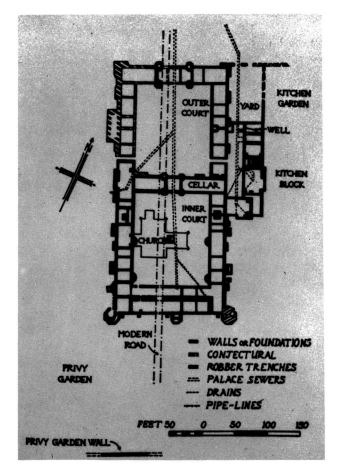

*35  Nonsuch Palace. Plan of Henry VIII's building of 1538–47 as excavated in 1959–60.*

planned great court and the more random placing of ancilliary buildings, which spread wherever necessary.[18]

However, Kip's view of Rycote is a highly sophisticated image from a later period. A particularly rare contemporary record of another Tudor house, Shurland, on the Isle of Sheppey, is rather closer to the original idea of a Tudor multi-court-yard house (see colour plates). Today only the entrance range to the main court remains, until recently in a ruinous and very sorry condition. The view drawn for the royal survey of 1572 is particularly significant because of what we know about the circumstances in which it was done. The house and estate had been neglected since the death of the builder, Sir Thomas Cheyney, in 1558, and so it is likely that the house as depicted has been very little modified since it was first built in the 1520s. Documentary evidence also tells us about the size of the early Tudor household at Shurland. Cheyney is said to have kept 'ordinarilie eight score serving men, besides retayners, gentlemen and others that

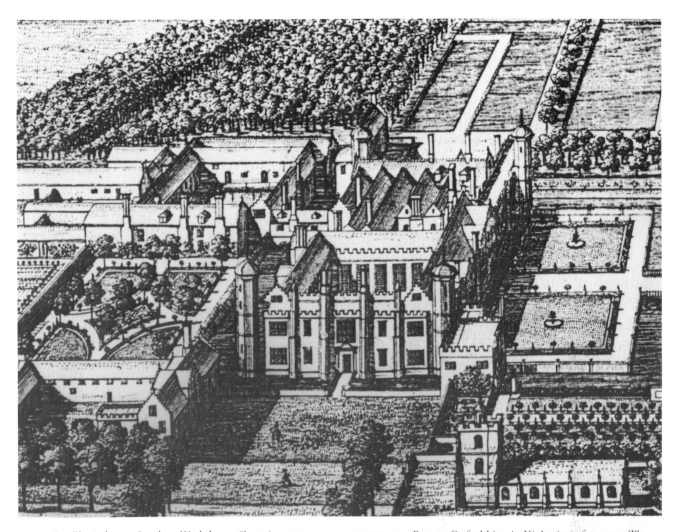

*LEFT 36  Charterhouse, London. Wash-house Court is a rare survival of a Tudor service court. The mixture of brick and stone suggests it may have been incomplete at the surrender of 1537 and finished by Sir Edward North.*

*ABOVE 37  Rycote, Oxfordshire, in Kip's view of c. 1720. The basic plan of the early Tudor house clearly remained, with original doorways and chimneystacks, though the formal gardens are seventeenth-century.*

were ready for all types of service, or danger of invasion, numbering at least 400 persons'.[19]

The view illustrated here, looking from the west, shows how so large a household was lodged, partly in base court lodgings beyond the gatehouse range, but also in large secondary courts to the north of the house (at the left of the illustration). The number of 'informal' approaches and entrances to the house, both internal and external, is also striking. Apart from those leading into and between the courts to the north of the main axis, there is also one on the south side (in the range on the right-hand side of the main courts, just at the point where the survey-maker stops filling in the brickwork and it becomes blank walling). The lodgings in the first court beyond the gatehouse seem to be accessible not just through the main gatehouse but also from side entrances outside the enclosing wall of the forecourt (in the two gable-ended ranges to the left and right of the gatehouse). These side entrances suggest that the gatehouse with its lodge was not the only point of entry to the house and that not every Tudor visitor would have approached Shurland along the axis shown in this bird's eye view. It is true, however, that the main gatehouse would have had a certain prominence because it was built on rising ground.

The last chapter looked at the way in which the trappings of defence remained a telling sign of attitudes to past values whilst no longer of themselves providing any real, practical protection against attack. But even if the need for self-defence was less urgent, the courtyard house still expressed something of the singular nature and self-sufficiency that had been true of the great house as a community in medieval times. Each household was an important network of allegiances between those within it and demonstrated on a small scale the hierarchy of people in society at large. Later in the sixteenth century the courtier and political theorist Sir Thomas Smith was to define the household as 'the man, the woman, their children, their servants bond and free, their cattle, their household stuff and all other things which are reckoned in their possession'.[20] All these had to be sheltered and found a place in or around the courtyard house.

The lord of the house was judged by his social peers according to his ability to keep his house in order. In 1534, Sir Francis Bryan wrote to Lord Lisle, the Deputy at Calais: 'as I am informed, you are no good husband in the keeping of your house, which is a great undoing of many men; therefore I would advise you to look upon it, and to consider that in taking good heed, you may do yourself

pleasure and your friends also.' (Bryan was inferior to his correspondent in rank of nobility, but effectively superior to him as one of the most favoured Gentlemen of the King's Privy Chamber.)[21] The lord was the moral guide and head of his household just as his apartments stood at the head of the courtyard plan. This was a time when governmental decrees were increasingly having a direct effect on everyone's life and the royal will was transmitted to the servants of a household through the authority of the lord. In October 1538, Lord Lisle received a letter from John Hussee, his agent in London, enclosing certain articles that 'shall be requisite to set up in every place within your house: as, hall, chamber, gate and other offices in the house, to the end that your lordship, being head, may be a light to the inferiors'.[22] Hussee here indicates what were considered to be the key places of communication within the great house and the symbolic importance of the role of the lord.

The various occupations within the household are revealed in surviving household regulations and certain day-to-day accounts which list wages, provisions and clothing for all servants as well as making very clear the specific duties attached to each position. Inventories also tell us a great deal about the subtleties of relative status. The quality of a servant's lodgings, their privacy or lack of it, and the value and material comfort of the furnishings which they enjoyed were a very fine measure of the perceived pecking order. There was clearly a recognized difference between the lower servants, whose tasks were menial and repetitive, and those who served the lord and his family directly; this distinction to some extent echoed the division at the Court itself, where the household below stairs (of cooks, accountants and waiters at table), was distinct from that above stairs (where the personal attendants to the King were members of his Privy Chamber and were amongst the most powerful in the land).[23]

In some inventories, the rooms slept in by the lower servants are named after the function of the occupant, such as the 'room for the porter', whilst the rooms of the upper servants are given the personal names of the people concerned. Usually the lowest and youngest of the servants, and often all the women (except the personal attendants of the lady of the house) shared rooms. In fact large Tudor households still consisted mainly of men, a vestige of days when great houses were principally military strongholds. Men still invariably did the complete range of domestic tasks, with the general exception it seems of the laundry.[24] According to the inventory of 1542 the women servants at

Sutton Place all shared a room and so did the 'lads' of the kitchen, along with the fool who bedded down with them. The porters who looked after the gatehouse entry were not classed among the higher servants, even though their job was crucial in guarding admission to the lord's house. However, they were far from being the most menial of all; inventories invariably inform us that the porter was better housed than other servants who tended the house and grounds. In the 1575 inventory of Lacock Abbey, the porter's bed was valued more highly than that of the gardener, at one shilling and sixpence as opposed to one shilling, and he also had more bedding and other furniture. Sometimes houses had a permanent maintenance staff; in early Tudor times there was a resident joiner at Sutton Place, a glazier at Compton Wynyates and masons at both Sutton Place and Hornby Castle, Lancashire, the newly reconstructed home of the Stanleys, Lords Mounteagle.[25]

The disposition of rooms within the courtyard originated in the basic division of the household in medieval times. The life of the lord, his family and guests (increasingly made more private by the provision of separate rooms) was quite distinct from that of the servants. This division is apparent in the reconstruction of Temple Newsam in Yorkshire (Fig. 38), where the house is centred on the conventional hall with upper and lower ends. In the great courtyard house these 'state' and 'service' sides were extended into projecting wings that eventually turned at right angles to run parallel to the hall and meet at the gatehouse.

No house today can show us a complete interior with anything like its original room spaces and furnishings to demonstrate this basic division. Even at Compton Wynyates, a rare survival of a complete brick courtyard, the rooms within have been altered somewhat in later centuries as needs changed. In some instances, however, a part of the building still demonstrates well one particular aspect of the composite nature of the house and its operations. At Haddon, for example, we can still see the room that must have been the most frequently used of the early Tudor set of family apartments, the panelled and painted low parlour off the high end of the hall. By contrast, at Holme Pierrepont in Nottinghamshire (Fig. 39), probably built in the first years of the sixteenth century for Sir William Pierrepont, only the brick entrance range of the original Tudor courtyard house still remains. Recent restoration work within this range has uncovered almost identical sets of lodgings set one above the other.[26]

Quite a number of houses retain enough archi-

tecturally and internally to be very instructive, notably Hengrave in Suffolk and Cotehele in Cornwall. The plan of Cotehele (Fig. 40) shows how the house grew over two generations of the Edgcumbe family in the early Tudor period ending up as a main courtyard with two subsidiary courts. The building becomes relatively more showy and ambitious; Sir Piers Edgcumbe's post 1500 new block with parlour below and solar above presses up against and overshadows the east end of his father's chapel (Fig. 41). Where surviving architectural evidence of whatever kind is matched by a contemporary inventory, we can get closer still to the daily lives of those who lived in these buildings.

Inventories were generally drawn up at the death of the owner, but would usually also be compiled if he were charged with treason, since a traitor's goods were forfeit to the Crown. These documents are lists of contents; they are useful for architectural history simply because it was usually convenient to list contents under the name of each room and also, to facilitate the task of the cataloguer, leading from one room to another. So we can often assume that the order of rooms as listed in the inventory reflects the actual order of rooms in the house and this helps to reconstruct the plan. It is not always clear where the inventory moves on to a different floor since stairs, having no 'contents', are not usually mentioned, though they may be referred to incidentally in a description such as the 'chamber at the stair head'.

Among the group of courtyard houses newly built for great courtiers, five in particular can be said to match sufficient surviving architectural evidence (in one case a reconstruction from archaeological work) with an inventory, and are usefully placed in different regions of the country: Sutton Place in Surrey, in the Thames Valley region and within the orbit of London; Ingatestone in Essex; Thornbury Castle in Avon; Compton Wynyates in Warwickshire; and Temple Newsam in Yorkshire.[27] Three of these were inventoried very soon after they were completed. The other two, Ingatestone and Temple Newsam, were inventoried later in the sixteenth century, but the names of the rooms used suggest that their internal layout had not altered very much as the century progressed. At several other houses enough architectural evidence survives to reconstruct their basic internal arrangements. The main courtyards of all these houses show the expected division between state and service sides. However, as none of the service courts has survived, it is sometimes unclear in some cases whether the inventory leads off into a secondary court.

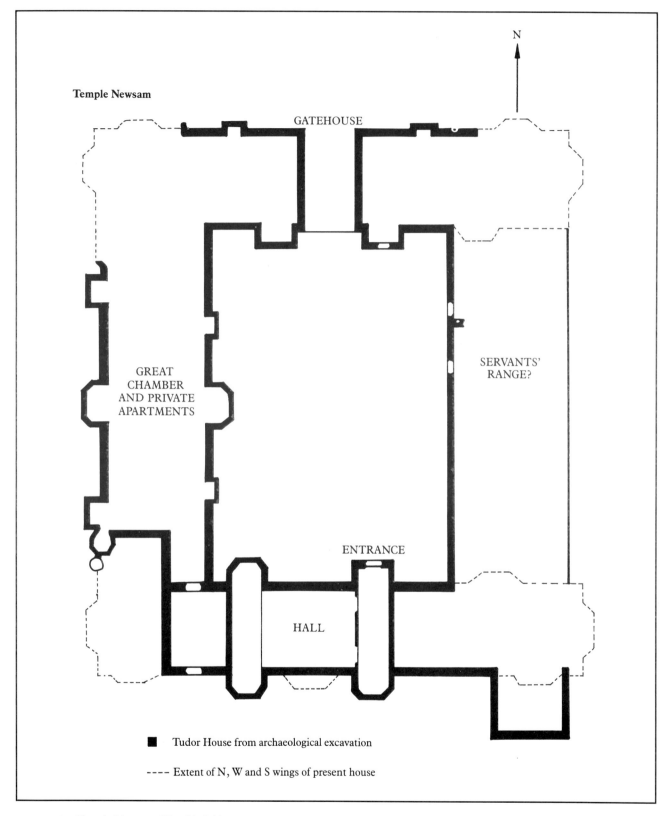

**Temple Newsam**

N

GATEHOUSE

GREAT
CHAMBER
AND PRIVATE
APARTMENTS

SERVANTS'
RANGE?

ENTRANCE

HALL

■ Tudor House from archaeological excavation

- - - - Extent of N, W and S wings of present house

*ABOVE 38  Temple Newsam, West Yorkshire, c. 1520–35.
Conjectural plan of Lord Darcy's pre-1537 house based on
excavations and the inventory of 1565.*

*RIGHT 39  Holme Pierrepont, Nottinghamshire. The early
sixteenth-century lodgings, with brick parapets added in c. 1800,
when the front was also stuccoed (removed only in 1975).*

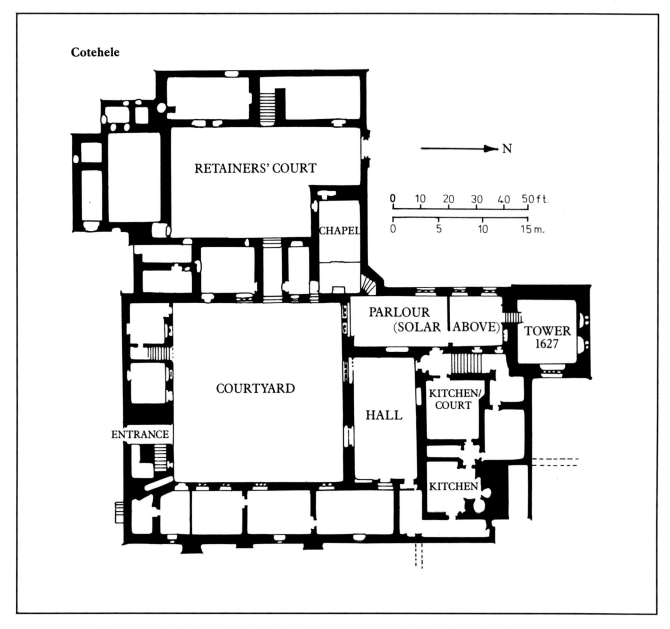

Cotehele

RETAINERS' COURT

CHAPEL

N

0  10  20  30  40  50 ft.

0      5      10      15 m.

PARLOUR
(SOLAR ABOVE)

TOWER
1627

COURTYARD

HALL

KITCHEN/
COURT

ENTRANCE

KITCHEN

ABOVE 40  Cotehele, Cornwall. The house of Sir Richard and Sir Piers Edgcumbe, 1485–1539. Sir Richard remodelled and expanded the two main courtyards of the thirteenth- to fourteenth-century house, moving the entrance to the south side. Sir Piers completed the hall, the parlour wing and the buildings around Kitchen Court.

RIGHT 41  Cotehele, Cornwall. The northeast corner of the main court, with the chapel on the left. The granite is cut very fine (ashlared) around the parlour and solar windows.

At Thornbury (Fig. 42), the state/service divide is more emphatic than at the other houses. The apartments for the Duke and Duchess of Buckingham take up the upper and lower floors of the south side of the inner court, leading off from the upper end of the vanished great hall, and also look outwards on to a privy garden as if to stress their sense of 'separateness' from the communal life of the court behind them.[28] Inventories can sometimes be helpful in clarifying the likely disposition of rooms within the sixteenth-century house. It is unlikely, for example, that the present upper-floor long gallery in the east range at Sutton (Fig. 43) is original in any way. No gallery is mentioned in the inventory of 1542 and the circuit of the east side of the house described in this document lists a great many upstairs rooms between what was clearly a staircase from the 'upper' end of the great hall and the porter's lodge by the gatehouse, allaying any suspicion that a great gallery has somehow been omitted.

Of these five houses, the interior of Compton Wynyates is one of the most interesting (Fig. 44). Though the usage of rooms has changed, the house preserves many original internal room spaces. At the time of the inventory of 1522 the south side of the court led from the 'upper' end of the hall through a parlour (with a chamber above it) to the chapel chamber (leading into the chapel projecting on the south side of the house). The inventory then refers to a nursery, probably on the upper floor, a 'white' chamber and two bed-chambers before the gatehouse was reached. On the north side of the house, starting from the gatehouse which we have just reached from the south, there was the porter's lodge. The inventory then refers to the master receiver's chamber, the steward's chamber, the wardrobe, the yeoman's chamber, leading finally to the kitchen and buttery and the 'lower' end of the hall. It is not clear whether the rooms mentioned after the porter's lodge are on upper or lower floors.

This clear division of the court is recommended by Andrew Boorde, whose writings on the practical and healthy house were quoted in Chapter 1. In his *Dyetary of Health* he wrote: 'Make the hall under such a fasshyon, that the parler be anexed to the heade of the hall. And the buttery and pantry be at the lower ende of the hall, the seller under the pantry, sette somewhat abase; kychen set somewhat a base from the buttry and pantry, commyng with an entry by the wall of the buttry, the pastry house and the larder-howse anexed to the kychen. Then devyde the lodgynges by the cyrcyute of the quadryuall courte, and let the gate-house be opposyt or agaynst the hall-dore (not Dyrectly) but the hall-dore standynge a base, and the gatehouse in the mydle of the front entrynge in to the place....'[29] Compton Wynyates and Sutton Place are exceptions in their period in that they did not reflect Boorde's advice that the hall door should be set out of line with the gatehouse in order to trap winds and draughts within the court so that they did not pass directly from the gate to the main door. In contrast, Cowdray House (Fig. 45) is a prominent example of a contemporary courtyard where the off-centring in the manner of Boorde's advice seems evidently deliberate. Planning of this kind raises questions about symmetry and the visual appearance of the courtyard house.

Some of the architectural features developed at this time to distinguish different parts of the house outlived the fashion for courtyard houses. One such feature was the change in the relationship between the ground and first floors with the upper floor becoming increasingly important. From medieval times onward great houses usually had at least one major room on the upper floor. This was at first called a 'solar', but by the early sixteenth century it was quite often referred to as the 'great chamber' and this became the common name for the main room of state in Elizabethan times. By then the great chamber often formed part of a complete sequence of upper-floor rooms (mirroring what was already normal practice in royal palaces by the early sixteenth century). At the same time the staircase hall emerged to provide a dignified means of approach to this sequence of state rooms. In some houses the once 'great' hall took on the role of a vestibule to the staircase hall on the ground floor.[30]

Two developments in the early Tudor period point to the demise of the great hall as the place where 'state' and 'service' met in the day-to-day life of the house. One was the emergence of what was later to be called the 'double-pile' arrangement, in which a complete sequence of rooms in the hall range provided access behind the hall itself and could be used to bypass it. This arrangement is the rational conclusion of a plan like that of Cotehele (see Fig. 40), where all the building ranges were only one room in depth but where the existence of a tiny court behind the hall suggests the need to circulate around the back of it. The plans of houses such as East Barsham in Norfolk and Hengrave in

42 *Thornbury Castle, Avon. Plan of the inner court of the Duke of Buckingham's building, 1508–21.*

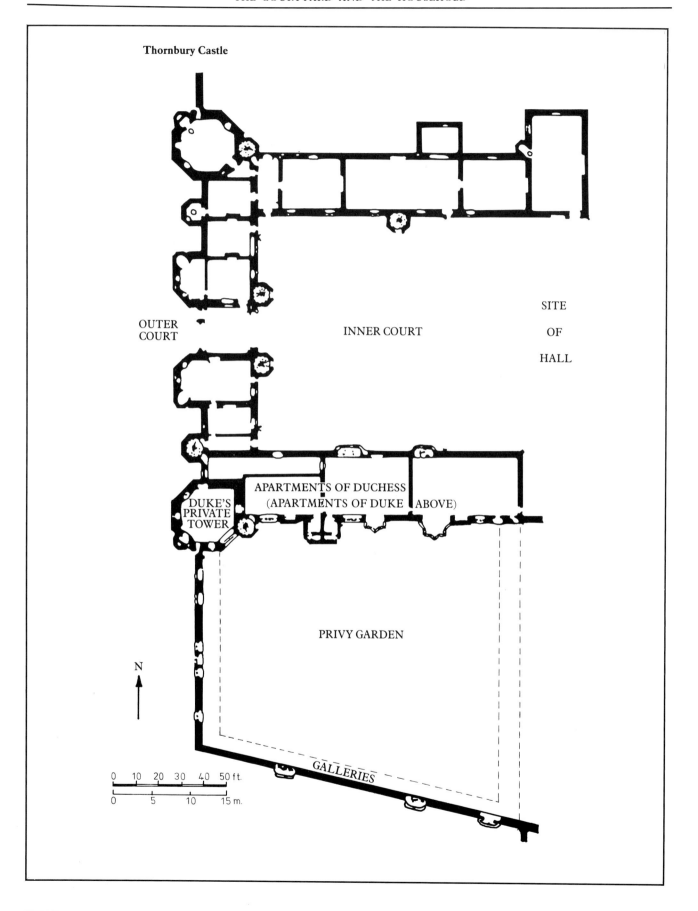

Thornbury Castle

OUTER
COURT

INNER COURT

SITE

OF

HALL

APARTMENTS OF DUCHESS
(APARTMENTS OF DUKE ABOVE)

DUKE'S
PRIVATE
TOWER

PRIVY GARDEN

N

GALLERIES

0  10  20  30  40  50 ft.

0       5       10      15 m.

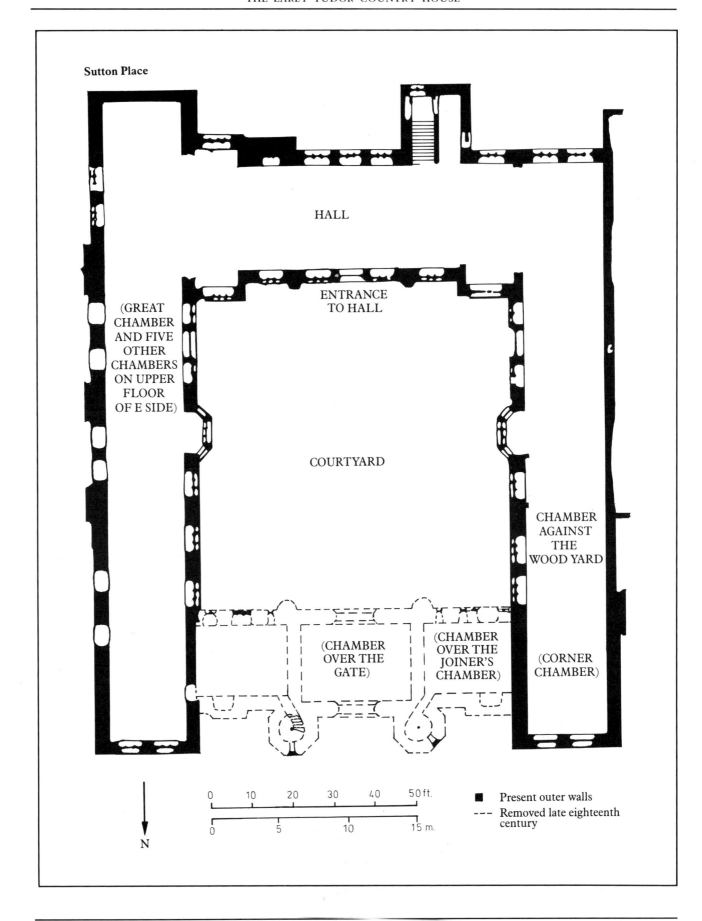

Sutton Place

HALL

ENTRANCE
TO HALL

(GREAT
CHAMBER
AND FIVE
OTHER
CHAMBERS
ON UPPER
FLOOR
OF E SIDE)

COURTYARD

CHAMBER
AGAINST
THE
WOOD YARD

(CHAMBER
OVER THE
GATE)

(CHAMBER
OVER THE
JOINER'S
CHAMBER)

(CORNER
CHAMBER)

0    10    20    30    40    50 ft.

0        5        10        15 m.

N

■   Present outer walls
- - -   Removed late eighteenth
century

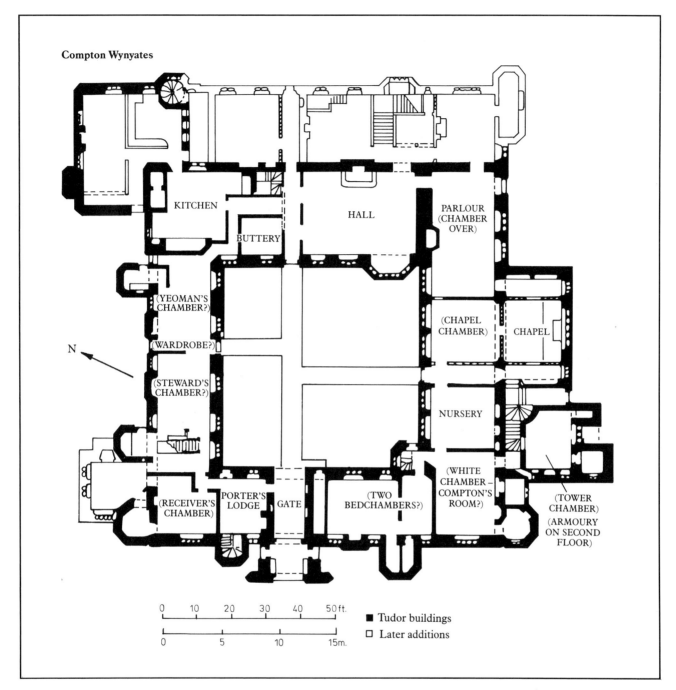

**Compton Wynyates**

KITCHEN

BUTTERY

HALL

PARLOUR
(CHAMBER
OVER)

(YEOMAN'S
CHAMBER?)

(WARDROBE?)

(CHAPEL
CHAMBER)

CHAPEL

N

(STEWARD'S
CHAMBER?)

NURSERY

(RECEIVER'S
CHAMBER)

PORTER'S
LODGE

GATE

(TWO
BEDCHAMBERS?)

(WHITE
CHAMBER –
COMPTON'S
ROOM?)

(TOWER
CHAMBER)
(ARMOURY
ON SECOND
FLOOR)

| 0 | 10 | 20 | 30 | 40 | 50 ft. |

| 0 | | 5 | | 10 | 15m. |

■ Tudor buildings
□ Later additions

*LEFT 43   Sutton Place, Surrey. A conjectural reconstruction of Sir Richard Weston's house from the 1542 inventory. Upper-floor rooms are in brackets.*

*ABOVE 44   Compton Wynyates, Warwickshire. Conjectural plan of Sir William Compton's house from the inventory of 1522. Upper-floor rooms in brackets.*

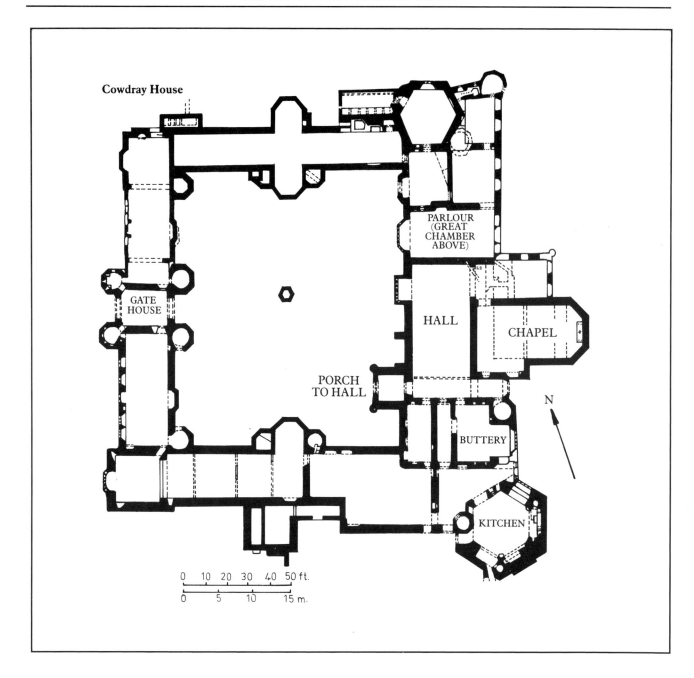

**Cowdray House**

GATE
HOUSE

PARLOUR
(GREAT
CHAMBER
ABOVE)

HALL

CHAPEL

PORCH
TO HALL

BUTTERY

N

KITCHEN

0  10  20  30  40  50 ft.

0      5      10      15 m.

Suffolk show this development to its fullest extent and in both these cases the double-pile was clearly intended from the start.[31] More frequently the final arrangement evolved more slowly from one or more projections at the back of the hall range. For example, a corner tower was added to the northeast point of the court at Compton Wynyates, and a chapel was constructed directly behind the hall at Cowdray, as if to emphasize that it was as important as the hall in the life of the house.

The second development was the increasing demand for halls of only a single storey (Fig. 46). There were still many great houses built with two-

*45  Cowdray House, West Sussex. The full extent of the house as completed by Sir David Owen, Sir William Fitzwilliam and Sir Anthony Browne, c. 1520–48.*

storey halls open to the roof, including Cowdray, Compton Wynyates, Cotehele and, judging from the visual evidence of what is now lost, Shurland and Rycote. But inventories and in some cases surviving evidence seem to indicate a number of single-storey halls at this time. (For example, a double chimneystack above a single chimney flue would suggest that there were originally fireplaces on two floors.) The inventories of Sutton Place, The Vyne, Ingatestone and the Duke of Norfolk's

*46  Deene Park, Northamptonshire. The sixteenth-century wing off the high end of the hall, with its bay window part blocked to accommodate the original floor between ground-floor parlour and upper solar.*

great house of Kenninghall in Norfolk all appear to record halls of one storey because other rooms are mentioned as being over them. At Kenninghall, space above the hall was reserved for 'the great and chiefest Lodging' (or guest apartments), whilst at Ingatestone the room over the hall was used as a dining chamber by 1600 (when the inventory was taken), if not before. Illustrations of lost houses can sometimes also indicate single-storey halls, as is the case with records of Lord de la Warr's house at Halnaker, in West Sussex, and of the house built for Sir James Worsley, Captain of the Isle of Wight, at Appuldurcombe.[32]

As the sixteenth century wore on, access to grand upper-floor rooms was increasingly dependent on a prominent staircase. As with so many domestic architectural features that introduced a new note of size and magnificence, the taste for great stairs seems to have originated in the royal houses. At Henry VII's Richmond there was a large stair tower giving access to the upper floors of the royal lodgings, described in the seventeenth century as 'a chiefe ornament unto the whole fabric of Richmond Court'. The Richmond tower may

well have been influenced by the large and often highly ornamented projecting staircase towers that were a familiar and prominent feature of French royal building, a slightly later example being the famous staircase tower in the Francis I wing at Blois (Fig. 73). At Nonsuch, the 'generous winding steps magnificently built' up to the King's apartments were noted by several later visitors. Still to be seen is the impressive straight stair up to the great hall at Hampton Court, from the inner gatehouse giving on to Clock Court. But though stairs in private houses developed with some ingenuity in the early Tudor period, the idea of a staircase in a splendidly decorated room to itself had yet to become the norm even in the great houses of the nobility.[33]

Before the emergence of the great stair there was little distinction between the various stairs serving different parts of the building. Traditionally, stairs were placed in a turret and the way these stair-turrets were disposed could be used to separate one part of the house from another and make each part self-contained. In earlier times, the ability to seal off parts of the house was important for defensive reasons. Even in the early sixteenth century the turret stair remained the most common form of moving from one floor to another. Technologically, these stairs had become highly proficient. By the early Tudor period they could be made completely of brick, including the newel or central post and the handrail inset into the wall, as can be seen today at Oxburgh Hall (Fig. 47). Some stairs made entirely of wood had begun to appear; important early Tudor examples still to be seen include those in the gatehouse of Wolfeton House in Dorset and in the south gate of the former priory of the Knights of St John in London. Where these stairs were positioned in new and unusual ways this indicates radical rethinking about access to the house.[34]

Sometimes turret stairs were contained within the thickness of an inside wall, but these were difficult to light. More usually they were placed in one of three positions; first, at the angles of buildings (on the outer angles of courtyards or towers, or in the angle created at the junction of two walls within the court); second, in the turret projections of gatehouses; and third, protruding directly from straight walls, both inside and outside the court (Fig. 48). At any given house, there might be stairs in any combination of these positions, according to where they were needed. At Compton Wynyates, for example, there are turrets in several different places; there is one off the porter's lodge

*48   Cadhay, Devon. The east front of the house built for John Haydon, probably just after 1545. The stair turret at the centre connected private apartments on the upper and lower floors.*

which projects out from the entrance front to the main court and serves the tower at the northwest angle, while a second lies in the southwest angle of the courtyard and a third is incorporated into the northeast tower.

These stairs did not always link ground and upper floors directly; sometimes they were used to bypass the floor immediately above so that access from the ground might, for example, lead directly to the roof, with no door to first or second floors. Or they could link two upper floors only, with no stairs in the ground storey of the turret. The gate-house at Coughton Court in Warwickshire, for example, has a turret which is hollow at ground-floor level.[35] At Laughton Place in Sussex there was probably access from the ground to the first floor in Sir William Pelham's tower (see Fig. 22), but not it seems from the first floor to the second; this second floor was effectively isolated from the floors above and beneath it and access to it was only possible from the second floor of the main body of

the house to which it was attached. From what we know of other towers and the use of their upper floors, it could be that this second-floor room was some kind of strong room for Pelham's muniments and valuables. A turret stair at the angle of the tower led directly from the ground floor to the third, probably reflecting the fact that the tower was used as an outlook or vantage point, either for military purposes or to spot quarry for the hunt. So someone on watch could pass from ground level to the top without passing through the private parts of the tower. At Laughton, therefore, stairs were an essential part of the complicated arrange-ments for privacy and security, controlling access to different parts of the building.[36]

There is some evidence that turret stairs con-tinued to be seen as the best way of preserving the privacy of the most important people in the house. At Thornbury Castle, a turret stair at the angle between the huge southwest polygonal tower and the south front gave the Duke of Buckingham

*LEFT 47   Oxburgh Hall, Norfolk. Turret stairs in the 1480s gatehouse. Steps, newel and handrail are all in brick.*

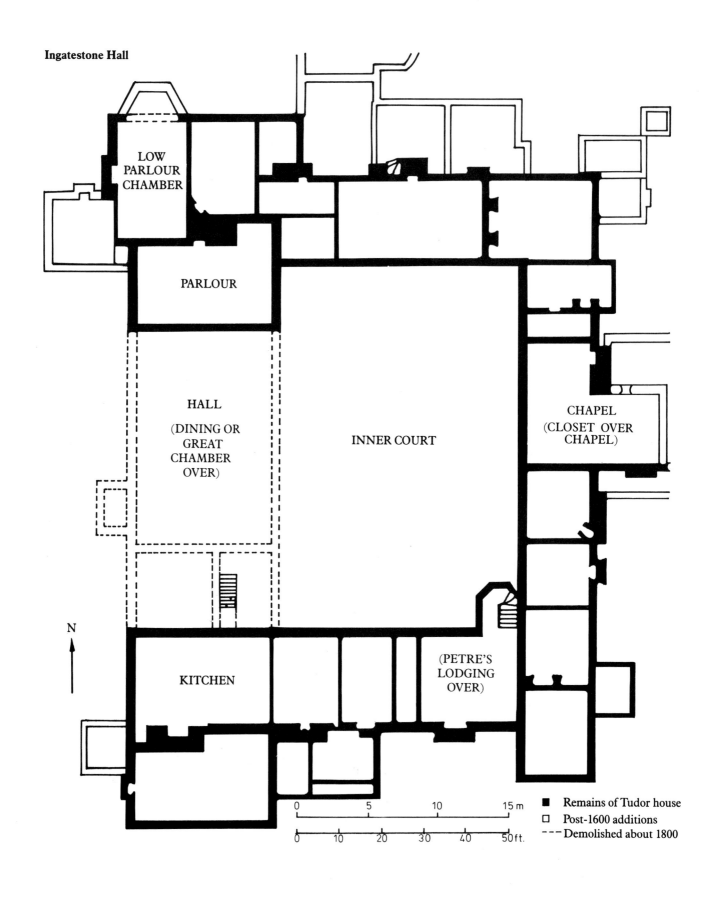

**Ingatestone Hall**

LOW PARLOUR CHAMBER

PARLOUR

HALL
(DINING OR GREAT CHAMBER OVER)

INNER COURT

CHAPEL
(CLOSET OVER CHAPEL)

N

KITCHEN

(PETRE'S LODGING OVER)

0   5   10   15 m

0   10   20   30   40   50 ft.

■ Remains of Tudor house
□ Post-1600 additions
--- Demolished about 1800

direct access to the privy garden from his apartments on the upper floor of the south range. In buildings where a straight stair, or a series of straight stairs was the principal means of access to upper floors, a special turret might serve just the private rooms. This was particularly true of collegiate buildings, which were important precedents for the planning of courtyard houses. The straight stair built between sets of lodgings within the body of the range, with a door at the foot of the stair to give access to the court, is a familiar feature of collegiate architecture. At the Cambridge colleges of Queens' and Christ's, straight stairs served sets of lodgings in the fifteenth and early sixteenth centuries, but a turret stair still provided the Master of the College with private access from the dais, or

upper end of the hall, to his lodging. In private houses, too, this principle is sometimes evident; at Ingatestone (Fig. 49), the house built for Sir William Petre, a turret stair in the southeast corner of the inner court gave access to the 'Master's Lodging' (as it was indeed called in the 1600 inventory) on the upper floor.

Turret stairs were obviously an intrusion in the courtyard plan if they had to be irregularly placed or if they broke up the visual unity of a facade. Sometimes they were deliberately centred on the external face of a courtyard house, as can still be seen at Littlecote, in Wiltshire, in the first completed range of a new courtyard planned by Sir Edward Darrell before 1530. A centred staircase turret also features in the 1540s range of private apartments at Cadhay in Devon (Figs. 48 and 50).[37] Straight stairs within the body of the building did not pose problems of this kind. At Sutton Place, where the internal facades of the court were visually more unified than those of possibly any other known country house of these years, straight internal stairs are likely to have been the main form of

*LEFT 49   Ingatestone Hall, Essex. The plan of Sir William Petre's house of 1539–55, as conjectured by F.W. Emmison from the 1600 inventory. Upper-floor rooms in brackets.*

*BELOW 50   Cadhay, Devon. The house of John Haydon, which he rebuilt 1545–50, although the south wing may possibly be later.*

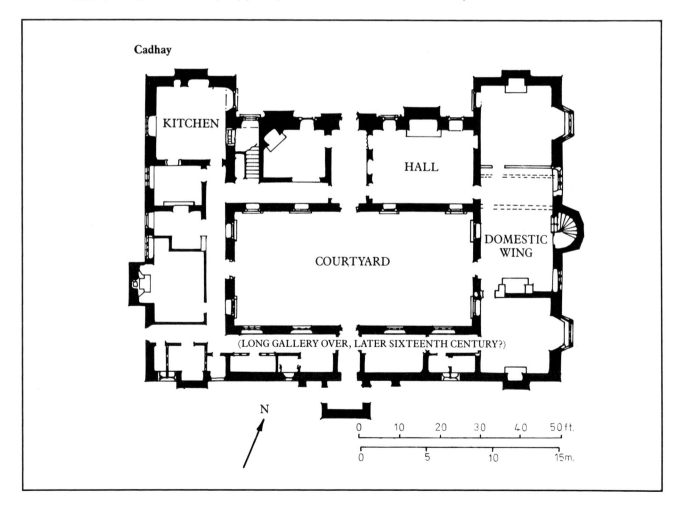

access before fires and other changes in the eighteenth century altered the interior of the house completely. We know that Sutton had one turret stair on the outer face of the gatehouse, but there is no certain evidence for any others in the original building.[38]

It has sometimes been suggested that the increased use of the internal corridor was the principal reason for the disappearance of a proliferation of turret stairs in great houses. Corridors fronting a series of rooms or apartments gave shared access while at the same time preserving privacy, because each room could be reached without going through any of the others. But the evidence suggests that corridors and turret stairs co-existed in many houses in early Tudor times and that passages used as a means of communication and access have a long history; what happened in the late fifteenth and sixteenth centuries was that they became more fully integrated into the body of the great house. They were also used more inventively during this period and some passages slowly took on more recreative functions and developed into splendid rooms of state, the 'long gallery' of great Elizabethan and Jacobean houses (see Chapter 5).[39]

Because they were commonly built of wood, much of the medieval evidence for corridors is lost, but three types of wooden corridor can be discerned from documents about late medieval buildings. First, there was the wooden 'pentice', built up against a stone or brick range to provide access along it so that it was not necessary to pass through the rooms within. This was a forerunner of later, more rationalized corridors or passages that were built into the main house from the beginning and were constructed in the same, more permanent materials. Second, covered corridors were sometimes built as free-standing structures to link isolated parts of a complex of buildings (Fig. 51). Third, by the fifteenth century, there were corridors or 'alleys' circulating gardens. One of the best documented is Henry VII's work at Richmond, where the corridors are known to have been two-storeyed. Another example is the wooden galleries around the garden of Poulteney's Inn, the Marquess of Exeter's house in London, which were reconstructed in 1530. At Thornbury Castle, covered ways around the garden allowed the Duke and

*51   The Hospital of St Cross, Winchester. This rare survival of an early sixteenth-century wooden gallery with a brick oriel linked the infirmary building of the hospital to the church.*

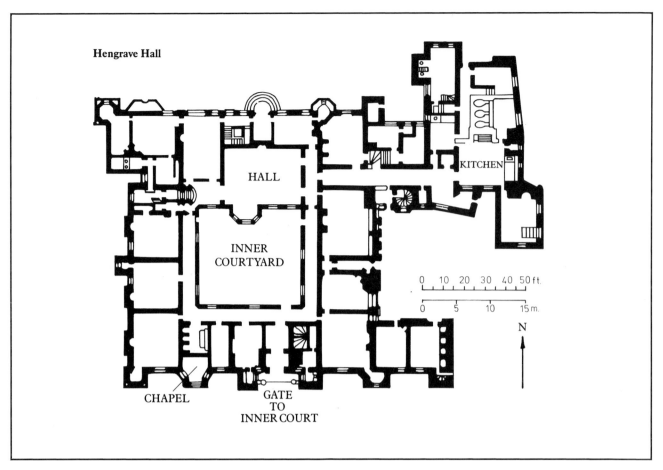

Hengrave Hall

HALL

INNER
COURTYARD

KITCHEN

0  10  20  30  40  50 ft.

0    5    10    15 m.

N

CHAPEL

GATE
TO
INNER COURT

Duchess of Buckingham to pass from their apartments in the south range to the churchyard, without having to go through the main courtyards of the castle. A common feature of these garden corridors was that they were invariably open on at least one side so that those using them would look on to the garden. It can therefore be assumed that their function was partly recreative as well as practical.[40]

The corridor reached its full potential in the courtyard house where it formed a circulating passage around some or all sides of a courtyard, enclosing and looking on to the space of the court just as the Thornbury passages looked on to the privy garden. Corridors used in this way first appeared to serve courtyards that were principally made up of single-room units occupied by different people, in other words where a 'public' space was needed to provide access to the 'private' rooms off the corridor. Collegiate buildings therefore probably led the way, though, as we have seen, the 'cloister' arrangement common at Oxford with what was effectively a corridor open on one side to the court was rare in domestic architecture. Herstmonceux Castle had an open 'cloister', with gallery above, around Green Court, the largest of its courts, by about the middle of the fifteenth century. At Shurland House, the survey view of

*ABOVE 52  Hengrave Hall, Suffolk. Sir Thomas Kytson's house of 1525–38 with a corridor around three sides of the inner courtyard. The kitchen wing was demolished in the eighteenth century.*

*RIGHT 53  Hengrave Hall, Suffolk. The northwest corner of the courtyard, built 1525–38. The window lower left lights the corridor running around three sides of the court.*

1572 seems to show that the early Tudor house had a ground-floor open corridor, with rooms (or perhaps a closed corridor) on the floor above in the courtyard behind the great hall. This corridor looks as if it gave access to buildings at the rear of the house, one of which is surmounted by a cross and was therefore the chapel. It also appears that there were continuous corridors, of timber, around Archbishop Bourchier's courtyard (now known as Stone Court) at Knole in the third quarter of the fifteenth century.[41]

The closed-in corridor fronting ranges of lodgings with doorways and windows giving on to the court was clearly more suitable for domestic buildings. This feature appears in Wolsey's palaces, particularly at Hampton Court, where corridors still give access to lodgings in base court. Some houses had a continuous corridor giving access around the entire inner court, the very heart of the house, and this arrangement was particularly signi-

ficant in the development of the courtyard. At Hengrave (Figs. 52 and 53), built for the wealthy merchant Sir Thomas Kytson, there is a corridor around just three sides. Interestingly, however, the corridor continues along the eastern side of the hall, and thus effectively serves as the equivalent of a screens passage. Another corridor at right-angles to it leads off eastwards into the kitchen wing. Kytson must have used much of the inner court as his own domestic space, since we know that there

was once an outer single-storeyed and moated court in front of the present house as well as a separate kitchen wing. Using his corridors Kytson could have passed directly to rooms in the east or west ranges or to his chapel.[42]

Across the country, at Melbury Sampford in Dorset (Fig. 54), Giles Strangways, an important king's man in these parts, had built a new house, completed shortly after 1540, when Leland described its 'loftie and fresch tower'. As the plan shows (Fig. 55), the original house at Melbury had a corridor running round all four sides of the court, giving access to each of the rooms and opening out naturally into the vestibule before the tower stair-case. In this house, corridor and stairs have truly come to be an integral part of the house rather than

*LEFT 54 Melbury House, Dorset. The prospect tower of Giles Strangways' house, c. 1540.*

*BELOW 55 Melbury House, Dorset. The known extent of Sir Giles Strangways' house of c. 1540.*

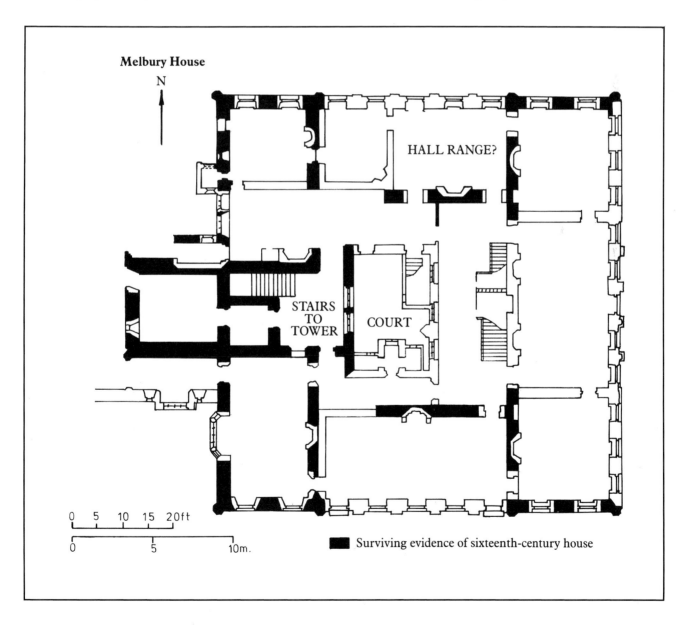

**Melbury House**

N

HALL RANGE?

STAIRS TO TOWER

COURT

0  5  10  15  20ft

0          5          10m.

■ Surviving evidence of sixteenth-century house

the appendages they were in previous generations.[43] What is also perhaps particularly noticeable at both Hengrave and Melbury is the way in which the courtyard itself has become subsidiary, in overall ground area, to the mass of the buildings around it. The ratio of building to open space has shifted in favour of the former. Ranges of buildings no longer bounded a vast open space, as they once did at Otford, for example, and still do today in the surviving base court of Hampton Court and in the great court of the ruins of Cowdray. It is equally interesting, however, that visual appearance remains important; for all the compactness of the interior of his house, Kytson obviously still wanted a long and impressive facade to his main court at Hengrave, so this extends eastwards beyond the end of the east range (see Fig. 16). The gate on the outer facade is thus not at all in line with the centre of the square plan of the court.

From the earliest documentary evidence it seems that these corridors were often called 'cloisters', particularly at collegiate establishments. The most sophisticated corridor access of all was developed in the monastic cloister, a lesson not lost on secular patrons who took over these buildings following the dissolution (see Chapter 7). In a monastic cloister the open arcades on all four sides lend a sense of unity to the whole court, concealing the very disparate functions of the four ranges they serve. They block out the different rooms and appear to push them back, ensuring that no windows in the ground-floor rooms will look into the court; it is the cloister in front of these rooms that is lit. It seems that no early Tudor courtyard house quite took the step of unifying an inner court by means of a continuous cloister, at least not until the conversions of the monasteries themselves sometimes dictated the preservation of the monastic arrangement. The relatively sophisticated visual unity usually found in the cloisters of monastic establishments contrasts with the generally informal (though not to say visually unsatisfying) arrangements in great houses.

In the majority of early Tudor houses there were only tentative attempts to unify the appearance of the building around the court, or as approached from the outside. It is really only in Elizabethan times that it seems to have become common practice to apply regular architectural ornament to the exterior as a whole. Decoration of this kind was used at Longleat (Fig. 115), for example, in its final form of the 1570s, when every external face of what is still a courtyard house was covered with a highly organized expression of the classical orders of architecture (or at least a very Anglo-Flemish version of them). There is little indication that early Tudor builders expected their houses to present a visual entity. Discussion of qualities such as symmetry, a term often applied to houses of later periods as a way of expressing the harmony of the parts of the structure, is hardly relevant at this time. A sense of the order of a building might rest with words like 'semely', which the commissioners used in their letters to Thomas Wriothesley, when they wrote to persuade him to pull down the tower of Titchfield Abbey church. It is clear that the tower broke the skyline of the entrance facade of the house that was being created for him out of the abbey cloister.[44] The four-square Tudor plan of Melbury, with a gable end at each corner of the exterior facades, is therefore highly unusual (Fig. 56). Yet even here, although the gables provided a common point of punctuation, other architectural features and the off-centred tower may have destroyed any exact kind of symmetry in the original form of the house.

On the contrary, most surviving buildings suggest that courtyard houses were still seen as collections of individual ranges; certainly the entrance and parallel hall ranges were considered more important and might carry most of the significant heraldry whilst the side ranges, usually lodgings, were not always thought worthy of much decoration or even a dominant architectural feature. The use of building materials too might underline the distinctions between different parts of the house. As we have seen, the royal apartments block at Richmond was built in stone, while the buildings around it were of brick and timber. At Thornbury, similarly, the outer court was built in a rougher stone than the smooth ashlar finish of the inner court, immediately distinguishing the service quarters from the state apartments. Such contrasts were evident even in the most sophisticated buildings for the Court, as in the difference between the two courts at Nonsuch already described (see pages 68–9).

Three of the most important courtyard houses of the period show clearly how concern and awareness of visual order varied from casual informality in the first example to the imposition of a unifying decorative scheme in the third. The informality of the entrance front at Compton Wynyates seems orderly, but the impression of a unified design does not bear analysis. The turrets and towers do

*56 Melbury House, Dorset. The Tudor gable end at the southeast corner of the house, which is repeated at all four corners of the Tudor courtyard. All the window openings are later.*

not balance each other and there is no order in the size and spacing of what remains of the early Tudor window openings, or in the levels at which they are placed. Within the court, the line of approach from gate to hall is off-centre, doorways to the ranges at left and right are placed asymmetrically and are not in line with each other. The hall bay, virtually in the corner of the court, is the main focus of interest. There is, though, a quite subtle underpinning to these disparate elements, which is often overlooked in discussion of this house. Without the projections, the outer walls form just about a perfect square, and the inner walls of the courtyard form a square also (though the square of the court is placed a little west of centre, because the hall range was made wider than the gatehouse range). The originally moated site on which the inner court was rebuilt was clearly cut in medieval times to exact dimensions and these continued to determine the shape of the later house.

In contrast, some visual order was clearly intended at Cowdray, in West Sussex, as shown in Grimm's beautiful eighteenth-century watercolour (Fig. 57). The architectural motif of the gatehouse with its turrets on either side is virtually repeated in the turrets which flank projections in the wall in the side ranges. We cannot know how useful these turrets were in the original house, but it seems

their positioning was partly for aesthetic reasons. There were galleries on the upper floors of these ranges by the eighteenth century and, if these existed in Tudor times, it would seem extraordinary to provide turret stairs that led to the upper floor half-way along a gallery (unless of course they led directly to the roof, isolating the first-floor rooms, as was done elsewhere). Cowdray is a very important example of a house where visual symmetry in the court seems to have been superimposed on to a structure otherwise expressing the usual disparate arrangement of the great Tudor house, with its emphasis on accentuating important points of reference like the gatehouse, the hall porch and the great bay window to the hall.[45]

The one surviving house where visual order is expressed most cogently is Sutton Place (Fig. 58),

*RIGHT 1 Fulham Palace, London. The porch to the great hall in the courtyard of 1510–20, showing the creation of brick patterning, or diaper work, by setting darkened headers into the red brickwork.*

*BELOW 57 Cowdray House, West Sussex. Grimm's eighteenth-century view looking towards the gatehouse, showing the semblance of symmetry in the court with bay windows flanked by stair turrets facing each other. (London, British Library)*

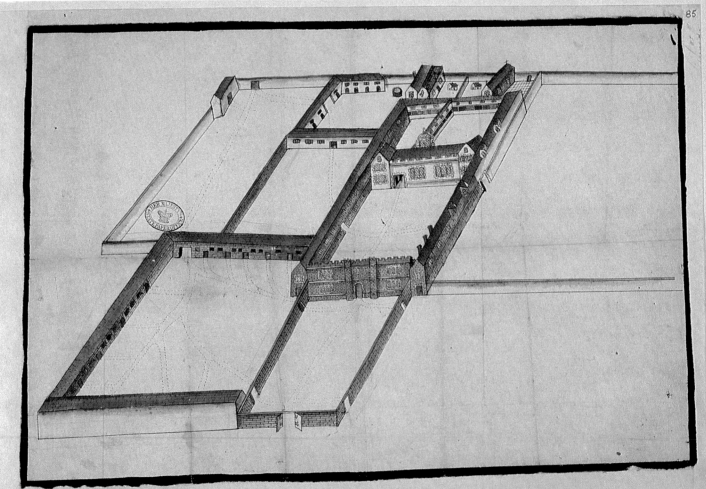

LEFT 2 *The south front of Grimsthorpe Castle, Lincolnshire, built by Charles Brandon in the late 1530s to rival the new house of the gentry family of Thimelby at Irnham a few miles away. Most of the window openings are eighteenth-century.*

BELOW LEFT 3 *Shurland, Isle of Sheppey. The view drawn for the 1572 survey, looking at the house from the west. It shows how complex Tudor houses often were, with the main house surrounded by walled enclosures and service courts. (London, Public Record Office)*

BELOW 4 *Buckland Abbey, Devon. A view from the south showing the crossing tower of the monastic church. Sir Richard Grenville made his house out of the nave space, building on the projecting range to the right.*

FAR LEFT 5   Newstead Abbey, Nottinghamshire. Looking into the cloister from the southeast angle. The original medieval cloister window openings were re-used in the construction of a two-storey corridor around the courtyard. The original location of the conduit is not certain; it once stood before the front of the house.

ABOVE 6   Smithills Hall, Greater Manchester. The solar ranges, with the timber bay to the new parlour of the early sixteenth century and the chapel at the left.

LEFT 7   St Osyth's Priory, Essex. Stone chimneystacks on the tower built by Thomas, Lord Darcy, in his conversion of the former monastery after 1553.

ABOVE 9   Gosfield Hall, Essex. The west range of the house, originally the entrance front, probably of the 1540s–50s.

LEFT 8   Sandford Orcas, Dorset. The south side of the house probably built in the 1540s, with the bay window to hall and great chamber at the right.

ABOVE 10  Poundisford Park, Somerset. The remarkably compact H-shaped house built for William Hill in the 1540s.

LEFT 11  Newark Park, Gloucestershire. The Doric doorway to the hunting lodge of Sir Nicholas Poyntz, possibly built during the 1540s.

58,59  Sutton Place, Surrey, built between 1521 and 1533. The bay window in the courtyard (RIGHT) is decorated with terracotta work, linking its design to that of the flanking walls. By contrast, the anonymous seventeenth-century view of the north front of the house (OVERLEAF) shows the austerity of the original gatehouse range, demolished in the eighteenth century.

but significantly this unity is achieved by subordinating elements of architecture to an overall decorative order and one which operates only within the court itself. Sutton displays emphatically something that must have been common to many courtyard structures, a contrast between a plain, unadorned exterior and sumptuously decorated interior facades around the court. This effect is now lost at Sutton since the gatehouse range is gone and the interior facades are visible when the house is first approached, the building as a whole appearing like later, open-sided Elizabethan houses. We know what the gatehouse range looked like from two eighteenth-century views of it illustrating the outside (one showing the collapsing structure being shored up), and from a seventeenth-century drawing (Fig. 59). These show its rather stark, unadorned appearance and something of this character is still evident on the east side of the house where the irregularly spaced chimneystacks destroy any impression of a balanced design. (This side of the house has been considerably 'softened' in recent years by the addition of a modern moat and gardens.)

The interior face of the gatehouse range is preserved in a coloured drawing in the Bodleian Library, showing how the plinths either side of the entry were covered with terracotta, thus echoing those flanking the main door opposite. The terracotta decoration in the courtyard is what lends it unity, with a continuous frieze and plinth moulding that would originally have been on all four sides. The terracotta emphasizes the lack of dominant projections and blends well with the basic building material of brick, ranging in colour from buff to pink-red to purplish-red. Sutton Place is the courtyard house at its most glittering, demonstrating a surface quality that must have seemed truly glamorous in the eyes of sixteenth-century visitors.[46] Within the courts, and more especially within the walls of these houses, inventories reveal that the lifestyle of the socially and financially privileged was becoming increasingly comfortable.

*RIGHT 60 Chenies, Buckinghamshire. The other side of the range shown in Fig. 32. In contrast to the oriels and windows of the courtyard facade, this plain exterior wall has only the brick projections that served as privies and closets.*

# 'A Fayre New Parlor':
# The Evidence of Inventories

WHEN THOMAS WEST, Lord de la Warr, was forced to relinquish his house at Halnaker in West Sussex to Henry VIII in 1540, he pleaded with the King to give him another house in exchange. His second property, the old house at Offington, near Broadwater, which had been in his family since 1387, was, he claimed, impossible to use no matter what sums he might be prepared to spend on it because 'it is so near the sea coast and . . . not very wholesome'.[1] Finding himself having to make the best of Offington, however, West clearly contrived to live there in subsequent years in some comfort. By the time of his death in 1554, when an inventory was taken, the old house had been enlarged to almost seventy rooms, including several well-appointed parlours, a great chamber, various galleries and a guest chamber tricked out in velvet. There were individual bedrooms for members of West's family and also for all his more important servants, including his steward, clerk of the kitchen, housekeeper, cook, baker and armourer. The inventory also tells us that many of the principal rooms led into smaller rooms which acted as antechambers or closets. In this way, each important room was surrounded by private, less formal space; rooms such as 'the gallery at my lord's chamber door', 'the chamber within the velvet chamber', 'the inner chamber within the said parlour'.[2] So, despite West's initial misgivings (or had he simply exaggerated the disadvantages of Offington to get what he wanted?), he seems to have re-established his household with dignity and privacy in well-appointed surroundings. In this he was certainly typical of the courtier class of his time.

The inventory of West's goods illustrates the increasing value placed on privacy in this period and the architectural changes that made this possible, particularly the developments in the use of corridors that were described in the last chapter. On a more general point, the inventory shows that the sheer number of rooms in the houses of the wealthy was increasing. Activities that were once all concentrated in one place, making large spaces such as the hall multi-functional, were happening now in rooms specially built and furnished for one purpose. This move towards greater privacy and towards rooms with particular functions seems to have been accompanied by a decrease in the amount of ceremonial in great houses, certainly by the end of the sixteenth century. Ceremonial had once been important as a means of defining which function a multi-purpose room was to be used for at any one time. But as many more rooms became available, the 'public' life of the house (communal dining and the reception and entertainment of visitors) was clearly separated from the 'private' (parlours for the family, the rooms for sleeping, closets and study chambers). The lives of the members of these households were also distinguished by an interest in leisure pursuits, which might include the more cultivated arts of learning and collecting, in contrast to a medieval retinue, whose chief, and in some cases only function had been to serve as a private army.[3]

Inventories such as that of Thomas West are particularly valuable because there are very few surviving interiors from early Tudor England, and practically none in an unrestored state or with much in the way of original furnishings. Only in rare instances have early sixteenth-century interiors remained structurally unaltered, primarily where houses became the second or third properties of later owners and were therefore not extensively modernized or redecorated. All old houses tend to be periodically remodelled and modernized according to the tastes of later generations, but early Tudor interiors were fundamentally rejected in the centuries that followed. It was not until well into the nineteenth century that there was a revival of interest in the interiors of this period accompanied by an appreciation of their particular qualities, seen as a blend of the informal, the cosy and the traditional. The nineteenth-century version of Tudor England is expressed in Dickens' description of the Maypole Inn in *Barnaby Rudge* — 'Its windows were old diamond-pane lattices, its floors were sunken and uneven, its ceilings blackened by the hand of time, and heavy with massive beams.' — and it lives on today in the fake woodwork and open fireplaces of English public houses. The élite of Stuart and Georgian times did not value this quality of cosiness, which could not be transformed to provide settings for their grand and formal life-style.[4]

One of the major problems was that Tudor rooms were not large enough. Though the interiors of great houses of the early sixteenth century were often richly, even garishly, decorated, the majority of the rooms were still quite small. They lacked the scale and grandeur that appealed to later generations and had two particular characteristics which together conspired to ensure that so much of England's early Tudor heritage of interior decora-

tion was destroyed, particularly in comparison with the immediately following Elizabethan and Jacobean period. First, apart from the hall itself (and then only where it was still a two-storeyed room open to the roof) and perhaps the great chamber, early Tudor rooms were low-ceilinged and lit by long, low windows. In contrast, the chief apartments of later sixteenth-century houses generally enjoyed higher ceilings with taller windows to match. As a result, when high-ceilinged rooms of classical proportions were the norm in the seventeenth to nineteenth centuries, Elizabethan rooms might be tolerated whilst early Tudor rooms were not. Later commentators made constant reference to the meanness and darkness of late medieval and early Tudor houses, encapsulated in Horace Walpole's comment about Halnaker that 'some parts within are as modern as the time of Henry 8th. The rooms are low and bad', or his equally disparaging remark about the long gallery in the entrance range at Gosfield Hall, Essex, that it was 'a bad, narrow room'.[5]

The second feature of these rooms that made them anathema to later owners was to do with the fact that their decoration lacked any expression of what might be called 'internal architecture'. Some early Tudor rooms were hung with tapestry or cheaper forms of wall hanging, but otherwise they were panelled, a practice that had quite functional origins. As William Harrison wrote in his *Description of England*, panelled rooms are 'not a little commended, made warm, and much more close than otherwise they would be'.[6] Panelling was certainly becoming more ornate and decorative at this period and people were increasingly prepared to import it from abroad. The merchant John Johnson purchased Flemish panelling for his master Anthony Cave, a merchant trading at Calais, in 1549, and was so impressed with it that he arranged for a further hundred panels to be shipped over to King's Lynn for his own house at Glapthorn in Northamptonshire. He paid 5s 4d for it to be set up in the winter of 1550.[7] But this internal decoration was carried out with a conscious lack of concern for the overall visual effect. Panelling was bought by the piece and it was applied from floor to ceiling rather like wallpaper to cover as much wall surface as possible. It could be cut about to fit corners and it was often later removed in bits and used elsewhere (Fig. 61). Panelling from the domestic quar-

61 *Panelling of the 1520s from Boughton Malherbe, Kent. This fragment of early Tudor 'anticke' wood carving has been removed from the house and is now in the USA.*

LEFT 62   Deene Park, Northamptonshire. This upstairs room with original early Tudor fireplace and linenfold panelling, though re-arranged, is a rare example of a period interior. The royal arms were set up here in the seventeenth century.

ABOVE 63   Cowdray House, West Sussex. The ruined great hall of the 1530s–40s, with its three raised windows and a bay for the dais. The bays next to this served parlour (ground floor) and great chamber (above).

ters at Faversham Abbey, for example, was re-moved at the Reformation and placed all around the lower walls of the great hall at Dorney Court in Buckinghamshire. Many fragments of this kind of panelling survive, but very few complete interiors (Fig. 62).

In contrast, by the Elizabethan period fitting a room with wooden panelling was for the first time regarded as having some aesthetic importance. The panels were made up into much larger sections and were fixed with an eye to the height and width of the wall as a whole. Classical pilasters were intro-duced to punctuate the panelling and give it pro-portion and grandeur. Stuart and Georgian pat-rons could at least relate to this kind of interior decoration and were more likely to preserve it.[8]

Given that there are only a handful of examples of early sixteenth-century interiors close to their original state or with much of their original con-tents, the evidence of contemporary inventories is of great importance in reconstructing the use and

appearance of the rooms of a great house and in deducing how the lifestyle of the occupants was changing.[9] In the case of the great hall, the first room a Tudor visitor to a great house would have seen, inventories reveal something of its changing functions. As Chapter 4 described, houses where the traditional plan had been quite radically changed now had single-storey halls. Though these were no longer the focal central point of the house in the sense of being the place where all communal activi-ties were concentrated, halls were clearly still used for certain ceremonial functions. Continuity with the past was of greater importance to those who had their new houses built with two-storeyed halls open to the roof according to older conventions, so suggesting these rooms had all the significance of their medieval predecessors. Beddington, in Surrey, built for the Carew family, and Cowdray in West Sussex (Fig. 63), built for Sir William Fitzwilliam, were given two-storey halls with splendid hammer-beam roofs, rivalling the magnificence of that at Hampton Court, though these rooms were principally intended to emphasize social status by their size and built-in fittings rather than be used on a daily basis. An undated sixteenth-century inventory for Beddington values the movables of the hall at only 13s 6d, a mere fraction of the value of the contents of the parlour or the great chamber, both of which exceeded £20.[10]

In some houses the presence of tables and forms for dining shows that the hall had not lost all its original functions. In 1509 the London house of Edmund Dudley, Chief Minister to Henry VII, had a long board, two trestles and two joined forms in its hall. At Sir Richard Fermor's house at Easton Neston in Northamptonshire in 1540 trestles and forms to the tables were mortised into the ground. But inventories mention little by way of minor furnishings in the halls of these houses and in some places not even the barest provision for dining existed. This suggests that the necessary furniture was carried in when needed from elsewhere in the house on those rare occasions when the hall was used. At the Bishop of St David's manor house at Lamphey, near Pembroke, a house on which considerable sums had recently been spent, the hall had no furniture at all when inventoried in 1536, save three pieces of old saye (a sort of serge material) on the walls with mats under them.[11]

Off the high or the lord's end of the hall there was usually access to the parlour through a low door, and perhaps along a short passageway. Parlours were comfortable, low-ceilinged rooms and many older houses were given new ones in the early sixteenth century. Two notable surviving examples are at Smithills Hall, near Bolton (Fig. 64), and at Haddon in Derbyshire (Fig. 65). Smithills is a largely fifteenth-century house whose east, domestic wing was refitted and possibly extended by the owner, Andrew Barton, in about 1516.[12] The panelling of his new parlour has been brought back to this room from elsewhere in the house and it shows a familiar mixture of panels of linenfold combined with others with profile medallion heads. This room and the parlour at Haddon both feature a large bay window area which was clearly almost a room to itself; many inventories refer to cushions for the windows in rooms such as these, implying that there were fixed benches or stools in the embrasures. The low parlour at Haddon was restored in the 1920s, yet it remains a remarkable example of a room of the period. It has panelled walls displaying royal and familial heraldry and also a painted ceiling, similarly decorated with heraldic emblems, which here appear on a painted

64 *Smithills Hall, Bolton. The new parlour made in c.1516. Some of the original panelling, with its mixture of linenfold and medallion heads, has been returned to this room.*

ground of chequered and lozenge (diamond-patterned) work.[13]

Parlours were used for a variety of purposes. In some houses they were slept in, as at Bramall in Cheshire in 1541 where William Davenport's 'parlour chamber' contained a feather bed and four mattresses, or at Markeaton in Derbyshire in 1545, where there was a bed with a tester with yellow and green taffeta curtains.[14] Generally, though, the parlour had come to be used as a private dining room. At both Easton Neston and Lamphey the parlour had become the usual place for eating on a day-to-day basis, certainly as far as the head of the house and his immediate family or followers were concerned, and the hall was rarely used for this purpose. Similarly, it is the parlour, of all the main rooms in the house, that seems to be equipped for dining at Compton Wynyates in 1522, for the in-

65   *The low parlour, Haddon Hall, Derbyshire. The painted ceiling recalls the temporary decorative work undertaken for festivities at Court, recorded only in documentary sources.*

ventory records two tables of oak and elm, each 12 feet long. Sir John Gage's parlour at Firle in East Sussex in 1556 had a long table in the more unusual soft wood of fir, probably imported from the Baltic or Scandinavia. [15]

In some houses belonging to people of the highest social class, rooms called 'parlours' are found all over the house and were clearly sitting rather than dining rooms. In 1540 Lord Lisle, the King's Deputy in Calais, had a parlour without tables or forms; its furnishings consisted of a stool covered with black velvet, a joined chair and two joined stools, cushions of carpet work and others woven with his arms, and a wicker screen. In a well-appointed house such as this, we know that there were separate rooms called 'dining chambers'; 'my ladyes dyning Chambre' in the Lisles' house had a long table with trestles, six joined stools, a chair covered with crimson velvet and an abundance of cushions 'of dyvers sortes'. It is largely these courtier houses where dining chambers are recorded that also had 'withdrawing' chambers, as noted in 1547 and 1549 at the Duke of Norfolk's houses of Kenninghall in Norfolk and Chesworth in West Sussex, and at

Lord Paget's house at West Drayton in 1556. These withdrawing rooms were clearly not the simple, poorly-appointed spaces sometimes found in medieval houses, into which servants could 'withdraw' from their duties in an adjacent state room. They were rooms of leisure for the lord and his family, presumably found in these courtier houses because people of this class were more likely to have important guests and so needed rooms set aside for dining and retiring which would always be available. [16]

The main parlour was normally on the ground floor and the great chamber was often sited above it. Indeed the parlour and great chamber at Haddon were created by putting a floor into the former two-storeyed solar. Since medieval times the great chamber had developed into an important room of state which, like the hall, may only have been used for special occasions. By the early Tudor period, however, it appears to have been possible to transform this room, increasingly the most expensively decorated in the house, to fulfil whatever function was needed in order to entertain or accommodate guests. It could certainly be used as a formal dining room, and inventories often suggest that it could be the state bedchamber for the most distinguished visitors. A great bed is recorded in the great chamber at Edmund Dudley's London house in 1509, with a 'testar of bawdiken embrodrid' and a profusion of carpets, hangings and coffers full of expensive clothes. The great chamber was also the setting for important events in the life of the family, such as marriage celebrations, or the lying-in-state before burial.[17]

The great chamber of a house would usually be signified by a prominent upper-floor window, perhaps an oriel, looking into the court. Another point of reference within the courtyard might be the chapel. Indeed Andrew Boorde recommended that as many of the rooms that looked in to the court as possible should have a view of the chapel. Not all houses had private chapels and only a handful of original early Tudor examples survive. Some retain part of their original wealth of decoration, but none have very much of their former contents, which largely disappeared after the Reformation. Here again, inventories provide valuable evidence. Country house chapels in the period up to mid century were expensively equipped with plate, vestments, altar furnishings, hangings and panel paintings. At the time of his fall from power in the winter of 1546–7, the Duke of Norfolk had a wooden retable of great size (some 12 by 5 feet) in the chapel at Kenninghall, with a gilded Passion of Christ sequence 'wrought upon wainscot'. The chapel also contained six pieces of counterfeit arras (tapestry), again depicting the story of the Passion. These were each of 9 square yards, an indication of how large the chapel must have been.[18]

Something of the quality of a chapel of this kind is preserved at Towneley Hall, near Burnley in Lancashire, although the chapel here has been moved from its original position and only part of the original fittings survive. The Towneley family, like the Howard Dukes of Norfolk, adhered to the Roman Catholic faith after the Reformation and their chapel still has some of its original woodwork and the kind of imagery that was once common. Appropriately, an early sixteenth-century carved Flemish altarpiece, a multi-panelled depiction of the Passion sequence, similar in content to the lost altarpiece at Kenninghall, now stands over the altar. It was placed here at the end of the eighteenth century and is typical of the sort of expensive object that the wealthiest patrons of Tudor England commissioned for their devotions. As in the case of other expensive and fashionable furnishings for their houses, they looked to the Low Countries for the highest standards of workmanship and materials.[19]

At other houses, as the third quarter of the sixteenth century wore on, chapel fittings were removed and vestments, the more expensive items of plate and images over the altar disappeared. By 1566, the chapel of the Worsley family at Appuldurcombe on the Isle of Wight, a house built for the courtier Sir James Worsley in the reign of Henry VIII, had only cushions, forms, a Communion table covered by a carpet of dornax (a simply-patterned linen cloth, made at Tournai in Flanders), a large Bible and a Communion book. There is no mention of any images whatsoever and, in contrast to inventories fifty years earlier when the contents of the chapel would be more valuable than those of any other room in the house, the furnishings of the chapel at Appuldurcombe were estimated to be worth 24s 4d. This was just one sixth of the value of the contents of the owner's own chamber and less than the value of either of the two most valuable beds in the house.[20] Something of the Reformist zeal that overtook Tudor chapels can be seen today at Bramall in Cheshire. Here, in the chapel fitted out for the Davenport family in about 1500, the ghostly remains of the pre-Reformation painting of the Passion of Christ have been recently uncovered behind the text of the Ten Commandments that was painted over it in the later sixteenth century. There could not be a more eloquent or emphatic reminder of how the text displaced the image in the religious rituals of Tudor England.[21]

Despite the changes of the Reformation, two surviving chapels indicate the composite splendour of the early Tudor interior and reflect, one of them perhaps in a very direct sense, painting and craftsmanship at Henry VIII's court. The chapel at Ightham Mote in Kent, built for the courtier Sir Richard Clement, has a wagon roof covered with painted royal emblems. This woodwork may not, however, have originally been designed for the chapel; it is possible that it came from the store of the Royal Office of Works, and may have been first made for a wooden gallery or raised vantage-point put up for a great royal occasion like a joust or a tournament. It certainly matches the descriptions of decorative work commissioned by the Royal Works, work that would have been colourful, rapidly executed and designed to be used for only a short period of time.[22]

But even Ightham chapel is surpassed by the quality and range of early Tudor fittings at the chapel of The Vyne in Hampshire (Fig. 66), with its woodwork, imported tiles and stained glass. Instead of the painted work at Ightham, the ceiling here is made up of a typical early Tudor pattern of thin, wooden ribs. The floor tiles may have been intended for, or have been removed from, other parts of the house, for they were found in the grounds and laid here in the nineteenth century. They are believed to have been made at the workshop set up in Antwerp in 1512 by the Italian, Guido de Savino of Urbino. The windows were commissioned by Lord Sandys, the owner of the house, probably from Flemish craftsmen, and are closely related to a larger commission, now only known from fragments, for his burial chapel of the Holy Ghost at Basingstoke. They depict the Passion of Christ with Henry VIII, Katherine of Aragon and Queen Margaret of Scotland kneeling in prayer.[23] Both Ightham and The Vyne show that Tudor courtiers kept their loyalty to the ruling dynasty in the forefront of their minds, even in the part of the house dedicated to their devotions.

Chapels were not the only place where religious images were seen, as these might be depicted on wall hangings in other parts of the house. The Reformation did not, as might be expected, mark the end of religious imagery in private houses, but it did lead to a shift in the choice of subject matter. After the 1530s, the central themes of Christian worship, such as scenes from the life of Christ and the Virgin and representations of essentially spiritual ideas, feature much less prominently in inventories as subjects for hangings. But other religious subjects would not leave the owner open to a charge of image-worship in post-Reformation England. Old Testament subjects and the lives of popular, warrior saints were increasingly common and these, together with episodes from classical history, suited the well-established fashion for scenes depicting heroic and chivalric ideals. They feature in inventories both before and after the Reformation. The inventory of Lord Darcy's goods in 1520, for instance, included two hangings of St George and another of the story of King David. At Lord Sandys' Mottisfont, the great chamber and adjacent rooms had hangings depicting the story of King David and Solomon in 1541. At Kenninghall in 1547 there were fourteen counterfeit arras of the story of Hercules in the great chamber. The hangings in these three examples were all quite expensive and were in prominent rooms, but cheaper, painted

66 *The Vyne, Hampshire. The chapel of Lord Sandys' house c.1518–27. The ribbed ceiling and stained glass are original to the chapel. The early sixteenth-century floor tiles were also made for the house.*

cloths depicting narrative subjects were found all over sixteenth-century houses. An inventory of 1542 shows that even the joiner's chamber at Sutton Place had hangings of buckram.[24]

One thing that would strike a twentieth-century visitor used to the abundance of paintings in country houses of a later period would be the relative absence of easel pictures. Small, portable paintings on wood or canvas were usually found in only a few rooms, notably the hall, the parlour and perhaps the private rooms of the lord and lady of the house.[25] The price put on these in inventories was never very high since cash value was related only to size, rather than to any idea of a standard of quality that would be applied to such things in subsequent centuries, with the growth of collecting and connoisseurship. Generally speaking, the relative scarcity of paintings in private houses suggests that the élite of early Tudor England were only marginally concerned with collecting for its own sake. Most non-religious works were of course portraits, principally of the King or English historical figures. Only those of the courtier class would have had their own portraits on the walls of their houses at this time. However, there are one or two examples of groups or sets of pictures of famous people, usually of the kings of England, though sometimes of great European leaders or heroes of the past. These sets were to become more common in Elizabethan times. For example, there were twenty-eight portraits at Kenninghall in 1547, 'the vysenamies of divers noble persons' in the 'long gallery'.[26] Clearly so large a group of portraits must have needed a lot of wall space, but although long galleries were subsequently used for the display of pictures, this was not their principal purpose at this time.

The increasing significance of the gallery in sixteenth-century houses is a good indication of the growing importance of the provision of space purely for recreation and private pleasure. Some of the spaces known as 'galleries' were no more than corridors and contained few, if any, movable contents. In these cases, their existence is only recorded in contemporary inventories by reference to the room to which they gave access. For example, there are several recorded instances of galleries which simply served as rooms leading to chapels and these appear to have had few or no furnishings. The gallery at Offington quoted at the beginning of this chapter was clearly perceived simply as the means of access to 'my lord's chamber door'.

However, other inventories do list galleries with furnishings and hangings, suggesting that these must have been some of the earliest examples of the kind of room with which the term 'long gallery' has come to be associated. The question is to what extent these early sixteenth-century examples exhibited the characteristics commonly associated with the long gallery which is such a feature of later English country houses.[27] The archetypal long gallery was a room of great length and was usually elaborately decorated, as befitted its status as one of the state rooms of the house. It also had quite specific functions attached to it. The long gallery was not, like its corridor predecessor, simply, or even primarily, a room built for easy passage from one place to another, but somewhere that members of the household and guests might go to do particular things, especially for recreational purposes, such as walking and admiring the prospect from large windows. Access to the gallery was emphasized by a prominent stairway and perhaps by a grand and expensive doorcase.

This archetypal gallery was a characteristic feature of great Elizabethan and Jacobean houses. It was usually not only long but also wide, perhaps with windows on both of its long sides, and it often took up the entire wing of a house or most of the roof space. The long gallery clearly became an established fashion in the later sixteenth and early seventeenth centuries, as is shown by the determined effort to create gallery spaces in houses which previously did not have them. Sometimes this was done by converting a pre-existing building range, as at Haddon Hall in the early seventeenth century, or sometimes by adding another storey to the building in question. A notable example of this sort of addition was the extraordinary creation of a gallery over the south, gatehouse range of Little Moreton Hall, in Cheshire (Fig. 67), perhaps as early as 1559, but possibly later.[28]

There is, however, only fragmentary early sixteenth-century documentation about the decoration of galleries and what they were used for that could be used as the basis for assuming that every reference to a 'long gallery' indicates a room of the sort defined here. The fullest documentary evidence comes from the grandest domestic buildings, the royal and episcopal palaces. Cavendish's *Life* of Wolsey, one of the most valuable contemporary written records of the domestic routine of a powerful political figure, describes the Cardinal's galleries as 'good to walk in' and this writer also gives other instances of the long gallery's usefulness as a place for private conversation.[29] As for decoration, the length and splendour of Henry VIII's galleries at Whitehall and St James's were a point of particular rivalry with Francis I of France. This emerges strongly from the letter the ambassador Sir John Wallop wrote to Henry after he had been to see the decoration of the new gallery at Fontainebleau in November 1540; he had been personally conducted into the gallery by the French king who, like his English rival, kept the key to the room himself.[30]

The contents of what were described as galleries in inventories of courtier and other houses from the first half of the century suggest that these rooms had a variety of uses. One of the first references to a 'long gallery' in documentary

67 *Little Moreton Hall, Cheshire. The gallery over the south range. The arch-braced roof-trusses were designed to give maximum headroom.*

sources is the 1509 inventory of Edmund Dudley's London house, where a 'long galerre agayn the gardynne' was equipped with hangings of buckram, two 'stayned clothes of ymagerie' and various items of furniture. The 'galarre next to the great chambre' at the same house was similarly furnished as a comfortable room, but both the 'lowe galare by the gardeyn' and the 'gret galare at thende of that' were clearly storerooms for linen, canvas and (in the first of these two rooms) 'a cartlode of old lede'. Similarly, the gallery with pictures at Kenninghall was probably described as 'long' simply to distinguish it from other galleries at the house. There was a 'short gallery' on the topmost floor that led to a turret chamber, and also a 'presse gallery'. This was named after the press (a cupboard, usually for the storage of clothes) that stood there, and this gallery also contained the tester and valance of a bed of yellow Bruges satin and, curiously, the harness for a horse.[31]

The most famous contender for the distinction of being the earliest English 'long gallery' to survive in anything like its original condition is the Oak Gallery at The Vyne. This gallery almost certainly once led to a room in a tower at its south end that no longer exists and its construction and decoration are thought to date from no earlier than about 1515. The heraldry of the panelling, which includes the arms of Katherine of Aragon, suggests that it could be no later than 1527. We know that the panelling must have been moved around in the eighteenth century when the window openings were changed, but there seems little doubt that this remarkable survival of linenfold work, showing the arms and devices of Lord Sandys, the patron, with those of his friends and family and Court connections, was always intended for this room. In the 1541 inventory the room is well if sparsely furnished with red and green curtains at the windows and carpets beneath them, three tables and a Spanish folding chair. Yet there is no mention of hangings, whose absence would have been extraordinary in a room of this size and importance, unless they were unnecessary because the walls were already covered with the wainscot that can be seen today.[32]

All these rooms had an essentially public role; they were places where the owners of these great houses lived out their public lives and to which visitors and perhaps a great number of servants had necessary access. But the early Tudor house also had rooms set aside for purely private belongings and to these few would gain entry. For example, the tower room at Laughton Place in East Sussex (see p. 85) gave the lord of the house total privacy

and also conditions of the greatest possible security. Similarly, Sir William Sharington's room in his new tower at the converted monastery of Lacock Abbey had shelves specially made for housing his valuables and documents and these and his stone table can still be seen. The character of these tower rooms is summed up in a later description of the ideal 'strong room' written by a follower of the Earl of Northumberland: 'I wish the Earle to have in his house a chamber very stronge and close, the walls should be of stone or bricke, the dore should be overplated with iron, the better to defend it from danger of fire. The keyes therof the Earle himself is to keepe. In this Chamber should be cubbards of drawing boxes, shelves and standards, with a convenient Table to write upon; and upon every drawing box is to be written the name of the Manor or Lordship, the Evidence whereof that box doth containe ....'[33]

If they lacked a strong room, owners kept essential documents, together with their personal possessions, in 'closets' off larger rooms. At Edmund Dudley's London house in 1509 a closet off the great chamber contained the minister's evidences, bills and personal money. Lord Lisle kept his writings, along with a 'closse stole for a Jaques' and his 'chamber potte', off his 'chamber' (that is to say, his bedchamber, the full word being hardly ever yet used) at Calais in 1540.[34] These rooms also give us some of the earliest evidence for the possession of books, though even the greatest of Henry VIII's courtiers probably had only a few. The inventory of the goods of Sir William More of Loseley describes what he kept in 'myne owne closette', namely his maps (these would have been a rare possession), writing instruments and a large collection of books on a variety of religious and profane subjects.[35] One of the most valuable descriptions of private possessions of this period appears in the inventory of Markeaton, Derbyshire, and this is for a very special reason. Unlike the usual run of inventories, taken for probate when the owner died, or by royal commissioners at the time of attainder, the Markeaton document was drawn up by the owner himself, Vincent Mundy, a wealthy man of the local gentry, at the time of the birth of his son. It has the quality of a personal record of a kind not found in other inventories. Off the 'gret chamber wher we dyne' (another 'great chamber', presumably the true equivalent of other rooms of this sort discussed above, is separately listed) was his study containing his books, a red coffer for his evidences, a standing dish for pen and ink, and his weights and measures, including a pair of gold balances.[36]

A general deduction from the evidence of inventories is that those living in the country houses of the early sixteenth century enjoyed a high standard of living. By about 1550, this had become so noticeable that it was a matter for debate among pamphleteers who discussed the present state of society. Critics of the increase in luxury and comfort felt there was a moral question involved about the need for the governing class to act responsibly, spend less privately on themselves and more on the public good. For William Harrison, writing his *Description of England*, the argument was mainly one of economics. In his view, the rise in the standard of living of the upper classes was accompanied by greater exploitation, higher rents, a greater incidence of usury and inflation. But nevertheless, he felt it was commendable '. . . in a time wherein all things are grown to most excessive prices . . . we do yet find the means to obtain and achieve such furniture as heretofore hath been unpossible . . . . Certes in noblemen's houses it is not rare to see abundance of arras, rich hangings of tapestry, silver vessel and so much other plate as may furnish sundry cupboards, to the sum often-times of £1000 or £2000 at the least.'

Harrison's estimate is borne out by the total value of Lord de la Warr's movable goods in 1554, which came from Offington, from his much smaller house at Ewhurst and from his house in London. The total sum involved was a little over £1800. Moreover, for Harrison, it was not only the upper classes that had benefited. 'In the houses of knights, gentlemen, merchantmen and other wealthy citizens, it is not (uncommon) to behold generally their great provision of tapestry, Turkey work, pewter, brass, fine linen, and thereto costly cupboards of plate . . .' and 'it is now descended yet lower, even unto the inferior artificers and many farmers, who . . . have for the most part also learned to garnish their cupboards with plate, their joint beds with tapestry and silk hangings, and their tables with carpets and fine napery, whereby the wealth of our country . . . doth infinitely appear.'[37] Much of this abundance of household goods, as is obvious from some of the terms used above, was due to a thriving import trade in luxury goods. This raises important questions about England's connections with Continental Europe in the period that is conventionally called the Renaissance.

# 6

# 'The Anticke All Gilt': England and the Renaissance

THE SET OF joined panels from Beckingham Hall, Essex (Fig. 68), dated 1546, is typical of work that was being produced in many parts of Europe at this time. It is not known where exactly in the house these panels came from, but they are most likely to have been in a very prominent position, probably over the hall fireplace. Like the use of external heraldry, the purpose of these decorated panels was to promote the social position of the owner of the house under the King, and here the family arms in the lowest panel are juxtaposed with the royal arms at the top. Heraldry is an exact science and the coats of arms themselves have to be unambiguous, but whoever produced these panels indulged in a great deal of artistic licence in the decorative fantasy which surrounds the shields. It has sometimes been suggested that the semi-profile heads are actually portraits of members of the Beckingham family, but this is difficult to prove. And even if they are, they were clearly inspired by German woodcuts and by classical portrait busts, as shown by the dress of the central figure.[1] This sort of decoration, whether in wood and plaster for the interiors of houses, or in terracotta and carved stone for exteriors, marks the most widespread and immediate response to forms of classical ornament ultimately deriving from Italy. This type of decoration is conventionally described as Renaissance, but is this an appropriate word to use in an English context?

Whenever the term 'the English Renaissance' is mentioned in discussing the visual arts, it is invariably used rather imprecisely to indicate a period in early modern history when English art came under the influence of Continental Europe. Styles in architecture and the applied arts that had originally developed in Italy are said to have come to England through such centres as France and the Low Countries, being somewhat transformed and sim-

plified in the process. In a literal sense, the word Renaissance does not seem applicable to England. Whilst there is cause for arguing that there was a 'rebirth' of interest in the art of the ancient world in Italy, through a new awareness of the remains of the Roman Empire (although the basis for this argument has been substantially revised in recent years), in England this was impossible since practically nothing from classical times could be seen above ground.[2] So the question arises of how best to describe the early Tudor fashion for foreign styles of ornament and applied architectural decoration.

The word that occurs countless times in contemporary letters, contracts and payments is one or other variation of 'anticke'. (The conventional modern spelling 'antique' was sometimes used in the sixteenth century and is invariably used in later transcriptions of documents from the Tudor period.) 'Anticke' is often used without qualification in contemporary sources so it seems likely that

*68   Panels from Beckingham Hall, Essex, dated 1546, now in the Victoria and Albert Museum, London.*

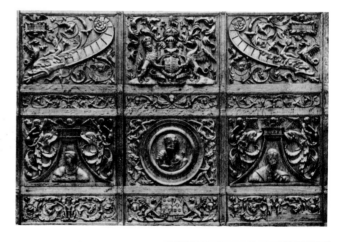

it was commonly used and understood. For example, Leland writes of the interior of Sir John Russell's house at Chenies that it is 'richely paintid with antique workes of white and blak', and a merchant writes to his Antwerp agent to order tiles 'drawn with antiques of the latest fashion', both clearly taking familiarity with the term for granted.[3] At the end of the century, Henry Peacham, in his *Art of Drawing*, listed the common features of the 'anticke', by then seldom used, and stressed its essentially inventive quality: 'The forme of it is a generall and ... an unnaturall or unorderly composition for delight sake, of men, beasts, birds, fishes, flowers, &c without (as wee say) Rime or reason, for the greater variety you shew in your invention, the more you please .... You may, if you list, draw naked boys riding and playing with their paper-mills or bubble-shels uppon Goates, Eagles, Dolphins, &c: the bones of a Rammes head hung with strings of beads and Ribands, Satyres, Tritons, apes, Cornucopias, Dogges yockt [yoked] &c drawing cowumers [cucumbers], cherries and any kind of wild trail or vine after your owne invention, with a thousand more such idle toyes, so that herein you cannot be too fantastical.'[4]

Though the original sources of this form of ornament were the classical remains of Italy, 'anticke' in sixteenth-century England referred to 'antics', in

69 *Oxburgh, Norfolk. Detail of the terracotta screen in the Bedingfield chantry chapel, c.1525–30.*

the sense of ornament as something playful and capricious, rather than to the ancient world. This vocabulary clearly supplanted a heavier form of ornament in which designs based on simple vegetable shapes featured prominently. This is often described in contemporary documents as 'savage' work, though early Tudor patrons might have seen the development of 'anticke' simply as a refinement on what had gone before and certainly old and new styles were used together. In the construction of the great hall for the Revels at Greenwich in 1527, 'Iawe pieces [a form of cornice] and crestes were karued wyth Vinettes and trailes of sauage worke, and richely gilted with gold and Bise [a bright blue colour, usually obtained from smalt]' and to these were attached candlesticks of 'antyke woorke' to light the room.[5] The terracotta screen from the Bedingfield chapel at Oxburgh (Fig. 69) shows how dense 'anticke' ornament could be applied; the 'invention' of which Peacham writes here emphasizes the surface of the object and inhibits any understanding of its architectural structure.

Although the élite of early sixteenth-century England had a common interest in, even a passion for the 'anticke' as ornament, there is little indication that there was anything more than a superficial understanding of what was going on in Italy. It is likely that the style was perceived at Court to be associated with what might be described as the use of art for propaganda, in this case to celebrate military and diplomatic victories. 'Anticke' ornament was used to decorate temporary structures put up for great occasions at Court, just as it was used in classical times on triumphal arches and columns erected to glorify the might of Roman emperors.[6] But there is little evidence to show that Henry VIII's courtiers were able to make the intellectual leap from an awareness of how ornament was used to a knowledge of Italian ideas about proportion in architecture, or of the Italian concern with the sort of ornament that was suitable for each type of building. For the English, 'anticke' ornament, lavish, colourful and gilded, was an end in itself. Historians have perhaps inappropriately interpreted the occurrence of this fashion in England as indicating the beginning of a more profound awareness of European developments.

Until quite recently, the development of architecture in England was seen in evolutionary and deterministic terms. In other words, it was seen as inevitable that the Renaissance or classical style would eventually triumph in England in its most developed form, just as it did elsewhere in Europe. So the 'anticke' ornament of the early Tudor period was seen as a crude copying of the sophisticated worlds of Italy and France, a superficial application of classical decoration to buildings that were basically medieval in construction and purpose. This lack of sophistication, it was argued, inevitably gave way to a deeper understanding of classical proportions which reached final fruition only in the seventeenth century, in the age of Inigo Jones and Christopher Wren. By this time, England was becoming a cultural colony of Europe and was in a position to contribute to the further development of the prevailing style.[7]

A more recent view of English developments sees them as forming a more irregular and erratic pattern of false starts, each deflected by the changing course of the Reformation, which affected English attitudes towards the use of pagan and religious imagery, and towards things foreign (and particularly things Italian and Catholic) in general. The English response to Continental developments in the sixteenth century is therefore more usefully envisaged as a succession of 'Renaissances', each with a different character and purpose, rather than as a gradual purification of one style. Looking at architecture and its allied art forms, the first res-

ponse to Continental ideas was indeed to combine these with native traditions in a new vocabulary of ornament that was applied to the surfaces of objects. This development was stimulated by the trade in foreign, luxury goods because it was small objects, such as metalwork and jewellery, that encouraged the fashion for 'anticke' decoration. Few examples in these media survive today, but the remaining terracotta and wooden fragments suggest that the native output of 'anticke' ornament was neither sophisticated in style nor of high quality workmanship.

The second phase of development is seen as beginning around 1550 and is marked by the first consistent use of the classical orders. A group of courtiers, centred on Edward Seymour, Protector and Duke of Somerset, built houses on which ornament was used with much more sense of visual unity and which reveal a deeper understanding of the need for order and proportion in the basic design of the house, such as the layout of windows and doors. These developments are evident in certain avant-garde pieces of tomb sculpture as well as in architecture. The third phase was the extraordinary compromise between English and foreign ideas (now chiefly imported through the pattern books of Flanders) that resulted in the individuality of Elizabethan architecture.[8]

Yet even this recent view of English developments perhaps does not fully come to grips with why and how English architecture changed, and especially with the peculiar and quite individual character of the initial phase of foreign influence. This is to some extent because the useful parallels that can be drawn between England and Europe at this time have been interpreted too narrowly and have been looked at almost solely in terms of stylistic criteria. Also, surface ornament has been taken very much at face value, with a tendency to see its superficial nature as somehow echoing the purposes and intentions of those who commissioned it; shallowness of relief somehow equals shallowness of taste. This view neglects the fact that the popularity of 'anticke' ornament raises several interesting issues about the relationship between patronage at Court and in the country at large and about how the relative qualities of different materials for building and ornament were perceived. There is also the question of what 'anticke' ornament tells us about the rivalry between English courtiers and their Continental counterparts.

One of the reasons why the architecture of countries on the fringe of mainland Europe, like England, has often been thought provincial and inexpert by comparison with Italy has been because the Italian Renaissance is epitomized by its most famous buildings, notably churches and palaces, which were mainly constructed in the expensive and permanent materials of stone and marble. Similar comparisons have been made between Italian sculpture and that of the rest of Europe, seen as peripheral to Italian leadership. It is certainly true that Italian buildings and objects made of the highest quality materials, whose expense and fine workmanship invoked awe and appreciation, raised the general standard of production. But these palaces in stone and marble were only the tip of the iceberg when it comes to considering Italian buildings of this time in general. In Renaissance Italy, the common awareness of fashionable ideas, whatever stylistic label they were given, would have been just as conditioned, as elsewhere in Europe, by people's everyday experience of the superficial application of ornament and the use of sham or inexpensive materials.

Through close study of records and surviving evidence, it has recently been shown that the basic building material of Florence, the city said to have given birth to the Renaissance, was brick.[9] Only the wealthiest families could afford to build completely in stone, or with a complete stone facing, like the famous palaces of the Rucellai or the Strozzi. Elsewhere, people employed the architecture of disguise, with brick covered so as to suggest that the building is of a different material. For example, the large Florentine palace built for the Canacci family (Fig. 70) in the fifteenth century is basically a brick construction, covered with grey-brown *intonaco* or plaster, which is scored to look as if the wall is built of small pieces of dressed, cut stone. Below the level of the first cornice, the *intonaco* is richly decorated with *sgraffito* work, in which motives of dogs and chains are blended in an heraldic visual pun on the name of the owners (*cane* = dog; *catenaccio* = door-chain). Only doors and windows are surrounded by stone, thus emphasizing the important architectural features of the building.[10] Although the decorative elements of the Canacci palace are crafted with a delicacy and richness rarely found in English attempts at this kind of ornament at this time, the parallel with similar work in England is nevertheless very marked. A basic and relatively cheap building material has been used. It was locally manufactured and it has been covered with a surface overlay to enrich it and suggest that it is more expensive than it really is. It cannot be necessarily assumed that contemporary Florentines saw the result as artistically second-best.

Any comparison between England and Italy at

70 *Palazzo Canacci, Florence, built in the late fifteenth century. In the angle between this and the adjacent palace, the smooth rendering has disintegrated to reveal the rougher brick surface beneath. (The ground floor of Florentine urban palaces such as this would invariably be used for storage and a courtyard; the family rooms would be on the first floor.)*

this time should be based on comparing like with like. It is also worth looking closely at who was responsible for those buildings in which fashionable 'anticke' ornament was used and considering a wider geographical picture than has usually been the case. In particular, were the patrons from different countries of a similar social class and how far was the 'anticke' mode a deliberate choice over more traditional forms of ornament? England was not alone among European countries in the way in which a new, mixed élite gained a new prominence in the workings of government. Newly-created posts evolved to meet the changing needs of the time. The post of secretary to the King, for example, took on an increased importance in European courts to become one of the chief executive offices of State.[11] Throughout Europe the new

'anticke' style was patronized both by sovereigns themselves and also by people of relatively obscure origins who had a point to make about their hard-earned wealth and power and who were most anxious to reflect the outward splendour of the sovereign who had made them what they were.

It is particularly interesting to look at France in comparison with England because this was the country with which England had the most diplomatic contact and the one courtiers were most likely to visit. In fact, the French response to Italian ideas has remarkable parallels with what happened in England, allowing for the fact that French contact with Italian sources was more direct than English connections following the French invasion of Italy in 1494. To some extent, the assumption of Italianate motives of decoration in French architecture reflected an attitude of conquest and appropriation. As in England, the evidence for the employment of foreign craftsmen is largely documentary, since there are few identifiable remains of the work for which they were paid.

While it is true that the case for attributing particular buildings to Italians is stronger in France

than in England, it would seem that in both countries it was local craftsmen who were instrumental in finally determining and creating the hybrid style that overlaid medieval traditions of building with a new and fashionable skin of ornament.[12] In both countries, too, the pace for large-scale domestic building activity was set by leading churchmen. In France, the chief figure was Georges d'Amboise, Archbishop of Rouen. Like Wolsey, he was Chief Minister to the King, was given the cardinal's hat at his sovereign's express wish and aspired to the papacy itself. His great Normandy château of Gaillon (Fig. 71), the major part of which was probably built in the years immediately after his failed bid for the papacy in 1503, was certainly a key building. It helped to ensure the spread of Italian craftsmen within France because a large group of them moved here from their initial base of operations in the Loire valley in order to work on the château. Their repertoire of ornament was then more generally introduced to the northern part of France from here. Gaillon, in particular the great gatehouse with its applied Italianate ornament, was undoubtedly a prototype for Wolsey's own building projects.[13]

France was also similar to England in the way in which the King took the lead in patronizing Italian craftsmen, both in terms of the sheer numbers he employed and in the choice of individuals for their particular skills and merits. Royal patronage in both countries and the rivalry between the two kings resulted in buildings whose individuality far surpassed even the most ambitious works of other patrons. The programme of external decoration in stucco and slate devised for Henry VIII's Nonsuch

*LEFT 71   The château of Gaillon, Normandy, c.1503–10. The great pitched roof and the dormer windows are not original, but are replacements erected in recent years based on the first design.*

*BELOW 72   Nonsuch Palace, built 1538–47, in a late sixteenth-century print based on Hofnagel's drawing of the palace from the park. The exterior of this inner courtyard was covered with slate and stucco decoration, designed by the Italian Nicholas Bellin of Modena.*

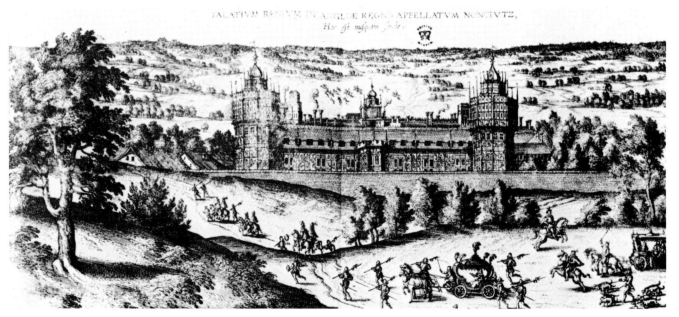

Palace (Fig. 72), begun in 1538, displayed a complex understanding of classical literature and history and was used to advertise the virtues of the King and the power of the Tudor dynasty. Its immediate impact in England was minimal, for such a programme was beyond the financial reach (and possibly beyond the understanding) of many of Henry's courtiers.

Similarly, Francis I's building works demonstrate a confidence in applying classical forms in a three-dimensional way that transcends the surface quality of other French buildings that adopted the Italian style. This is seen, for example, in the sculptural boldness of the staircase at Blois (Fig. 73), which attempts to merge the French tradition of a stair tower with the notion of a pierced screen of classical ornament. A similar boldness appears in the deep window reveals at Saint-Germain-en-Laye, which suggest the form of a classical loggia. The presence of Italians at the French and English courts, whether they can be held directly responsible for these buildings or not, possibly inspired these schemes to some degree, but the end results are ultimately solutions firmly in the tradition of the indigenous architecture of each country.[14]

In the case of the courtier class, the parallels between France and England are even more marked, though again more through a shared concern to express social position than in the sense of direct stylistic comparisons. The new fashion for Italianate ornament was taken up most avidly by the group of men whose position in society devolved from their role as king's servants in central or local government and who were therefore essentially first generation and *nouveaux riches*. A number of families from Tours in the Loire valley, whose banking and financial expertise made them close counsellors of the French kings, were particularly prominent in France. They included men like Florimond Robertet, who built the château of Bury, Gilles Berthelot, who was responsible for the château of Azay-le-Rideau (Fig. 74), and Thomas Bohier, who built the earliest parts of the château of Chenonceaux (which was later to become a French royal palace).[15] Although their buildings varied in the way they adopted classical or Italian forms, and although they still reflected French traditions of building and basic design, they all demonstrated a preference for the Italianate forms of ornament and used them to embellish peculiarly French architectural features, such as dormer windows (lucarnes) and round angle turrets. The English royal household became increasingly modelled on that of the French kings during Henry VIII's reign, so it is interesting to consider to what

extent English courtiers saw and copied the social pretensions of these buildings and how far their efforts were instrumental in introducing the French version of Italian ideas to England more generally.[16]

Early Tudor patrons might have had direct experience of foreign styles of architecture and architectural ornament in three principal ways; first, by the direct employment of foreign craftsmen in England; second, by travel on diplomatic or other missions when they could have seen new buildings at first hand; and third, as previously indicated, by the import of foreign, luxury goods that used the same vocabulary of ornament as architecture and might have prompted new ideas.

As far as the employment of foreigners is concerned, there is very little evidence to go on. Both Henry VIII and Cardinal Wolsey used foreign craftsmen (some of them with architectural experience), most notably a distinguished series of Italians, but they seem mainly to have been employed on work that was basically decorative, in particular the temporary structures erected for Court celebrations.[17] Some were used to more immediate advantage in the 1540s, when the need for new, technologically advanced fortifications against the French led to their employment as military engineers. Girolamo da Treviso, who was sent out to the Pas-de-Calais as an adviser in siege warfare, was killed at the English assault on Boulogne in September 1544.[18] An exceptional case of Italians being employed by a courtier was in the decoration of a house at Whitefriars, London, which belonged to Thomas Cawarden. In his privileged position as Master of the Revels at Court, he was able to draw on the services of Bartolommeo Penni, brother of Gianfrancesco and Luca Penni who were pupils of Raphael in Rome, though there is no record of what Penni actually did at Whitefriars.[19]

Estimating the significance of foreign travel is as difficult as assessing the employment of foreign craftsmen. There is in fact no general correlation between those courtiers who travelled widely and often, whether as students, soldiers, diplomats or resident ambassadors, and a particularly Italianate or French character in the buildings they were responsible for.[20] It would be in any case wrong to assume that those who travelled, even for the ostensible purpose of education, would necessarily be visually curious and they would almost certainly have been unskilled in recording

*73  Blois, France. The staircase tower in the Francis I wing of c. 1515–24. English royal palaces were also being built with great staircase towers at this time, but without the Italian-influenced decoration seen here.*

what they had seen, whether visually or verbally (see Chapter 1).[21] One pertinent example will demonstrate both the potential for making connections between English and foreign patrons and the difficulty of proving the degree of cross-fertilization.

Richard Weston's Sutton Place has often been directly compared with French examples of domestic architecture, particularly with regard to its plan. Weston had certainly travelled extensively in France before 1521, the earliest possible date on which work on Sutton Place could have started. An extended journey in 1518 took him through the Loire valley as far south as Cognac in Angoulême.[22] Francis I's building works in the Loire were barely under way at this date, but Weston is likely to have seen the houses of leading courtiers. At the château of Chaumont, for example, he could have seen the way in which the arms of Charles d'Amboise, Great Master of the Household to Louis XII, and those of his uncle, the Cardinal-Archbishop of Rouen, cover a plinth to the visitor's left on going through the entrance arch to the courtyard. The treatment is very similar to the terracotta facing Weston later commissioned on the plinths either side of the entrance arch and the main door at Sutton Place (Fig. 75).[23]

The château of Bury (Fig. 76), begun in 1511 for Florimond Robertet, Secretary of State to Louis XII and Francis I, was built to a plan that was to set a pattern for later French architecture and that at first sight appears to foreshadow the design of Sutton Place. The château had a symmetrical courtyard in which the entrance range faced the principal suite of rooms. The door to the hall lay centrally in the facade and was emphasized by the fact that the central third of the range was raised into a high pavilion.[24] Sutton Place shares these features. But, apart from the extra height of the hall facade, the comparison is principally based on the plans of the two buildings, rather than on their appearance; the visitor to Bury would have seen a building that looked in every way different from Sutton. Most importantly Bury was built in stone,

while Sutton Place was of brick and terracotta. Bury had a low entrance screen, above which the principal range could be glimpsed from a distance, a feature that was not to be adopted in England for some generations to come. There could hardly have been a greater contrast with the severe brick

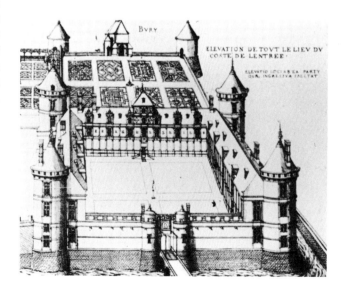

LEFT 74  *Azay-le-Rideau, France, from the southeast. Building on this French courtier house was begun in 1518 and work on the court side was complete by 1524.*

ABOVE RIGHT 75  *Sutton Place, Surrey, c.1521–33. Plinths with RW for Richard Weston and his personal device, the tun, are typical of the play on words in architectural decoration favoured by Renaissance patrons.*

BELOW RIGHT 76  *The château of Bury, France, begun 1511– 12, of which only a fragment now remains. From the print by Du Cerceau.*

entrance facade of Sutton Place, which gave no indication of the courtyard within. The supposition that this English house is indebted to a French prototype is very interesting, but it rests on the paradox that the feature which would have impressed Weston's fellow courtiers, the novel appearance, was not immediately apparent and certainly not French.[25]

Attention has also been drawn to the fact that the *putti* (or cherubs) in the terracotta panels over the external doorways at Sutton are very similar in style to French examples (Fig. 77), particularly those in the compartments of the stone vault of the chapel of the Hôtel Lallement at Bourges.[26] It would clearly be stretching coincidence to suggest that the same craftsmen worked both at Bourges and for an English royal courtier in the Thames

valley and such similarities must have arisen from some more widespread influence. This is most likely to have been the use of similar books of patterns and designs, as workshops of this period were dependent on much the same sources and presumably these were also what building patrons were looking at. The simplified and rather crude quality of much contemporary woodcut illustration and the frequent repetition of motives from book to book would explain the naïve and vigorous design and execution that is such a feature of the ornament at both Bourges and Sutton. French Books of Hours, for example, have been identified as the source for similarly robust figurative work on the de la Warr chantry chapel at Boxgrove Priory in West Sussex (Fig. 78), commissioned by Thomas West, Lord de la Warr, in about 1532.[27]

The third source of contact between England and the Continent was through the import of goods. The fashion for covering the exteriors of houses with 'anticke' decoration, and particularly the use of terracotta, makes sense only if it is seen

*77 Sutton Place, Surrey. Putti over the door on the south side of the house, with darker terracotta for the balusters flanking them. Tudor heraldic glass can be seen in the windows on either side.*

as an extension of the highly ornamented hangings and other goods that were imported as furnishings at this time. The dominant port of entry for goods was London, though it is clear that other south and east coast ports also shared in this traffic, particularly because of their importance in the transference of goods between London and other parts of the country by sea (a carrying trade that is often neglected in studies of this period because of the lack of documentation).[28] These trade routes may also have been used by foreign craftsmen and the pattern of trade may explain localized examples of Continental styles. The most important of the inland areas where foreign workers may have been active was that part of southern England north of Southampton. This is where the so-called 'Winchester School' was responsible for a group of tombs and chantry chapels in Winchester Cathedral and was also influential in West Sussex and Hampshire. Similarly, the notable use of terracotta in East Anglia (mainly for tombs, but with possibly related architectural work) may have originated

from a workshop of foreign craftsmen based at Norwich.[29]

The term 'terracotta' can be literally translated as 'burnt earth', but the basic material is essentially different from ordinary earths used for baking bricks. Terracotta was known as 'burnt pot earth' in early sixteenth-century England, a term which suggests its affinity with the fine-textured clays used for pottery. Terracotta was fired for longer than bricks and usually at higher temperatures and the compact quality that resulted meant that it could be used for fine detail that was not possible in any other material.[30] Terracotta was widely used in England only for a short period in the early sixteenth century, and again in the eighteenth and nineteenth centuries. It was used fairly extensively for architectural ornament in East Anglia from

78 *Boxgrove Priory, West Sussex. The naked* putti *on this detail from the de la Warr chantry chapel are in the spirit of* anticke, *the decorative surrounds closer to older 'savage' work. Pattern books are known to have been the source for the figurative work.*

79  *Layer Marney, Essex. Detail of a window with brick and terracotta work of the 1520s.*

about 1515 to 1535 and was favoured by high-ranking courtiers and local gentry families alike. The gate-house and adjoining ranges of Layer Marney, in Essex (Fig. 79), are surviving examples of its decorative potential. This house was begun for Henry Marney and his son, John, who successively held the title of Baron Marney and were leading figures at Court in the first years of Henry VIII's reign.

Less prominent work in terracotta, but figurative rather than simply decorative, survives on top of the turrets of the gatehouse of West Stow, in Suffolk, the home of Sir John Crofts, who was Master of the Horse to Mary Tudor, Henry VIII's sister.[31] This house may be connected to what a written description makes clear was one of the most ambitious programmes of terracotta decoration of this period. This was devised for Mary Tudor and her husband, Charles Brandon, Duke of Suffolk, for their house at Westhorpe, in the same county, known to us only through an eighteenth-century description of its demolition: 'The workmen are now pulling it down, as fast as may

be, in a very careless and injudicious manner. The coping bricks, battlements, and many other ornamental pieces are made of earth, and burnt hard, and as fresh as when first built. They might, with care, have been taken down whole, but all the fine chimnies and ornaments were pulled down with ropes, and crushed to pieces, in a most shameful manner. There was a monstrous figure of Hercules, sitting cross-legged with his club, and a lion beside him, but all shattered to pieces ....'[32]

This record of what appears to have been figurative and presumably large-scale terracotta work is interesting in the light of another commission in which Charles Brandon was involved. When preparations were under way in 1520 for the Field of Cloth of Gold, Brandon was asked to send 'divers of the Kinges armes and bestes cast in moldes, which wold doo great ease and furtheraunce to the Kynges busynes'. More than one contemporary reference to the temporary building constructed as the royal palace at the Field of Cloth of Gold describes the gatehouse as having brick towers on each side, defended by figures of men casting stones and shooting iron balls from cannons. Hall's *Chronicle* in particular mentions statues of ancient princes, including Hercules and Alexander, above the gateway.[33] If pieces of terracotta work prepared originally for Westhorpe, or second versions of pieces designed for that house, found their way to the Court celebrations in the Pas-de-Calais, this emphasizes again the close connection between the decoration of Court festivities and that of courtier houses. The similarities lay not only in the use of materials (which in this case could be painted and gilded for splendid effect), but also in the selected images and, as we shall shortly see at Sutton Place, in the speed of assembly.

Patrons of lower social standing than these members of the court aristocracy also commissioned fine terracotta work, as is shown by the windows made for Shrubland Old Hall in Suffolk. One of these can still be seen at the house, whilst others were subsequently moved to the nearby churches of Henley (Fig. 80), Barham and Barking.[34] In Norfolk, terracotta is found on the fragment of the once much larger house of Great Cressingham, built for the Jenney family, and possibly dating from as early as 1509–14. It is also seen in this county at Great Snoring, on the remains of the house built for Sir Ralph Shelton; at Wallington Hall, built for the Coningsby family; at Denver, built for the Willoughby family; and at East Barsham, built for the Fermors.[35]

Although all these East Anglian houses employed terracotta, they in no sense form a stylistic group, since not all the terracotta ornament can be described as in the 'anticke' style. They have all often been dated to about 1525 (this is the date when the untimely death of the young John Marney halted work at Layer Marney), on the assumption that the same terracotta workshop was responsible in each case, but the range of motives suggest that this was unlikely. The decoration of Layer Marney arguably shows the deepest understanding of classical ideas of architecture, since the window transoms in terracotta have been designed as elongated colonnettes with capitals. Of perhaps greater importance is the fact that there is no correlation between sophistication of ornament and sophistication of technique. At East Barsham, where a large range of semi-classical and older, medieval motives are used alongside each other in both terracotta and cut brick, the technical skill displayed in the terracotta ornament is visibly greater than in the stylistically more sophisticated work at Layer Marney.

A second area where terracotta was used to add ornament to architecture in the 'anticke' style was the Thames valley. Here there is direct evidence that terracotta moulds were passed from one building project to another, for the same ones appear to have been used for the window surrounds and plinths at Weston's Sutton Place and at Wolsey's Hampton Court. (Though it has to be admitted that the Hampton Court connection is based on fragments of terracotta that were clearly made from the Sutton Place moulds discovered in the foundation rubble of Wolsey's buildings — none have been found applied to any wall surface.) Terracotta fragments were found in the area of the inner gatehouse during the excavation of Nonsuch Palace in 1959–60 and from Wyngaerde's view of London it is also likely that terracotta was extensively used in the decoration of Charles Brandon's Suffolk Place in Southwark, perhaps employing the same moulds as were used at Westhorpe (see Fig. 15).[36] Finally, there are two other isolated instances of the use of terracotta outside the main areas of East Anglia and the Thames valley, presumably the direct result of Court connections. At Laughton Place, East Sussex, terracotta was used on the new brick tower and other buildings within the moat built for the Pelham family and dated 1534, while undecorated terracotta forms part of the structure of the small lodge of Kneesall, Nottinghamshire, built for John, Baron Hussey (one of the northern lords executed for not supporting the King's cause in the uprising known as the Pilgrimage of Grace in 1536).[37]

The quality of terracotta decoration outside East Anglia is variable and ornament is again often quite

ABOVE 80   Henley Church, Suffolk. The terracotta window of the 1520s taken from Shrubland Old Hall and set incongruously into flint walling.

81   Sutton Place, Surrey. Detail of the terracotta mouldings from a window facing into the court. These mouldings were not inserted with very great care for on other windows they are sometimes upside down.

82  *Horton Court, Avon. The stone doorway of William Knight's house of the 1520s with a mixture of classical and heraldic motifs found on no other house of this time and more specific and detailed than those at Sutton Place (see Fig.81).*

crude and summary. At Sutton Place (Fig. 81), two of the three patterns of ornament used in the hollow chamfers of the window mouldings seem to have been designed to resemble trophies carried on poles, a characteristic 'anticke' motif. There is a suggestion of banners and quivers of arrows but the forms are simplified to the point where it is difficult to describe them as figurative at all. They appear especially bizarre where they have been inserted upside down. Even though some of the window mouldings at Sutton have been replaced at various times by copies, if the embrasures are examined clockwise around the court it is hard to avoid the conclusion that the terracottas were put in place with increasing speed and neglect and that errors were not checked for. As for quality and fine detail, none of this architectural terracotta can compare with custom-made examples by a leading

Italian craftsman such as the famous series of roundels of Roman emperors made by Giovanni da Maiano for Wolsey's Hampton Court in 1521.[38]

The payments for these roundels are recorded; we know that they cost £2 6s 8d each (or 3½ marks). However, they were clearly a very special commission and for this reason should not be compared with the architectural terracotta of a house like Sutton Place. Since no other payments for work in terracotta are known (other than further specialist work by Giovanni da Maiano for Wolsey, notably a 'history of Hercules', now lost), it is impossible to calculate relative costs which would indicate whether this material was a convenient, interchangeable and cheap means of decoration which was a viable alternative to stone. Certainly the widespread use of terracotta in East Anglia must have stemmed partly from the lack of local building stone, although it probably also reflected trading contacts with the Low Countries and the Baltic Coast, where the material was also popular.[39] East Anglia's close connections with the Continent have often led to the suggestion that many works in terracotta must have been imported, but this is unlikely to be the case. Apart from Kneeshall,

*83   West Drayton, London. The doorway to the surviving range of Sir William Paget's house with its fine brick mouldings.*

Weston's initials and repeated rebus motif at Sutton Place, to the fine detail of the paired arms of the Swillington and Booth families in the windows from Shrubland (Figs. 75 and 80). Collectively, these examples do not support the idea that terracotta was an easily distributed commodity that was imported ready-made. Its manufacture might, however, have depended on foreign expertise and the apparent disappearance of terracotta on a wide scale from the mid 1530s may be connected with the events following the Reformation which would have affected the availability of foreign craftsmen.

Apart from this question of foreign expertise, there were also more general considerations which were probably of greater significance. The popularity of terracotta ornament coincides with the great period of Henry VIII's lavish court entertainments, up to the coronation of Anne Boleyn in 1533. These were the years when Henry's need to impress the fellow-sovereigns of Europe was paramount and 'anticke' ornament, lavish and gilded, expressed his perceived status in the most celebratory way. The courtiers whom we know to have followed the royal example were all men who were prominent in the King's younger years, and were a generation older than the administrators of the later part of the reign. The houses of the men who surrounded the King in the 1540s are noticeable for their lack of external ornament; West Drayton, Standon and Ingatestone, built in a kind of commuter belt around London for Henry's hardworking Secretaries of State, were remarkably plain, the only variety in the texture of the wall surface being provided by brick mouldings (Fig. 83). Houses such as these marked a stylistic pause before a new approach in the perception of how foreign styles could be used was experimented with around the middle of the century. The other significant development of these years, the conversion of the monasteries, also marked a lessening in the concern for architectural ornament, but suggested important new approaches to planning the country house.

where the terracotta is structural and undecorated, all the known examples on courtier and other houses contain or contained at least some personalized heraldry, suggesting that this form of decoration was individually commissioned. The detail and extent of this heraldry ranges from the simple initials on the small blocks supported by dolphin scroll forms on the parapets of the gatehouse at Layer Marney, through the higher relief of

# The Conversion of the Monasteries

THE DISSOLUTION OF the monasteries by two Acts of Parliament in 1536 and 1539 not only aroused strong emotions at the time but has continued to do so amongst historians of the Tudor period. During the time of the Reformation itself certain leading scholars, whilst not daring to challenge the King's authority or purpose in bringing about the end of nearly one thousand monastic establishments, expressed regret that great repositories of learning were to be dispersed and called for their refoundation as schools and colleges.[1] One of the chief reasons for Leland's journeys was to record what was left of monastic libraries. In the seventeenth century, when it was clear to the radical politicians of the age that landed and established classes had done rather well out of the dissolution, there emerged a stream of invective in all kinds of literature against families in possession of former monastic property, fuelling the legend that all such families were somehow cursed.[2] In recent times, modern historians have often kept up the sense of indignation, seeing the attack on the monasteries as part of the wider plunder of the lands and goods of the Church (identified by these historians as co-terminous with the interests of the common people) by a comparatively small group of the privileged and powerful.[3]

It is true that a great deal of calculated destruction of holy objects and buildings did take place, and that the greed shown by many was human nature at its worst. However it is also true that, as far as the buildings were concerned, the process of dissolution was in many places less wilfully destructive than traditionally described and indeed the self-interest of the beneficiaries ensured that as much was preserved as was destroyed. In the popular imagination, monastic remains are typified by the ruins of great abbeys like Tintern, Glastonbury and Haughmond (Fig. 84). But there are probably even more former monasteries still surviving at the cores of buildings now put to all manner of other uses in both town and country; of these, country houses undoubtedly form the largest proportion.

Attitudes to monastic remains have changed over the centuries and not always to the benefit of their preservation. The sense of regret so well orchestrated in the seventeenth century was not then followed by an unbroken thread of care and concern. At the same time as some eighteenth- and early nineteenth-century landowners were turning monastic ruins on their estates into picturesque eye-catchers in the artfully-conceived landscape, just as many allowed them to decay and disappear or sold them for industrial use; Neath Abbey, in Glamorgan (Fig. 85), converted into a mid Tudor house by the Williams family, related to Thomas Cromwell, was the site of a copper-smelting works by the eighteenth century.[4] When nineteenth-century archaeologists first began to survey and ensure the protection of monastic sites, they were understandably initially concerned to identify the medieval church and monastery amid the standing buildings and record their findings. Only towards the end of the last century did attention begin to focus on what was subsequently made of these buildings by their secular, post-dissolution owners.

*ABOVE RIGHT 84   Haughmond Abbey, Shropshire, looking southwest from a point just beyond the east end of the monastic church. The abbey buildings spread over two cloisters.*

*BELOW RIGHT 85   Neath Abbey, West Glamorgan. View of the west face of the dormitory range with post-dissolution windows of the 1540s–50s inserted.*

William St John Hope (who wrote many learned articles and books on archaeological matters of all kinds between about 1880 and 1925) and, later, Harold Brakspear (whose work overlapped with that of Hope and continued into the 1930s) were pioneers in this field. But modern techniques of exploration are revealing much more. It is clear that the conversion of monasteries into houses presented a set of interesting challenges that helped to reshape approaches to the planning and appearance of the country house.

There has been much debate about the extent to which the dissolution created a new property-owning class and how far it simply concentrated more land and resources into the hands of those already well endowed. Several important local studies have been undertaken in recent years to see how many new fortunes based on land ownership were created at this time. By general consent, the answer has usually been that the already well-established families did very well. In addition, a few new families in each county or region successfully bargained for ex-monastic land and thereby staked a claim to an important place in local society for the first time. Beyond these groups, the theory of plunder by the few seems to hold good, for although the dissolution did change the pattern of tenant-farming, it caused no great expansion of the property-owning class.[5] This concentration of property in the hands of the few was particularly crucial for the fate of the buildings, because many of the new owners made their first great house out of the monastic buildings. The interesting question is whether they did this with a sense of doing something new, or whether they consciously converted them into something that looked and functioned like the established Tudor house.

In any event, it does seem that the disposal of monastic property was used by the Crown to get support for its actions among those who mattered. Certainly by the late sixteenth century it was perceived that government policy had resulted in some degree of what in the twentieth century we would call 'social engineering'. As an anonymous Elizabethan writer put it, Thomas Cromwell had 'caused the King of the abbes possessions to make suche dispersion, as it behoved infinite multitudes for their owne interest to joyne with the King in hollding them downe'. By 'divers' means, the writer goes on, the King sold and exchanged properties, 'preferring many sufficient persons to the Kinges servis who were some raised to the nobilitie and to worshippe and good calling, and all indewed [endowed] with maintenaunce out of the revenues of the abbays'.[6]

Yet it seems that no such coherent policy prevailed at the time of dissolution and that there was initially no clear plan about the future of monastic sites. Following the Act of 1536 that dissolved the smaller monasteries with revenues of under £200 per annum, there were official denials as late as the winter of 1538–9 that the larger establishments were also to disappear.[7] At the same time as denials were being issued, the larger monasteries were being subjected to increasing government interference in their management; in some cases, where the post of abbot or abbess fell vacant, men and women who would co-operate with the process of dissolution were appointed to these positions. Thus the second Act of Dissolution in 1539 often simply legitimized acts of surrender that had already taken place.[8]

The King certainly aimed to realize the cash value of monastic property, but in the first instance this was done by seizing valuables, such as the holy objects from monastic churches and the lead from the roofs, rather than by realizing the full capital value of land and buildings. As the years passed, the conditions for transferring seized monastic sites from the Crown to individuals were tightened up. Higher prices were demanded of those seeking to purchase and future obligations were imposed on the new owners. Selling was certainly more organized after the foundation of the Court of Augmentations to supervise the upkeep and disposal of this property on behalf of the Crown. Very few monasteries, contrary to popular belief, were actually given by the King to favoured courtiers, although it is certainly true that those in privileged positions at Court got first choice and were best able to obtain remarkably advantageous deals. But it is noticeable that the kind of sites which courtiers were securing for under £1000 in 1538–9 were fetching three or four times as much in subsequent years. In 1553, for example, Thomas, Lord Darcy had to pay £4000 for the former Augustinian house of St Osyth's in Essex.[9]

Similarly there seems also to have been no consistent policy on the question of how far to deface or destroy the monastic fabric at the time of the dissolution itself. The aim of destruction was primarily to prevent the monastic community from re-assembling within the buildings and to realize the immediate value of the most saleable materials; 'I pulled down no house thoroughly at none of the friaries' wrote Royal Commissioner Dr John London to Cromwell in October, 1538, 'but so deface them that they should not likely be friaries again.' Other commissioners noted how costly extensive demolition could be; systematically pulling down the great Cluniac priory of Lewes, in Sussex, for example, was highly labour-intensive. Where building stone was scarce, it does seem that monastic buildings were robbed of stone more quickly and extensively than elsewhere, as might be expected; in his letter of August 1536 John Freeman suggests to Cromwell that the quickest way to be rid of the churches of the Lincolnshire houses was to remove battlements, stairs and roof, and then to leave the walls as a quarry.[10] Significantly, where a great courtier had earmarked a site for his own use, very little destruction might take place, especially if he took immediate possession. In 1539, William Sharington was left in possession of the site of Lacock Abbey (Fig. 86) when the commissioners left, although his purchase was confirmed only some months later, and the buildings were left virtually intact here. Sir Thomas Wriothesley had stone shipped from Caen to Southampton in readiness for his work at Titchfield Abbey some months before the surrender, thus anticipating that the suppressed house would fall into his hands.[11]

As far as the domestic buildings of monasteries were concerned, it seems that it was expected these would continue to be used from the beginning. Many monasteries were of course at the centre of prime farming estates and it was essential that the productivity of the land be maintained. The 1536 Act called for every person or institution granted former monastic property 'to keep or cause to be kept an honest continual house and household in the same site or precinct, and to occupy yearly as much of the said demesnes in ploughing and tillage of husbandry'.[12] It was probably anxiety about complying with this Act that led Lord Lisle's agent in the west of England to write to him in Calais early in 1538. The letter was about the priory of Frithelstock in Devon, which Lord Lisle now owned but had sub-let to a Mr Wynslade, who 'hath sold all the alders and birch within the barton, with other fuel. . . . He doth not keep nor maintain such houses as he occupieth there tenantably. Your lordship may now lay all this to his charge when he commeth to Calais.'[13]

Not only were the domestic parts of the monastery often left intact whilst the church was defaced, it was also clearly perceived that the finest domestic buildings were fit only for the highest social classes. Sir Richard Rich surveyed the monastery at Abingdon in Berkshire as a possible royal residence. Glastonbury was similarly reported by royal commissioners to be 'the goodliest house of that sort we ever saw . . . mete for the King's Majesty, and no one else'. As we shall see, quite a number of monasteries in fact became royal residences. When

Dr London was looking over the monastic houses at Reading in Berkshire in 1538, he appealed on behalf of the townspeople that the church of the Grey Friars be used as a new town hall, but he pointedly took account of the fact that the domestic buildings were already earmarked to be used as the house of a powerful courtier: 'and if it please the Kinges grace to bestow that howse upon any of hys servantes, he may spare the body of the churche, wiche standith next the strete, and yet have rowme sufficient for a great man'.[14]

It is sometimes suggested that the new owners of monastic property desisted from radically altering and defacing their new possessions for fear of a reversal of government policy, or from religious scruples. But much of the evidence points to highly opportunistic and forthright action on the part of most beneficiaries. Both radical courtiers who were later to espouse Protestantism and those who secretly nourished a spiritual allegiance to Rome bought monastic properties and developed them. Instances of regret are rare, though Sir William Petre bothered to obtain absolution from the Pope during the reign of Queen Mary for the monastic sites he had obtained in the scramble after the dissolution; amongst these sites was the Essex manor belonging to the nunnery of Barking on which he had by this time almost completed his new house of Ingatestone.[15] Where regret was expressed, it could be tinged with opportunism. For example, although Lord de la Warr petitioned Cromwell to save Boxgrove Priory, he made it clear in his appeal that, if the religious house disappeared and his family's chantry chapel with it, and if the building could not subsequently be put to educational use, then his own material advantage would be some compensation: 'and if it might not stand so with his Grace's pleasure, then I would lowly beseech his Grace to have the preferment of the farm, with all such other things as the prior in his time had for the provision of his house'.[16]

Often, it was the most sacred part of the structure, the east end of the church, that suffered immediate demolition in the planning of a new house on the monastic site. The cynicism induced by the results of the visitation of the monasteries before the suppression, which had supposedly shown the extent of superstition and lack of moral standards at many of the houses, left little room for scruple. In the early days of the conversion

OVERLEAF 86 *Lacock Abbey, Wiltshire. The cloister of the nunnery, preserved by Sharington as corridors around the ground floor of his house, with new work of 1540–53 (windows and chimneys) above.*

87  *Samelsbury Hall, Lancashire. A window from Whalley Abbey placed here in the 1540s.*

of Titchfield Abbey in Hampshire, royal commissioners wrote to the new owner, Wriothesley, that their sale of 'marble stones, aulters, ymages, tables (pictures)' on his behalf was following in the steps of one recent bishop of Rome (Pope Alexander VI), who had also sold such things for profit. They also reminded him that 'as for plukyng downe of the church is but a small matter myndyng (as we doubt not but you woll) to buyld a chaple'.[17] The Southworth family took an entire window (probably from Whalley Abbey) for the chapel of their house at Samelsbury (Fig. 87) some

eight miles distant, and there it remains, embedded in sixteenth-century brickwork.

This lack of scruple stemmed to a great degree from the fact that secular patrons had long played an important part in the life of the monasteries and to a considerable extent already felt themselves proprietors, and certainly benefactors, as indeed they, or generations of their family before them, certainly were. The popular image of the monastery as a closed community without links with the outside world is of little relevance to the religious houses of England in the period just before the Reformation. Many had originated as spartan institutions in the early Middle Ages, built and equipped in a simple way for a dedicated spiritual life. But most had soon become dependent on rich local families, both for financial support and endowment and for representation at Court, where decisions were made about land disputes or the setting of taxes. Appeals to Cromwell for the grant or purchase of particular sites in the years after the suppression often played on the fact that the suppliant's family had endowed either the original church or some rebuilding that had taken place since. A strong sense of to some extent owning these buildings and their contents was therefore already rooted in the minds of the wealthy families of England. It led to some undignified scenes at the dissolution, like the occasion when Lady Cockayne's daughter retrieved her mother's velvet gown, given some years previously for the making of a vestment, from the nunnery of Polesworth in Warwickshire. As a result of their involvement in monastic affairs, many of the wealthy nobility and gentry had assumed the post of steward of monastic lands and revenues in the days before the dissolution. Just as we saw in connection with similar posts at the royal palaces in an earlier chapter, this entitled them to considerable rights of residence.[18]

Monasteries had always been places of hospitality, a duty enshrined in one of the principal texts of monasticism, the *Rule* of St Benedict, and extended to the rich and powerful as well as the destitute and needy. On occasion, hospitality was given so frequently to a particular patron that he or she might pay for new buildings and virtually use them as a private house. The Crown itself acted in this way; in the early 1530s, Henry VIII paid for his own royal lodging within the precincts of the Dominican friary of Guildford. At the Cistercian monastery of Tilty in Essex, the lay steward, Thomas Grey, Marquis of Dorset, who had great houses of his own in Leicestershire at Bradgate and Groby, reserved the right to use lodgings at the abbey whose construction he had paid for. Some months after the dissolution and the dispersal of the small monastic community in 1536, the aged Marchioness of Dorset was still in residence and proving difficult to dislodge. Further difficulties were caused by the fact that such patrons felt that these rights of residence were theirs to bestow and bequeath much like any other goods and chattels. Sir John Sharpe had lodgings and a garden next to the monastic infirmary at Coggeshall in Essex, with exclusive right to the use of a chapel in the monastic church. In his will he left all these privileges to a female relative.[19]

In some cases the use of monastic property on a temporary or seasonal basis continued after the dissolution. Thomas Wriothesley bought the former Cistercian abbey of Beaulieu in Hampshire in 1538. He already had two major houses in the county, one at Micheldever and the other at Titchfield, another former monastery. Beaulieu was let in subsequent years, but Wriothesley retained rights to hunt and fish during his short visits.[20] What is apparent from all these examples of lay involvement in monasteries is that there was more continuity between the pre-dissolution situation with regard to monastic buildings and their post-dissolution history than is sometimes imagined. But the total transformation of monastic buildings into private residences could only happen *after* the suppression. These conversions sparked off a new ingenuity in house-building that took the architecture and design of the Tudor house in new directions.

The conversion of monastic sites into private houses provides significant evidence of contemporary expectations of domestic comfort in great houses. Many former monasteries were transformed into houses at great speed; the kind of changes that were made, such as where doorways and windows were inserted, and where fireplaces were put in, are clear indications of the minimum standards that new secular owners were prepared to accept. Moreover, because monasteries were built to a basic standard plan and, with very few exceptions, were built in stone (even in those areas where the stone had to be transported great distances), new owners throughout the country faced common problems that cut across local traditions of design and availability of local building materials. These circumstances are unique in the history of English domestic architecture. The influence each monastery had on the planning of the country house was, of course, proportional to how much of the monastic fabric was retained. When a tenant farmer turned a small part of the monastery into a modest house, the resulting building was probably comparable to other vernacular dwellings of modest but comfortable size. For example, the refectory building of the priory of Horsham St Faith, in Norfolk, became a modest farmer's house in the later sixteenth century.[21] But when great courtiers tried to use more than one range of the complex of monastic buildings to create a house of some size and pretension, greater challenges had to be faced in the planning of these houses and the initial monastic layout was of much greater importance in influencing what was done.

The Crown was first off the mark in converting monasteries to domestic use. A choice selection of religious houses in the southeast of England were reserved as staging-posts for royal progresses. In the north, suppressed houses at York and Newcastle became the seats of the King's Council in the North and the Marches toward Scotland respectively. But in this area of royal building activity the results were probably less impressive and had less influence on domestic architecture generally than was the case with the royal palaces. None of the monastic conversions undertaken by the Crown remained royal property beyond the seventeenth century, with the exception of the King's Manor at York (still surviving today), and even this building was allowed to pass out of direct royal control by a series of leases during the reign of Charles II. Radical alterations to monastic buildings were usually necessary in order to meet the usual royal requirements, particularly the need for parallel sets of apartments for the King and Queen. At St Augustine's, Canterbury, where it proved difficult to carve these apartments out of the existing buildings, a completely new range was built for the Queen, ignoring the monastic plan entirely. Royal use of these buildings was of course highly sporadic. Generally, monastic conversions initiated by the Crown were less sensitive to the prevailing plan of the monastery than those undertaken to produce some of the most important courtier houses.[22]

The decision about which part of the monastic complex would provide a house for the new owner was determined by a number of factors. If the whole site was to be used, the church might be the least easily adaptable building, for it would need radical alteration, including the construction of floors in the nave space where these previously did not exist, and the provision of new window openings where existing ones were unsuited to domestic use. On the other hand, though stripped of its lead, the church sometimes proved the most soundly-built part of the monastery and for this reason proved the most difficult or expensive building to remove. Also it was usually the case that new owners were forced to adapt what was in the best state of preservation at the time of purchase.

The condition of the buildings may explain, for example, the later, Elizabethan conversion of Buckland Abbey in Devon (see colour plates). Though the Grenville family took over this property shortly after the dissolution, it was a member of the next generation, Sir Richard Grenville, who seems to have seriously set about the task of adapting the buildings, work that was probably completed by 1576, the date over the remaining fireplace in his hall. Whatever condition the cloister was in by this time, it proved too small for Grenville's needs and he made a house out of the nave space, raising the walls of the church and rebuilding the upper part of the crossing tower. The arch that once led from the crossing of the church to the south transept is visible on the south side of the house today. Grenville must have blocked in the arch, inserted windows and probably had the rest of the wall rendered; later restorations of monastic buildings which sought to emphasize their origins (in contrast to the first owners who were keen to eradicate such things) often 'unpicked' areas of wall such as this for picturesque effect. The house has a porch to the great hall on the north side and on the south a new kitchen range was added at right-angles to the nave and choir. Yet essentially Buckland was a single-block house with equally important rooms on its two main floors.[23]

But it is the earliest conversions that are of greatest interest in looking at aspects of continuity and change in early Tudor building. Generally speaking, the best illustrations of different kinds of conversion come from buildings belonging to the most powerful men, those with office at Henry VIII's court. It was they who had the resources to carry out extensive works, who would have been able to use their privileged position to prevent the worst excesses of destruction and who wanted houses of the greatest size and pretension. A fortunate few took over monasteries where the domestic buildings were themselves extensive enough to provide a suitable house. In these cases there were usually not only well-appointed lodgings for lay guests, but also splendid lodgings for the head of the establishment.

Many heads of monastic houses in the late Middle Ages had followed the great bishops in building to high standards of comfort and had created their own lodgings separate from the rest of the monastery. Usually positioned in the western arm of the cloister, these were the equivalent of a contemporary modern house, with their own great

hall and kitchen. The new brick lodgings created for Abbot Vyntoner at St Osyth's Priory in Essex, for example, matched any of the great mansions of his day in their provision for domestic comfort. In a few cases, some idea of the internal luxury of these lodgings has survived. The parlour created for Abbot King at Thame Abbey in the late 1520s still displays the fashion for 'anticke' decoration in the delicately carved panelling and frieze and a concern for comfort in the provision of an internal porch against draughts. Both the heraldry in this room and the stone carvings on the new hall built for Abbot Chard at Forde Abbey in Dorset show that the heads of monasteries were not averse to displaying their personal heraldry alongside that of local great families, just as secular house-builders did.[24]

It was often tempting for the post-dissolution owners to live in such quarters as these and demolish everything else, or at least let the abbey church and cloister generally decay. This appears to have happened at several of the great Cistercian houses where, contrary to the convention at the houses of other orders, the abbot's lodging was sited in the southeast corner of the complex and was particularly self-contained. Important examples are Margam in Glamorgan and Whalley in Lancashire.[25] In other houses, parts of the abbot's lodging formed the nucleus of a new house; the fine late fifteenth-century abbot's hall at Milton Abbey in Dorset (Fig. 88) became the centrepiece of the conversion by Sir John Tregonwell, Commissioner for the Dissolution in the West Country. It remains the core of the courtyard house today, though many of Tregonwell's additions were swept away in the eighteenth-century remodelling.[26]

Battle Abbey, in East Sussex (Fig. 89), where the new secular mansion was formed around the nucleus of a splendid abbot's house, is a particularly interesting conversion. This was partly because the monastic orientation of the buildings was preserved but also because the new owner took over some of the monastic responsibilities for the community in the village nearby. When Sir Anthony Browne, Master of the Horse to Henry VIII, acquired the site in 1538 he used the abbot's house as the core of his own dwelling, preserving the former entrance to the monastery through the great outer court. The church to the north was largely demolished and the cloister to the south used partly as a service area behind the main body of the house. The house as Browne left it is in the background at the centre of the Bucks' eighteenth-century print of the site, flanked by two reminders of the past. Browne

preserved the thirteenth-century monastic gatehouse to the northwest (at the left of the print),
but extended it to include a courthouse for the
town of Battle which pressed against its gate. The
new range of guest lodgings, probably constructed
by Browne's son in later years, is shown to the
right of the Bucks' view. These lodgings also
represented continuity with the past, for they were
built over the undercroft of the earlier monastic
guest range. The whole ensemble of buildings,
though disparate in alignment and scale, was
given a form of unity by the common battle-
menting. Judging by other, more detailed visual
records of the former state of the now much-altered
abbot's house and by the evidence of the still-
existing gatehouse range, the windows also shared
a common design. The grouping of buildings at
Battle shows the courtyard idea interpreted in a
very practical but informal way.[27]

But the real challenges came with attempts to
adapt the complete cloister to domestic use, for
this procedure forced new owners to think about
orientation and about the shape, size and relative
position of rooms within the building. It might
seem that adapting the four basic ranges of a cloister
into a house would be relatively straightforward,
but this was not, in fact, the case. Whether the
cloister stood north or south of the monastic church,
all monasteries were laid out to the same basic plan
and it was this plan which presented the first
challenge. In the conventional courtyard house,
such as Compton Wynyates (see Fig. 44), the
entrance range faced the largest ground-floor space,
the hall, across the court, but in the monastery the
western, entrance range faced the subdivided
chapter-house range (Fig. 93). This included the
south or north transept, slype (or passage) and
chapter house on the ground floor, and also perhaps
the library and undercroft to the dorter, all fronted

THE SOUTH-WEST VIEW OF BATTE

To Sr. THOMAS WEBSTER Bart. Proprietor of this ABBY.

This Prospect is humbly Inscrib'd by his much Oblig'd Servts

Sam. & Nath. Buck.

BBY, IN THE COUNTY OF SUSSEX.

*THIS Abby standing on ỹ very Spot of Ground on which King Harold fell was founded by the Conqueror in Memorial of his Victory & that Prayers might be made for ỹ Souls of ỹ Slain. He dedicated it to St Martin & placing therein Monks of ỹ Benedictine Order bestow'd upon it his Royal Manour of Wye, which according to ỹ Chronicles of this Abby contain'd twenty two Hundreds, and granted it many ample Privileges, among ỹ rest Exemption from Episcopal Jurisdiction, which with all ỹ others not taken away by Act of Parliament it still maintains. It was a large & Noble Structure as may be judged from ỹ Gateway (still entire) and ỹ other Remains. At ỹ Dissolution it was much defaced. Soon after that St Anth: Browne & his Son Anthony Lord Visct Montacute built ỹ stately Pile on ỹ south Side now become ruinous. It continued in that Noble Family till lately purchas'd by St Thos Webster Bart It had the Honour of ỹ Mitre & was valued at* ⎰ 880:14:7¾ Du: ⎱ 987:0:a $ p.

*Saml & Nathl Buck del & sculp. Publisht according to Act of Parliament March 2d 1737.*

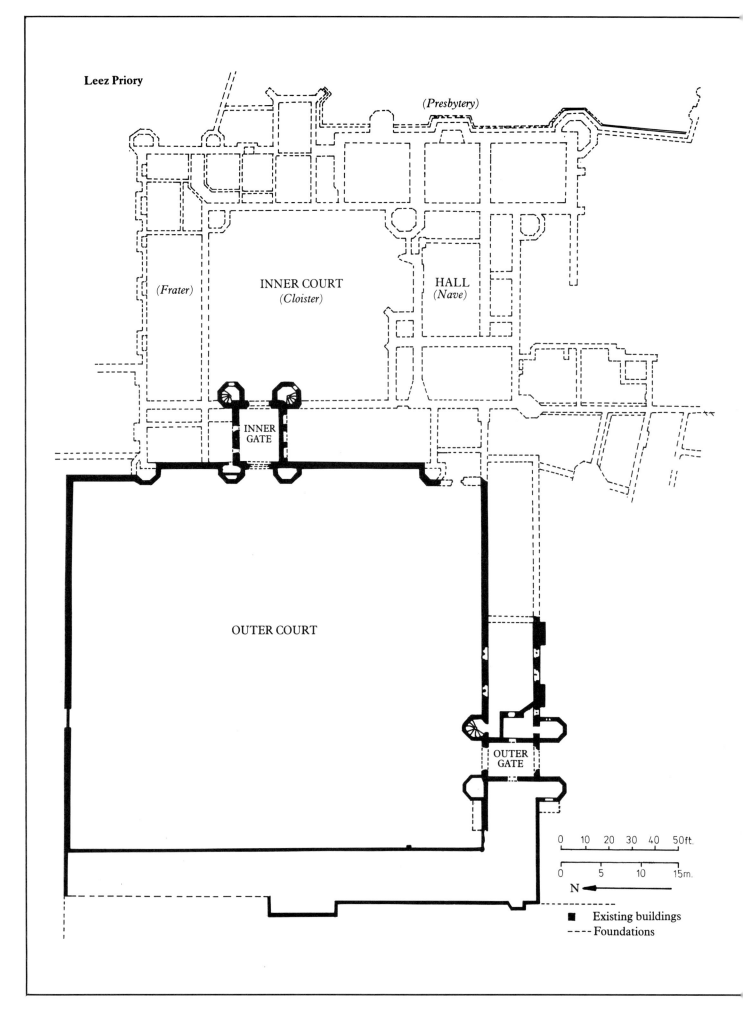

**Leez Priory**

*(Presbytery)*

*(Frater)*     INNER COURT
*(Cloister)*

HALL
*(Nave)*

INNER
GATE

OUTER COURT

OUTER
GATE

0   10  20  30  40  50ft.

0     5     10   15m.

N

■   Existing buildings
--- Foundations

by the eastern arm of the cloister. The second difficulty was that monasteries had a number of large room spaces placed upstairs, over under-crofts, or sub-vaults. Essentially, there were three spaces that could most conveniently be immedi-ately converted into the hall of the house; first, the nave of the church to the north (or south) of the cloister; second, the raised frater (where the monastic community ate together) opposite the nave on the south (or north) side; third, the dorter (where the monks or nuns slept), appropriately in the eastern range, but inconveniently upstairs and off-centre, stretching beyond the square of the cloister itself. Using any of these spaces involved rethinking the orientation of the house and de-ciding what spaces to use for different purposes.

It is of course true that placing the entrance range opposite the hall in the courtyard house was only the convention, not the rule; there are exam-ples where this did not happen. In some cases, therefore, the monastic plan was allowed to deter-mine the unusual arrangement of a hall at right-angles to the entrance. A significant example of this solution is Leez Priory, in Essex, shown in the plan in Fig. 90 and in the Bucks' view of the outer court in the 1730s in Fig. 91. Sir Richard Rich carved the hall of his house out of the former nave and as a result the visitor to Leez had to turn one right-angle to pass from outer to inner gate and a second right-angle from this inner gate to reach the hall. In the Bucks' print, the inner gatehouse range fills the centre of the illustration. The top of the pointed arch of the great window at one end of the hall can be seen in the centre of the picture, behind what is presumably a staircase tower (the hall seems to have once had an open hearth under a louvre in the centre of the roof, here exaggerated by the Bucks into a prominent construction). Other spaces of the monastery were also probably incorporated in the conversion, so the brick clad-ding with which Rich's converted house was faced (possibly in emulation of the splendid royal house of New Hall nearby) perhaps deceived historians in the past into thinking that this particular monastic transformation was more radical than in fact was the case. Indeed, the surviving fragment of walling that runs south from the inner gatehouse at Leez shows how brickwork was simply added to the

stone walls that were still standing when Rich took over the monastery.[28] Sir William Paulet's con-version of Netley Abbey in Hampshire (Fig. 92) resulted in a more conventional orientation. He also put the hall in the nave space, but moved the entrance range to face it, carving a new gate and flanking service rooms from the frater range on the south side of the cloister and demolishing the frater itself, which ran south from the range. The east, or chapter house range became the family and state apartments, and here Tudor brickwork, re-mains of fireplaces and large window openings can still be seen.[29]

One of the most radical conversions, however, was that of Titchfield Abbey (Fig. 93), where surviving correspondence about the conversion has enriched our understanding of what went on here.[30] The commissioners on site supervised the conversion for the absent patron, Thomas Wriothesley, over a period of just a few months at the beginning of 1538, immediately after he had been granted the property. It is clear from the letters that the first plan was to carve the great hall out of the east range, preserving the original entrance from the west. But this was quickly changed when difficulties surfaced and, at the instigation of those on site, the final plan retained the east range as a sequence of small room spaces (possibly the location of the chapel which the commissioners felt would atone for Wriothesley's destruction of the church). The hall was made out of the former frater and a gatehouse was forced through the nave of the church (Fig. 94). The axial re-orientation of the cloister, now courtyard, from west-east to south-north was complete. The need to complete the conversion quickly clearly deter-mined practical solutions; an extraordinary matter-of-factness about the whole effort and the assertive confidence that could drive a brutal wedge through the former church comes out in Leland's com-ment: 'Mr Wriothesley hath buildid a right stately house embatelid, and having a goodely gate, and a conducte castelid in the middle of the court of it, yn the very same place wher the late monasterie of Premostratenses stoode caullyd Tichefelde.'[31]

Speed of conversion was a prominent feature of building by leading courtiers, for they were the people with most foreknowledge of dissolution and could often, like Wriothesley at Titchfield, already have the necessary building materials to hand. But speed did not always result in a satis-factory house, or one that stood the test of time. At some sites, the succeeding generation had a rethink. At the former nunnery of Hinchingbrooke,

*90 Leez Priory, Essex. Sir Richard Rich's post 1536 house superimposed on the site of the Augustinian priory. (The house plan is shown in capitals.)*

now in Cambridgeshire (Fig. 95), the first owner after the dissolution was Thomas Cromwell's nephew, Richard Williams, who took his uncle's surname. He retained the monastic orientation based on an entrance from the west and, though the details of the plan of his house are not clear, he certainly had apartments built into the upper part of the former church (Fig. 96). A fireplace with his initials has been uncovered relatively recently on the upper floor here. But his son, Henry, who inherited the house in 1545, changed its orientation so that it was approached from the north, the direction of the town of Huntingdon. To mark this new approach he added bay windows to the north facade and built a gatehouse on this side, both of

which used material from his other monastic property of Ramsey Abbey. He also built a new service wing in brick to form a new forecourt.[32]

At Titchfield, the new hall in the raised frater space needed a porch with steps up to it to signify its importance, for the monastic entry from the ground floor at this point would have been too nondescript, covered as it was by the cloister walk. To build this porch and steps, and presumably for other reasons, the cloisters were demolished. In other houses, they were preserved as circulating corridors around the court and it seems that monastic conversions accelerated the development of the idea of using corridors to facilitate access within the great house (see Chapter 4). Access to

the important upper-floor rooms of the monastery-turned-house was sometimes provided by adding upper corridors over the cloister walks. Examples of this practice include the first post-dissolution house at Audley End, in Essex, fashioned from the abbey of Walden for Thomas, Lord Audley, and the lost Bermondsey Abbey, south of the Thames in London, made into a house for Sir Thomas Pope and recorded by Buckler's early nineteenth-century watercolours.[33] But three examples which survive in part or whole to this day are especially interesting.

The first of them is Mottisfont Abbey in Hampshire (Fig. 97), changed into a house for William, Lord Sandys, who appears to have moved here from his

other great house, The Vyne, by 1538. 'He makes a goodly place of the priory and intends to lie there most of his life' wrote the priest John Atkinson to Lady Lisle in that year. By the time Leland saw Mottisfont, probably not long after Sandys' death in 1540, work had stopped, for he records it as 'onperfecte'. Nevertheless, an eighteenth-century estate map demonstrates that Sandys managed to create, or at least begin, an ambitious double-courtyard house here. As at Titchfield (though oriented differently, with the church to the north rather than the south of the cloister), the frater was used for the great hall, but a new courtyard was built to the south to provide a court of entry for it. To the north of the hall, the nave formed the rear of a second court and was subdivided into two floors. There appear to have been both upper and lower corridors on the site of the medieval cloister serving this nave space and the rest of the inner court. If we look at the present entrance front of Mottisfont as it is today, we see the south side of what was once the nave space with the side wings of the inner court stretching before it, though these are now cut short and are rendered so that any sense of the extent and appearance of the Tudor courtyard has vanished. However, there are still relics of the Tudor arrangements. Each side of what appears to be a largely eighteenth-century centre-piece to the house there are brick turrets, conspicuous by their low roofline and tiny windows. Though the original function of these are uncertain, they were almost certainly constructed for Sandys' new house and mark the corners of the former cloister square. Between these turrets, behind the Georgian doorway and windows on ground and first floors, are fragments of the original circulating corridors.[34]

The second important example of a house with upper corridors is Newstead Abbey in Nottinghamshire (see colour plates), converted for Sir John Byron, Sheriff of the County in 1542–3 and ancestor of the poet Byron (who was to sell the house out of the family in the early nineteenth century). He retained the cloister walks but rebuilt them, perhaps for the very reason that he wished to extend them to the upper floor and the foundations needed strengthening. However, he re-used the original medieval window-openings in his new

*91 Leez Priory, Essex. Part of the Bucks' view of the outer court. The gatehouse and lower-floor lights are clearly early Tudor, but the shape and size of the upper-floor windows suggest they were Elizabethan alterations.*

lower cloister.[35] The third example is Lacock Abbey, in Wiltshire (Fig. 98), though here the sense of circulation on the upper floor is expressed in a more diffuse way. An upper cloister passage already existed on the south side of the cloister, connecting the abbess's chapel to the dorter in the former nunnery. The roof level of this corridor was raised by the new owner, Sir William Sharington, to match that of the chapel to which it gave access and he also created access corridors on the upper floor in the east and north ranges. The more impressive of these corridors was described as the 'longe stone chamber' in the 1575 inventory. The width of this room and what remains of its original fittings, including a fine stone fireplace and large window openings, suggest that it was truly a gallery looking out over gardens and countryside. On the uppermost floor of this range Sharington made a gallery, which seems to have been solely designed as a place of perambulation,

leading on to the roof and the uppermost room of his new tower.[36]

Though some evidence of the original post-dissolution room spaces remains at Lacock and Newstead, it is not clear how the internal arrangements operated in detail in the immediate period after the suppression. Some ground-floor rooms were clearly well-appointed domestic quarters; Sharington, for example, inserted a fireplace into the chapter house at Lacock and blocked up its openings into the cloister walk. At Newstead the chapter house may have served as the family chapel from the beginning, as we know it did later; the thirteenth-century interior, with nineteenth-century decoration, still survives. There is some evidence too that the southeastern end of the ground floor of Newstead may have provided living accommodation.[37] However, at both Lacock and Newstead the upper floor became the principal suite of domestic apartments whilst the lower floor,

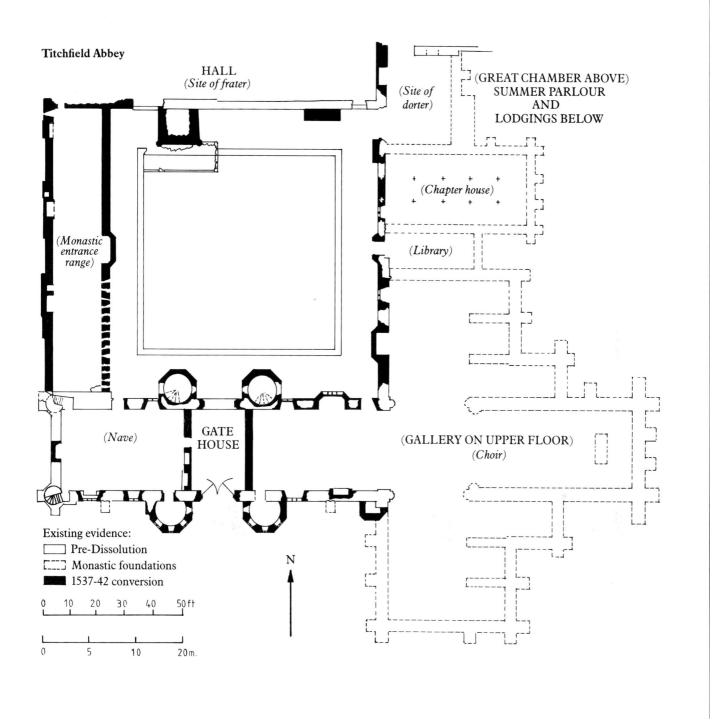

**Titchfield Abbey**

HALL
(*Site of frater*)

(*Site of dorter*)

(GREAT CHAMBER ABOVE)
SUMMER PARLOUR
AND
LODGINGS BELOW

(*Monastic entrance range*)

(*Chapter house*)

(*Library*)

(*Nave*)

GATE HOUSE

(GALLERY ON UPPER FLOOR)
(*Choir*)

Existing evidence:
☐ Pre-Dissolution
⌐⌐⌐ Monastic foundations
■ 1537–42 conversion

0  10  20  30  40  50 ft

0  5  10  20 m.

N

*ABOVE LEFT 92  Netley Abbey, Hampshire. Tudor doorway and windows of the entrance range of the post-conversion house, formerly the south range of the cloister. The frater block ran south from here and was demolished.*

*ABOVE 93  Titchfield Abbey, Hampshire. The final stage of Wriothesley's conversion superimposed on the monastic plan. (The house plan is shown in capitals.)*

ABOVE 94   Titchfield Abbey, Hampshire. Wriothesley's gatehouse
driven through the nave of the former church. It was probably
designed by the royal mason, Thomas Bertie, in 1538.

RIGHT 95   Hinchingbrooke House, Cambridgeshire. The Tudor
house of the Williams family superimposed on the medieval
nunnery. (The house plan is shown in capitals.)

**Hinchingbrooke House**

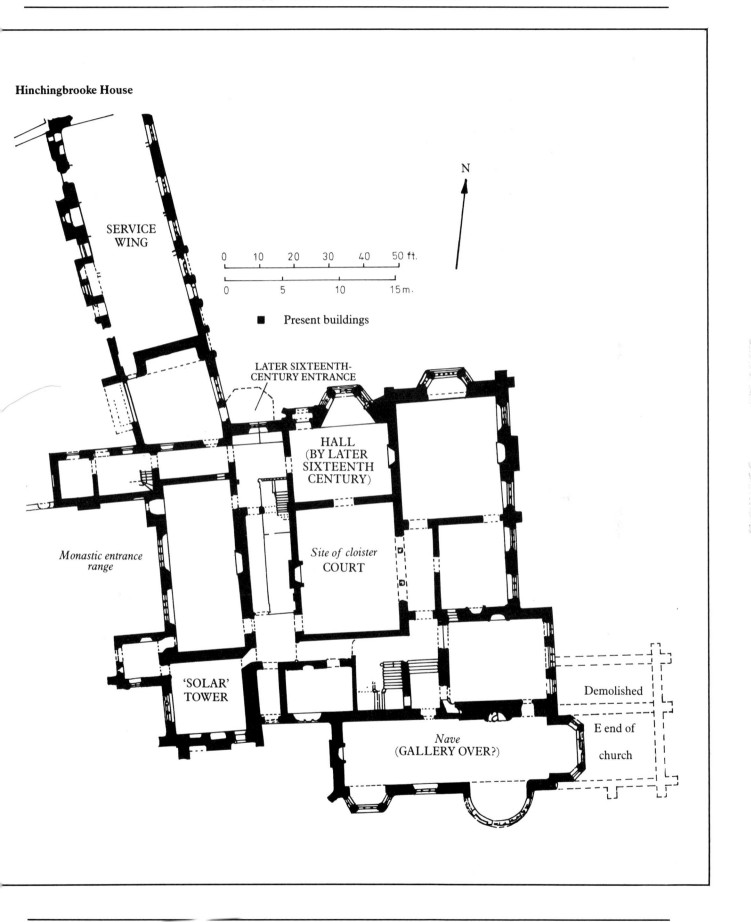

N

SERVICE
WING

0    10    20    30    40    50 ft.

0         5         10        15 m.

■    Present buildings

LATER SIXTEENTH-
CENTURY ENTRANCE

HALL
(BY LATER
SIXTEENTH
CENTURY)

*Monastic entrance
range*

*Site of cloister*
COURT

'SOLAR'
TOWER

Demolished

E end of

church

*Nave*
(GALLERY OVER?)

where many of the original undercrofts were incorporated in the new house, was used for service and storage. In both houses the hall was formed from the abbot's or abbess's lodging in the western range and in both cases the house was entered up steps to the hall on the external facade rather than from the courtyard. Tillemans' painting of Newstead in the eighteenth century shows steps and a raised porch clearly leading to the important upper floor (Fig. 99).

It would be pushing the point too far to suggest that monastic conversions first introduced the idea of a sequence of important rooms on an upper floor, not least because this concept was alien to the monastic layout. Medieval monasteries had many great spaces above ground, but they did not all connect with each other on the same level; the chief access to frater, dorter and the hall of the western lodgings would have been by individual staircases, emphasizing that the ranges around the cloister had been conceived and built separately. Moreover, as we have already seen, courtyard houses were already beginning to have important sets of upper-floor apartments before monasteries inspired new ideas about planning. But the monastic conversions undoubtedly accelerated the growing importance of the upper floor.

Newstead demonstrates a telling development in this process. At Hampton Court, where the state rooms were being finished for Henry VIII at just about the time of the earliest dissolutions in 1536, there is a clear disjunction between the upper-floor rooms in the palace; the floor levels between the great hall and watching chamber, for example, are not the same. In contrast, the floor of the Byron upper cloister at Newstead cuts directly across several points of monastic access on the lower floor, namely the tops of two processional doors that once led from the lower cloister to the church and those doors to the south transept and the chapter house. It is as if Byron were imposing a new and uniform floor level to what was effectively his upper state floor.[38] So Lacock and Newstead and houses like them do seem to show an important stage in the development of the great house with 'stacked' floors common in later architecture. John Chapman, mason at Lacock, later worked at Sir John Thynne's Longleat, the final phase of which was one of the first and most emphatic examples of the kind of house where stacked floors replaced the need for low and spreading courtyards.[39] Here the service floor was topped by the state floor with guest rooms and bedrooms on a further floor above. It is ironic that monasteries led to new sophistication in the devel-

opment of the courtyard whilst at the same time encouraging its demise as a useful formula for domestic architecture.

The significance of the monasteries in the context of the private house stands or falls to a great extent on their importance in the history of the planning of domestic buildings. In their physical appearance monastic conversions were not only

poor candidates for nominations as great architecture, but were in some ways throwbacks to the past. On the whole they were not constructed with any greater sense of symmetry or external order than the courtyard houses whose problems they redefined. Whilst Lacock has an important place in a discussion of the introduction of classical decorative elements into English architecture (see Chapter

ABOVE 96  *Hinchingbrooke House, Cambridgeshire. The converted nunnery from the west, the original entrance side of the house. The projecting range at the right was adapted from the former nave of the nunnery church.*

OVERLEAF 97  *Mottisfont Abbey, Hampshire. The present house from the south. The rising ground at the left covers a monastic cellar. The smaller, Tudor turret towers seen here between the centre range and the wings may have linked upper- and lower-floor corridors in Lord Sandys' conversion of 1538–40.*

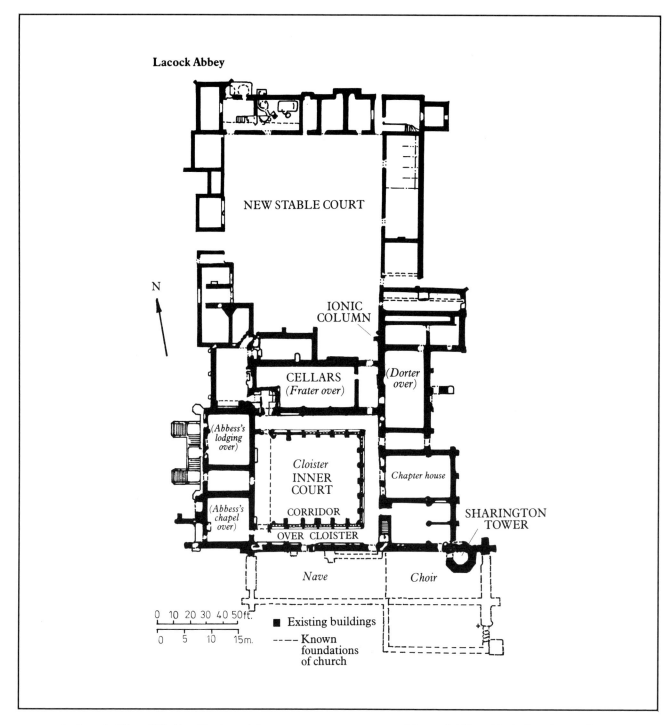

Lacock Abbey

NEW STABLE COURT

N

IONIC
COLUMN

CELLARS
(Frater over)

(Dorter
over)

(Abbess's
lodging
over)

Cloister
INNER
COURT

Chapter house

CORRIDOR

OVER CLOISTER

(Abbess's
chapel
over)

SHARINGTON
TOWER

Nave

Choir

0 10 20 30 40 50ft.

0   5   10   15m.

■ Existing buildings

--- Known
foundations
of church

ABOVE 98   Lacock Abbey, Wiltshire. Sharington's house
superimposed on the medieval nunnery. (The house plan is shown
in capitals.)

RIGHT 99   Newstead Abbey, Nottinghamshire. Tillemans' view
of the west front, c.1730, showing the steps leading to the hall on
the first floor. (Nottingham City Art Galleries)

9), this building can hardly be said to have shown much external order. On the west, or approach, front, much of the irregularly-spaced medieval buttressing was allowed to remain. Similarly, on the north front of Mottisfont the sixteenth-century window openings are interspersed among medieval buttresses that originally supported the north side of the nave. Only occasionally was there even any attempt to blend new buildings with old, one example being St Osyth's Priory, where the new range and towers built by Lord Darcy were covered with a septaria finish (contrasting squares of stone and flint) similar to that used on the monastic gatehouse.

Titchfield perhaps makes this point best of all, for it seems that the imposing gatehouse range about whose 'seemliness' the commissioners were so concerned did not match the other fronts to the house in terms of the appearance of the facade or even in its roof levels. In addition, the walling and even the windows of the monastic frater remained untouched on the north side of the hall until the extensive demolition of the house in 1781 (see Fig. 93). Titchfield conjures up not so much the conventional courtyard houses common at this period, but the castles of a bygone age. It has the same sense of a powerful, single entrance side which stands like a defensive front before the house

behind it, much like the show of the entrance facade at Bodiam and Herstmonceux. The twisted brick chimneystacks at Titchfield suggest internal comforts slotted in within old walls and recall the contemporary Tudor improvements to medieval castles like Framlingham (see Fig. 26).

Yet, whilst no one could claim that monastic conversions were visually sophisticated, they did involve interesting changes in where and how entry to the house was made. Turning once again to Longleat, one of its prime qualities is that it is outward-looking, with great windows on the exterior of the court and a main door that can be seen as one approaches the house.[40] By comparison, Titchfield is old-fashioned; the outside of the house is formidable, the stern gatehouse forbidding entry to the unwelcome. It is an essay in stone akin to the wall of barely relieved brickwork that once formed the gatehouse range to Sutton Place. Houses like Battle, Newstead, Lacock and the second phase of Hinchingbrooke all mark a move towards the emergence of the outward-looking house, even if they do not share Longleat's visual order and classical decoration. At all of these conversions, the outer gate of the monastery was used as the main gatehouse, thus taking it away from the house and setting it up as an isolated structure at the edge of what had been the outer court. Interestingly, a new outer gate was erected at Hinchingbrooke, symbolically created from monastic remains. In fact even the earliest visual records of Newstead give us very little sense of there being a gatehouse at all. In these buildings, the hall and entry to the house were not trapped within the court, invisible to all except those who were admitted. The entrance was there on the outside, with a porch or steps up to it. Tillemans' view of the west side of Newstead, with its extraordinary preservation of the west front of the monastic church, can hardly be said to show the formality of a classical facade in the manner of Longleat, but it does suggest something of the courtyard turned inside out and thus breaks new ground in the form of the great house.

# 8

# 'Withe Timbar, Brike and Flynte':
# Building Materials and their Regional Pattern

ONE OF THE fundamental distinctions made in the history of domestic architecture is that between buildings that are deemed 'vernacular' and those which are not. Certain kinds of buildings of the last few centuries, public buildings (like town halls and museums, for example) and, pre-eminently, country houses are termed 'polite' architecture.[1] The size of these buildings, their style and materials do not reflect the regional characteristics of their immediate environment. 'Polite' houses are usually associated with people whose political, economic and social interests are not confined simply to the area in which their respective houses are situated, and whose fabric and construction may well have ignored what was available locally and brought in fashionable building materials from elsewhere to ape the modish taste of London or the Court. As far as early Tudor England is concerned, the question is to what extent the great houses can be described as 'polite' and how far they were still fundamentally indebted to regional traditions in building materials.

Charles Brandon's move from Suffolk to Lincolnshire, discussed in Chapter 2, was accompanied by a complete change in the building material chosen for his house. The brick and terracotta of Westhorpe was replaced by the stone of Grimsthorpe (see colour plates). There are various reasons why Brandon may have made such a radical change at his new house. By the late 1530s when he was on the move it is arguable that brick and terracotta were no longer so fashionable as they had once been among the courtier class. More importantly, opportunist that he was, at Grimsthorpe Brandon could take advantage of stone that had become available as a result of monastic dissolutions; Leland tells us that he used stone from the dissolved abbey of Vaudey.[2] Finally,

it may simply be that a change of region inevitably meant a change in the available local materials and expertise. Brandon had moved out of East Anglia, where brick was the principal building material, and into Lincolnshire, an area that yielded fine building stone. Whatever the cause may have been, all these explanations raise questions about the regional quality of sixteenth-century architecture. They show that there was both continuity with the medieval past and the beginnings of a more general consciousness about style and fashion that challenged regional traditions.

Today we have detailed geological maps which show clearly that the country is crossed by a great limestone belt running southwest from the Wash to the Bristol Channel and then southwards to Dorset. We also have the advantage of being able to look back on centuries of stone quarrying and can identify those places within the belt where especially good building stone has traditionally been found. Those contemplating building in the sixteenth century would have had no such map and only fragmentary knowledge of the pattern of national resources. However, anyone with any experience of the logistics and practicalities of building, such as Brandon, would have had a relatively clear picture of the web of road and river transport. A good situation with reference to possible transport, coupled with the available resources for the project in hand, determined whether certain materials could be transported from one place to another.[3] Caen stone from northern France was a high quality material, particularly favoured for fine mouldings and other finishes and dressings, but the high costs of transport limited its use to places within short distances of the coasts and river estuaries of southern England. For example, Warblington (Fig. 100), the brick house built for Margaret, Countess of Salisbury, was near the Hampshire coast and so it was feasible to use a mixture of stone from Caen and from the Isle of Wight in the dressings around windows and doors and on the angles of the building.

Comments about building by contemporary writers raise two issues concerning the choice of materials. First, was there an established order of preference in which stone, the most expensive and permanent material, was thought to be most desirable, followed by brick which in turn was felt to be better than timber? Leland's comments on buildings always associate stone with strength and durability to the point where he implies that a well-built stone structure transcends architectural style; in his view, a castle built two hundred years ago was as good as one built a generation ago if it was constructed soundly. On the other hand, he always speaks of brick and timber in terms of their visual attractiveness and their inherent impermanence.[4] There is some evidence that buildings of brick and timber were sometimes finished to suggest they were of stone, or the prominent features were at least trimmed with stone. It is certainly true that temporary buildings of wood erected by the Royal Works were often painted to look like stone, most notably in the case of the temporary palace erected for the Field of Cloth of Gold (see Fig. 24). At some houses, the brick around doors and windows was disguised with plaster or paint to imitate stone mouldings; surviving examples of this practice include Ingatestone Hall, in Essex, and Eastbury Manor House at Barking, in East London (Fig. 101) (though crude cement was used in place of the original fine plaster when the house was restored).[5]

The second issue concerns the degree to which the increased use of supposedly better, more permanent materials reflected higher standards of living. In his *Description of England* William Harrison seems to assert that the use of stone was to be encouraged and that expense need not be a deterrent: 'The greatest part of our building in the cities and good towns of England consisteth only of timber, for as yet few of the houses of the commonalty (except here and there in West Country towns) are made of stone, although they may (in my opinion) in divers other places be builded so good cheap of the one as of the other.' In his description of the houses of the upper classes in particular, Harrison feels that there has recently been a definite shift away from timber construction: 'The ancient manors and houses of our gentlemen are yet, and for the most part, of strong timber, in framing whereof our carpenters have been and are

100   *Warblington House, Hampshire, c. 1514–26. A mason's mark on the stone dressings of the surviving gatehouse turret. Proximity to the coast meant that it was feasible to use stone from Caen and the Isle of Wight for this house.*

worthily preferred before those of like science among all other nations. Howbeit, such as be lately builded are commonly of brick, or hard stone, or both . . . . Those of the nobility are likewise wrought with brick and hard stone, as provision may best be made, but so magnificent and stately as the basest house of a baron doth often match in our days with some honours of princes in olden time.'[6]

However, although documentary evidence and the fragmentary residue of surviving early sixteenth-century buildings suggest that Harrison's assertions may be largely true, they also indicate that the picture is more complicated than simply that of one building material gradually and inevitably supplanting another, whether in the case of town housing, or in the country houses of the upper classes. At this period, for example, the centre of Northampton, a wealthy town in the middle of an area rich in building stone, was being reconstructed largely in wood.[7] In addition, it may well be that the choice of building material was influenced as much by what was available as by conscious choice. As the century progressed there was a serious shortage of available timber in many parts of England, particularly in coastal areas (where centuries of deforestation could not be remedied easily because new timber was slow to grow in these exposed places), in East Anglia (Harrison, in fact, acknowledges this) and in parts of northern England. The decision to build in a material other than wood may therefore have been simply due to lack of local supplies of timber. Certainly some timber was imported from abroad to mitigate this shortfall, but since the principal structure of a timber-framed building needed to be of unseasoned wood, taken from recently felled trees, the building of timber-framed houses was highly dependent on suitable wood being locally available.[8]

Sometimes, materials might be deliberately mixed for particular effect, or to distinguish different parts of the building. At Castle Acre Priory, Norfolk (Fig. 102), the walls of the new prior's lodging built in the early sixteenth century are basically of flint and stone rubble, with dressed stone for the angle buttresses and the windows, and flint and stone chequerwork topped by a timber framed gable over the main point of access. Sometimes a mixture of materials reflects different stages of building, or a change in fashion or the materials available (Fig. 103).

This diverse picture of the use of building materials was further complicated by the influences on individual patrons and the degree to which they were involved in the building process. Sometimes the key to the pattern of the use of particular materials seems to have been the familiar one of peer-group pressure, and this could obviously encourage a builder to follow local tradition if he was purely concerned with outclassing his local rivals. In the northwest of England and along the borders with Wales, in the counties of Lancashire, Cheshire and Shropshire, the sixteenth century saw the apogee of the development of the half-timbered house. Leland recognized its intrinsic identification with that region; seeing an unusually prominent half-timbered building at Morley in Derbyshire he describes it as 'al of tymbre after the

commune sort of building of houses of a(ll) the gentilmen for most of Lancastreshire'.[9]

The use of wooden-framing did not necessarily mean that the design of these buildings was inherently conservative, and indeed half-timbered houses built or altered at this time show sophisticated developments of plan similar to those being adopted elsewhere in the country. During the early sixteenth century, for example, half-timbered houses like Speke Hall, now in Merseyside, Bramall, now in the Greater Manchester area and Gawsworth in Cheshire were enlarged into multi-room court-yard houses similar to the brick courtyard houses of the south and east.[10] Those responsible for these buildings developed their own means of decorative display to rival the mouldings and ornament created in brick and stone and increasingly elaborate surface patterns of wood and plaster infill were devised (though it has to be admitted that in many cases nineteenth-century restoration has complicated these patterns in an attempt to make them look more picturesque and thus detracted from their former boldness of design). The proud inscription which the owner and carpenter added to Little Moreton Hall (Fig. 104) to commemorate the additions of 1559 is the equal in wood of heraldry on other houses in stone, or brick and terracotta. Regional materials still continued to be used even when the design of the house had changed fundamentally. As late as the 1560s the Shrewsbury woollen merchant Adam Otley built his large new house at Pitchford in Shropshire in the regional tradition of 'black and white' half-timbering, although it was designed on the then fashionable 'E' plan.[11]

The people responsible for all these half-timbered buildings that are such a feature of the northwest were principally men of local wealth and importance. In contrast, the buildings of those great men who had connections at Court were more likely to be in brick or stone, certainly where the major part of the house was concerned. Ridley in Cheshire, for example, was built of stone, as is shown by the only surviving sixteenth-century fragment, a gateway that was probably part of the original house. Leland gives us the clue as to why this material was used in an area still committed to timber-framing. Ridley was built, he writes, by Sir William Stanley, who was made Lord Chamberlain

*OVERLEAF 101 Eastbury Manor House, Barking, London, probably built in the 1550s. On the original house, the brick around the windows was covered with plaster to imitate stone, but plaster has now been replaced by cement.*

ABOVE 102   *Castle Acre Priory, Norfolk. Part of the prior's lodging, remodelled in the early sixteenth century, with a mixture of building materials to emphasize the domestic quality of this part of the priory.*

RIGHT 103   *Littlecote, Wiltshire. The projecting bay at the centre of the early sixteenth-century range, begun in stone and flint and later raised higher in brick.*

of Henry VII's household after his crucial support of the Tudor cause at the Battle of Bosworth. Another courtier, Sir Ralph Egerton, later lived at the house. Whichever of these men was responsible for what remains of the sixteenth-century building, it seems likely that they were primarily influenced by fashions at Court rather than by the local traditions of half-timbering.[12] Plaish Hall, in Shropshire, is another example of a house that reflects Court influences, being built towards the end of Henry VIII's reign in the late 1540s by the courtier Sir William Leighton. It is largely constructed of brick (apart from some stone walling which appears to have survived from an older house here) and this is the earliest known use of the material in the county.[13] Brick was by no means the only material used by royal courtiers but for some decades the momentum of the fashion for brick was difficult to resist.

Until recently, those writing about the use of brick in English buildings assumed that it virtu-

LEFT 104  Little Moreton Hall, Cheshire. The bay window of 1559, lighting hall and withdrawing room. Some of the decoration here is painted on plaster to imitate timber-framing. The inscription beneath the gables records the date and the owner.

ABOVE 105  Wormleighton, Warwickshire. The surviving range of the first great house of the Spencer family, probably built by 1522, with windows on a scale to rival Sutton Place.

ally disappeared between Roman times and the fifteenth century. In the last few decades, however, the discovery of documentary evidence for the use of brick, and in particular the restoration of later medieval buildings, has shown that brick was in fact far more widely used during the Middle Ages than used to be thought. There is documentary proof of the manufacture of brick in England from as early as the twelfth century, while investigation of surviving buildings has demonstrated that by the thirteenth century buildings were often principally constructed in brick and were then given a revetment (or covering) of stone or flint. Brick has been found to lie behind what are apparently stone walls in several East Anglian churches and even certain important, royally-endowed buildings which were certainly meant to be perceived as stone-built are in fact of stone-clad brick. Notable examples include the upper part of King's College Chapel in Cambridge and the spire of Norwich Cathedral.[14]

However, the use of brick as a basic building material did take off in new directions in the fifteenth century, when large houses and churches were specifically designed to display brickwork decoration on their external faces. On the other hand it is also true that the use of brick for major houses made only limited headway in those areas where building stone was plentiful, or easily obtainable. It has been estimated that there are about 500 surviving brick buildings dating from before the English Reformation of the 1530s, of which more than 350 are found in the East Anglian counties of Essex, Suffolk and Norfolk.[15] Where brick occurs west of the limestone belt, it tends to appear in bishops' or courtier houses from the end of the fifteenth century or the early decades of the sixteenth. Examples of such buildings include the house built by the Percy family, Earls of Northumberland, at Leconfield (in the East Riding of Yorkshire, now Humberside), John, Baron Hussey's lodge at Kneesall in Nottinghamshire, Sir Thomas Heneage's house at Hainton in Lincolnshire, the first house of the Spencer family at Wormleighton in Warwickshire (Fig. 105) (an important fragment of which survives), and, most emphatically of all, because it is the most important example remaining today, Compton Wynyates, also in Warwickshire (Fig. 1). All the people concerned held important offices at Court and clearly desired houses that reflected something of the brick splendour of the palaces of Henry VIII and Wolsey, but it is also likely that local deposits of clay suitable for brickmaking were what made the realization of these ventures possible. Investigations of the composition of the bricks used for Compton Wynyates have shown that the nearest source of clay is only six miles away.[16]

Brick production during the fifteenth and sixteenth centuries seems to have been largely devoted to providing material for individual building projects. The bricks themselves were manufactured at or near the site of the great building for which they were intended and there does not seem to have been the kind of large-scale commercial production seen elsewhere in Europe. Brick production was a seasonal activity because of the need to lay the clay through the winter months in order that it would be broken up by the severe weather before moulding and firing in the spring, but there is reason to believe that manufacture was sufficiently organized in some places to take on the character of a permanent industry. The Thames valley in particular seems to have had manufacturers who produced a regular supply and the royal building programme could not have been carried out so fast or so extensively without them; for example, bricks were bought in from local sources for the construction of Hampton Court, Oatlands and Nonsuch and for Henry VIII's conversion of the priory of Dartford.[17] The amount of early sixteenth-century brick building that survives might suggest that production reached new levels of quality as well as quantity at this time, but this is only partly true. If sixteenth-century houses are compared with their fifteenth-century predecessors, it is apparent that the standards of manufacture declined in some cases. This is most likely a direct reflection of the increased demand for brick, of the fact that the making of brick in England was probably no longer so dependent on foreign expertise, and of a general acceptance of lower standards in return for speed of construction and the chance to experiment.

Brick domestic buildings of the fifteenth century fall into quite distinct geographical groups, each of which can often be explained by the existence of a regional circle of patrons who all made use of the men, methods and materials of local brick workshops. Some of these houses show clear evidence of foreign influence. Brick buildings on the Continent may well have impressed many of those who fought in France in the period 1430 to 1450 and so inspired them to build in brick on their return. Leland points to several brick buildings which he claims were built in the fifteenth century from the profits of the French wars.[18] Bricks were also sometimes imported; the chronicler William of Worcester tells us that Sir Andrew Ogard, a Dane who was granted citizenship in England in 1433, imported bricks for his house at Emneth in

Norfolk.[19] Finally, there are documented references to foreign craftsmen working at several important sites. Although the demand for imported bricks slowly diminished as the century progressed and local output increased, foreigners often still supervised the manufacturing process. Two hundred thousand bricks for Stonor House, Oxfordshire, were made a few miles away at Cockernend in 1416–17 by 'les Flemynges'. At Tattershall Castle in Lincolnshire the chief brickmaker in the 1440s was Baldwin, 'the Docheman' (a term usually synonymous with German). What we know about the names of those who worked on the brick tower at Farnham, Surrey, for William Waynflete, Bishop of Winchester, in the 1470s, also suggests the employment of foreigners. By the early sixteenth century evidence for the involvement of foreigners disappears. Where documentation does survive, particularly in the case of the Royal Works, those involved in the making and use of bricks appear to have English names.[20]

This 'naturalization' of brick-making and building by the early sixteenth century was accompanied by a marked decline in the quality of the bricks themselves and by an apparent retreat from the willingness seen in the previous century to explore the architectural possibilities of the medium. At Rye House in Hertfordshire (Fig. 106), just north of London, there is a fragment of a fifteenth-century house built by the same Andrew Ogard who was an importer of bricks in the 1430s. Rye House is one of a small group of important brick buildings on the Essex-Hertfordshire border, all built between about 1430 and 1450, which also includes Nether Roydon, Faulkbourne Hall and Someries Castle. The Rye House fragment incorporates as many as fifty-eight different varieties of moulded brick. Each specially-made brick-type was employed for only one particular feature, so that putting this building together must have involved highly detailed planning and very careful control of the production process.[21]

The fifteenth-century ability to enrich the surface of a building with a multiplicity of brick mouldings, as if brick were essentially a sculptural medium, is much less evident a century later. By the sixteenth century the general increase in the size of houses demanded far more bricks and there is an apparent shift in what might be called the aesthetic use of the material. The available expertise

*106  Rye House, Hertfordshire. The surviving gatehouse to what was once a moated house, licensed for crenellation in 1443. Fifty-eight different types of moulded brick were used in its construction.*

*107  Temple Newsam House, West Yorkshire. The west side of
Lord Darcy's house, built by 1537. The 1565 inventory suggests the
great chamber and main apartments were here.*

is now deflected away from the building as a whole
towards a concentration on brick 'features', of
which the famous early Tudor brick chimneystacks are undoubtedly the most prominent survivals.[22] These chimneys were primarily conceived
as ornament rather than as an integral part of the
structure; they were often added to buildings that
were otherwise entirely constructed of stone or
timber, as can still be seen at Nether Winchendon
in Buckinghamshire and the castle of Framlingham
in Suffolk. At Framlingham, some of the chimneys
appear to be purely decorative, for they seem never
to have served actual fireplaces (Fig. 26).[23]

Rye House and the other brick houses in its
vicinity are characterized by the quality and complexity of the corbelling beneath the windows,
made with specially obtuse-angled bricks, a feature
that is rarely found in comparable sixteenth-century
houses. For instance, the (now heavily-restored)
corbelled upper windows on the court side of
Chenies, home of the courtier John Russell in
Buckinghamshire (see Fig. 32), are by comparison
much simplified in profile and depth. This trend
towards the use of simpler designs seems to have
extended to building technology in brick in general.
It may be significant that one of the very few
surviving early sixteenth-century examples of an
all-brick newel stair, that at Laughton Place in East
Sussex, built in the 1530s, is noticeably simple in
design when compared with a fifteenth-century
example of an all-brick stair. This shows in particular in the construction of its underside vaulting
and in the lack of finesse in its detailing, such as

the absence of a handrail incorporated into the brickwork.[24]

It was a different form of brick embellishment, diaper work, that was most fully exploited in the early Tudor period. This technique involved using vitrified bricks, often the result of over-firing, to create patterns on the surface of the brick wall. Diaper work was first used in the mid fifteenth century, appearing, for instance, on Herstmonceux Castle in the 1440s, but it became common from about the 1470s onward, about the time of Bishop Waynflete's commissions. It was particularly prominent on bishops' palaces, an excellent surviving example being the early sixteenth-century Bishop of London's palace at Fulham (see colour plates). Larger houses (and of course Herstmonceux itself was an early and, for its time, exceptionally large brick building) meant larger expanses of plain brick walling which in turn begged decoration. An example of just such an expanse of patterned diapering from the early sixteenth century is to be seen on Temple Newsam, Thomas, Lord Darcy's house in Yorkshire (Fig. 107), where the west face of the west range shows diapering to the height of three stories, an interesting reminder of the Tudor house that has been obscured by the later Jacobean rebuilding.

Sometimes diapering was used to create more sophisticated designs than simple patterns using lozenge and cross shapes. At the Archbishop of Canterbury's palace of Croydon, in south London, there are diapered cross keys and a small cross on a pedestal, showing that this form of decoration could be adapted to have some meaning and significance on an appropriate building.[25] Expanses of brick walling, whether diapered or not, might also be embellished with painted colour, as in the case of the tower at Farnham and the royal house converted from the remains of Dartford Priory in the late 1530s. This obvious concern with the surface of things underlines the early Tudors' desire to use ornament and the lavish application of colour and gilding to convey a two-dimensional splendour that was instantly impressive.[26]

William Thomas's *History of Italy*, written in 1549, is by inference disparaging about the quality and durability of English brick, as if acknowledging its recent inferiority. This comes out in his description of the wall encircling Rome: 'For notwithstanding it be builded of brick, yet it doth show such antique majesty (having 365 towers, agreeable with the number of days in the year) that he who seeth it must needs confess it could never be builded but in the time of the Romans' glory. Perchance some will marvel how brick should so

long continue, but their brick, whether it be of good making or of the heat of the sun that drieth much better than with us, is wonderful durable. For there be many buildings in Rome of brick that have continued these thousand years and more yet to this hour are nothing worn or decayed.'[27]

By the time Thomas was writing, brick was beginning to lose its attraction among the élite. Apart from houses in East Anglia, for which brick continued to be the principal building material for the rest of the century, most of the significant great houses initiated in the period c.1550 to c.1590 were built of stone.[28] Even in the southeast of England, where brick was evidently the most important fashionable building material of the first decades of the sixteenth century, isolated deposits of workable stone explain the incidence of small groups of great stone houses. Kentish ragstone, a limestone, had been employed quite often for important buildings in medieval London, simply because it was the nearest supply of stone that could be brought cheaply to the capital; it was used, for example, as early as the eleventh century for William I's White Tower at the Tower of London. In the early sixteenth century, there was a group of houses under construction in mid Kent where ragstone was employed. They were all associated with important ecclesiastical or Court figures, notably the Archbishop of Canterbury, who was responsible for Knole and Maidstone and Sir Edward Wotton, who built Boughton Malherbe.[29]

Despite its usefulness, however, ragstone is rough and brittle and not easy to work with. It is certainly quite unsuitable for the fine detailing on exterior stonework that was called for in an age of external heraldry and for the increasingly refined mouldings of windows and doors. The lead in using stone to its full potential undoubtedly came from the construction of an important group of West Country houses where the builders had access to older deposits of limestone (Fig. 108). This was more adaptable and more varied than a coarser stone like ragstone, giving the potential to design wall surfaces with the greatest possible range of texture and visual interest.

In the west of England, and particularly in the counties of Gloucestershire, Somerset and Dorset, access to local resources of good building stone had always prompted builders to employ refined exterior detail on major buildings, such as cathedrals

*OVERLEAF 108 Southam Delabere, Gloucestershire, the hall range. One of the largest surviving stone-built West Country houses of the early sixteenth century, a forerunner of the more innovatory houses built after 1550.*

and large parish churches. In the early sixteenth century this attention to detail was extended from ecclesiastical buildings to private houses. Some of this work suggests that local stone masons had access to pattern books or other sources which included Continental motives and occasionally the fineness of detail they achieved surpassed even the subtlest work in cast terracotta. A fine example of what was possible is Wolfeton House, just outside Dorchester (Fig. 109). Built for Sir Thomas Trenchard, only part of the first phase of sixteenth-century building work survives; this includes the gatehouse, which is incised with the date 1534, possibly marking the end rather than the beginning of the initial building programme. The details of the windows of this period show an extraordinary perception of the possibilities of using carved stone to express the depth of the wall. The mullions of the windows, set into deep reveals, spring from tiny pedestal bases which decrease in height inwards to give a perspectival effect. They show a use of materials that aspires to rather more than surface decoration. There may well have been a French source for this idea; a similar use of thin shafts on tiny bases, though without the perspectival effect of Wolfeton, can also be seen at the Normandy château of Fontaine-Henry (Fig. 110), built for the D'Harcourt family. Like Trenchard, the D'Harcourts were local officers of the King rather than from the highest courtier class.[30]

Both Trenchard and his son, Thomas II, married into the Strangways family. Giles Strangways was the builder of Melbury on the Somerset-Dorset border and this may well have been the first, chronologically, of an important group of houses in this region which extended the decorative potential of stone to its limits. They date from the period *c.* 1535 to *c.* 1560 and include Sir John Horsey's house of Clifton Maybank, the Bingham family's Bingham's Melcombe, Robert Morgan's house at Mapperton, Edward Knoyle's Sandford Orcas (Fig. 111; see also colour plates), and the new wing that Knoyle's father-in-law, Robert Martyn, built at Athelhampton.[31] Interestingly, the group responsible for these houses was not, in the strict sense of the word, from the courtier or metropolitan class, though all these men were loyal servants of the Crown in a local capacity. Strangways was the only one of them who served as a Member of Parliament and who was therefore likely to have spent extensive periods of time in London. Perhaps as a consequence of this, he was the only one to build a house to a strict courtyard plan and with a prospect tower. As a group, the builders of these houses parallel those men who

109  *Wolfeton House, Dorset. The bases to the uprights on the early sixteenth-century windows show the fine detail possible in West Country stonework of this period.*

were responsible for the half-timbered houses in the northwest of England. They were related by marriage, they shared local duties and, frequently, they were involved in bitter rivalries for land and local preferment. Their houses are likely to have been built by a common team of masons, so close are some of the details of construction.[32]

The use of materials in these West Country houses has two particular characteristics. First,

there was extensive use of ashlar facing, previously rarely employed except for the most important buildings, such as churches and royal palaces.[33] Secondly, though the stone prepared as ashlar was different in each case and local in origin to each house, Ham Hill stone was used for the dressings on all these buildings (at Sandford Orcas, the ashlar facing is also of Ham Hill stone). It could be finely cut and its golden brown patina was particularly suited to lending colour contrast to the wall it enriched. It was used to create surrounds for coats of arms and decorative panels, lozenge-shaped at Athelhampton, Bingham's Melcombe and Sandford Orcas, square at Bingham's Melcombe and Clifton Maybank (the entrance to the latter

*ABOVE 110    The château of Fontaine-Henry, France, built in 1535. Some details of the windows resemble those at Wolfeton House.*

*OVERLEAF 111    Sandford Orcas, Dorset, probably built in the 1540s. At the right is the gateway entrance, at the left the bay lighting hall and chamber.*

survives at the later sixteenth-century house of Montacute, to which it was moved). Amid the decorative vocabulary of this stonework, some interesting hints of new classical influences appear. The juxtaposition of small curved shapes, closely resembling a classical volute, suggests some

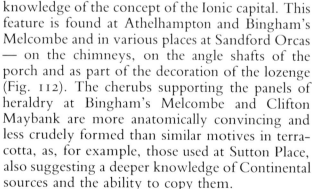

112   Sandford Orcas, Dorset. The upper part of the porch with decorated lozenge shield and shafts. The details of this decoration show some knowledge of classical forms.

113   Bingham's Melcombe, Dorset. The mid sixteenth-century oriel, with its sharp horizontal and vertical accents, shows a new awareness of architectural design on an otherwise unpretentious house.

knowledge of the concept of the Ionic capital. This feature is found at Athelhampton and Bingham's Melcombe and in various places at Sandford Orcas — on the chimneys, on the angle shafts of the porch and as part of the decoration of the lozenge (Fig. 112). The cherubs supporting the panels of heraldry at Bingham's Melcombe and Clifton Maybank are more anatomically convincing and less crudely formed than similar motives in terra-cotta, as, for example, those used at Sutton Place, also suggesting a deeper knowledge of Continental sources and the ability to copy them.

However, it is not only, or primarily, these finely cut decorative motives that give these buildings such distinction. More important is the sense of unity imparted to the whole house by the use of Ham Hill stone to dress and delineate the edges of all the major architectural features; it appears around doors and windows and along plinth mouldings and string courses, and was used for the polygonal angle buttresses to the gable ends of each building range, and for the caps and finials

which complete these buttresses. The mouldings are all simple and geometric in shape, giving a sense of sharp edging to everything. The great oriel at Bingham's Melcombe (Fig. 113) has a particularly strong suggestion of vertical emphasis and of expressing the wall surface as a grid of connected square and rectangular shapes, a feature usually associated with French Renaissance architecture and particularly the Loire châteaux; some sense of this can be gained from looking at the wall decoration either side of the staircase at Blois (see Fig. 73).[34] At Bingham's Melcombe it seems likely that squared-off architectural sections were designed in proportion to each other, introducing a new awareness that the building is made up of a set of related architectural features and is not just a wall surface for ornament.

Inventiveness and a concern for unity extends to the overall planning of these houses, for the social position of the owners meant that they did not require large courtyards to maintain the vast households of their courtier contemporaries and

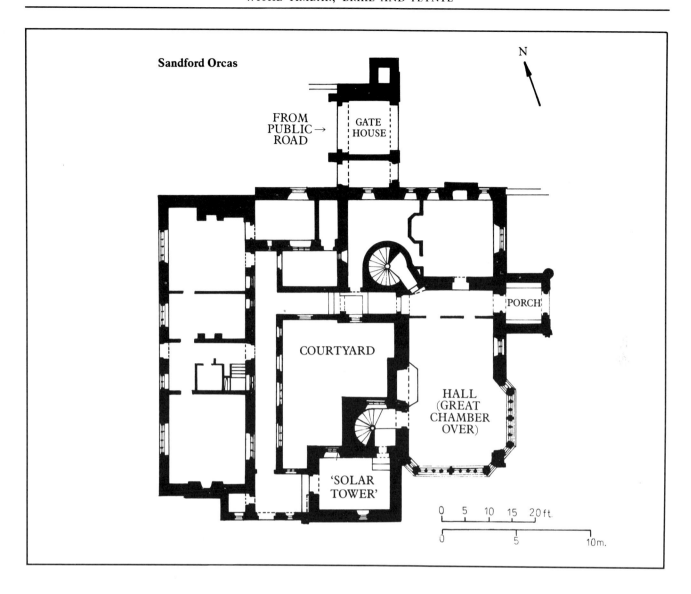

Sandford Orcas

FROM PUBLIC → ROAD

GATE HOUSE

N

PORCH

COURTYARD

HALL (GREAT CHAMBER OVER)

'SOLAR TOWER'

0  5  10  15  20 ft.

0                5              10m.

each of their buildings is characterized by a rather idiosyncratic compactness. Sandford Orcas (Fig. 114) enjoys the advantages of being an outward-looking house, but at the same time is designed to give privacy for the major rooms. It has its west, or back, side to the nearby road, but the main door faces east on to the garden, so that the visitor turns through 180 degrees to reach the porch to the hall.[35]

The major features of these houses and their location combine to determine their key importance for later developments. The characteristic buttressed gable end with finials recurs in the important group of quasi-symmetrical E-plan houses of the period after 1550, notably the houses of the merchants Robert Strode at Parnham and William Clifton at Barrington.[36] The strong suggestion of a re-assessment of classical design, still not fully understood, but potentially more sophis-

*114 Sandford Orcas, Dorset. The present plan shows the sixteenth-century layout, although there are only fragmented remains from this period in the west parts of the house.*

ticated than the earlier 'anticke' fashion in courtier architecture, heralds the new interest in Continental architecture that was pursued by a mid century group of patrons. In the light of this, it may not be accidental that two of the key buildings of the mid century period, Lacock Abbey and Longleat House, both in Wiltshire, are geographically close to the Dorset-Somerset border.

# 9

# 'A Farther and More Ample Discourse': The Somerset Group and a Change of Direction

FOR MORE THAN thirty years, beginning in the mid 1540s, Sir John Thynne was engaged on the building of his house at Longleat in Wiltshire, on the site of a former poor house of Augustinian canons. There were four successive stages of building, the most emphatic break coming in 1567, between the second and third stages, when fire virtually destroyed the house. What we see today, therefore, the final Longleat of the 1570s, bears little relationship to the first house that Thynne hastily constructed in the years 1546–9. These were the years of his Secretaryship to the most powerful man in England, Edward Seymour, Duke of Somerset and Protector of the kingdom from January 1547. Though busy and preoccupied with business in London, Thynne's involvement in the building of the first house was very marked; by letter, he concerned himself with every detail of construction. Compared with the dearth of information about other sixteenth-century houses, the survival of much documentation about Longleat helps us to follow the gradual emergence of a house that is said to epitomize the 'High Renaissance' of English architecture (Fig. 115).[1]

Two things are especially striking about the Longleat documents. Though there are no visual records of the first three stages of Thynne's house, it is clear that the house became more radical with each phase and at the same time more coherent in design. The first house was a piecemeal adaptation; Thynne's concern to remove buttressing and a large chapel window which upset the appearance of the house are reminiscent of the ad hoc decisions taken at Titchfield, where something serviceable and amenable was similarly created out of pre-existing walls and room spaces. Other alterations of the first phase included the construction of a battlemented tower and a staircase turret, similar to the kind of additions made to Laughton in the

previous decade. In these early stages there is little suggestion of novelty in style or construction. As time goes on, the records begin to mention details of stonework and internal fittings that imply a greater awareness of the new interest in the latest Continental, and particularly French, sources of design. This second building phase is also notable for the fact that Thynne increasingly employed masons from London, some of whom were French immigrants, and relied less on the local craftsmen whose skills had been adequate for his first house. The increasing awareness and new understanding of foreign ideas displayed at Longleat was characteristic of the circle in which Thynne moved. As a group, these men were also politically committed to the Protestant succession and to its successive leaders, the Duke of Somerset and John Dudley, the Duke of Northumberland. The remains of this short period of English architecture are if anything even more fragmentary and hard to elucidate than those of the 'anticke' phase, but the major buildings of this time nevertheless had a profound impact on the debate about the design and appearance of domestic architecture.[2]

A comparison with developments in France emphasizes the importance of the changes in architecture that were initiated around 1550 by this group of English patrons. In French architecture of this period, changes in the vocabulary of ornament can be used to support the idea that there were distinct phases in the absorption and understanding of Italian ideas. Particular events can be singled out as marking the starting-point of each phase. Italian styles make their first appearance in France in the

115 Longleat House, Wiltshire. The final house of the 1570s, with the consistent application of the classical orders on all four outer faces, has been described as the 'High Renaissance' of English architecture.

wake of the French invasion of Italy in 1494, after which many Italian craftsmen were brought to France to serve at the royal Court and elsewhere. The architectural ornament of this phase, known as the 'first' Renaissance, was intrinsically similar in design to that of the English 'anticke', with the same interest in using an established vocabulary of motives to create a shallow decorative surface (see Fig. 110). The second phase began in the 1540s after the arrival of the Italian architect and theorist, Sebastiano Serlio, and the return from Italy of the Frenchman Philibert de l'Orme. The subsequent decoration of buildings now showed a deeper understanding of the achievements of the High Renaissance in Italy: ornament became more rationalized, more simplified and in a sense more abstract. The previous fashion for motives based on a combination of fantastic animal and human forms with vaguely militaristic symbols, similar to the designs found in English architectural decora-

tion, was superseded by simpler patterns like the Greek key design. These changes appear most emphatically and consistently on new buildings, such as Serlio's château of Ancy-le-Franc and Philibert's work at Anet, but in some places one form of ornament can be seen giving way to another, as in the sequence of tombs for the Gouffier family in the church at Oiron, in Poitou. The important development in French architecture which underlies this 'second' Renaissance is a growing concern to use ornament as the vehicle of more profound ideas, especially about proportion and decorum in building design. However, in both phases ornament was often systematically applied over the surface of a building; to the untrained eye, it must have appeared that all that had happened was that the rich fussiness of the French form of 'anticke' had been replaced by a new simplicity.[3]

England differed from France in the sense that the 'anticke' form of decoration had never been used to unify all the architectural elements of a facade. When 'anticke' ornament was used, it might appear around windows, but not around doors; on parapets, but not on plinths; on the decoration of one courtyard, but not another. It was often heavily disguised by using it in such

*116   Cowdray House, West Sussex. The coat of arms over the porch. A purer form of classical ornament, seen here in the pilasters, was acceptable in small architectural details such as this before it could be applied to buildings as a whole.*

a way that it could be mistaken for a traditional form of decoration (perhaps the only form in which some people found it acceptable). At Layer Marney, for example, Italianate dolphin shapes form the heads to the window lights but they curve inwards in such a way that from a distance they appear to be a version of the familiar late medieval form of the cusp, or four-centred arch (see Fig. 79). The use of the classical orders was quite rare and tended to be restricted to one feature of the facade, most frequently coats of arms, which were applied to the building rather than an integral part of it. At Hampton Court, fluted columns with composite capitals flank the arms of Cardinal Wolsey, made in terracotta and now on the inner side of Anne Boleyn's gateway. Classical pilasters also flank the coat of arms in stone on the porch to the hall at Cowdray (Fig. 116). In contrast, mid century buildings are more ambitious in their use of classical decoration. This period saw some of the first attempts to apply classical orders across whole facades and to devise features that were more in keeping with classical ideas of proportion. The degree of understanding of classical and Italian ideas is perhaps less important than the new attempts at consistency.

John Shute's *The First and Chief Groundes of Architecture*, published in 1563, was the most important of the texts that underpinned the mid century interest in architecture. This was the first book by an English writer to examine, classify and illustrate the classical orders of architecture and its principal message was the importance of consistency and close attention to sources. Shute was sent to Italy in 1550 by the Duke of Northumberland, an indebtedness which he acknowledges in his dedication. The modest scope of Shute's book has been rather unfairly treated by many later commentators. It was, as the author states, intended as but the prologue to a wider and longer discourse on architecture, which probably never materialized because of his patron's fall from power in 1553. Shute makes a point of emphasizing that he thinks his book will be useful because of his personal experience of the orders in Italy and because he has measured surviving examples of Roman columns. In his view, although those who are interested in architecture will have read about the orders, their knowledge will be imperfect because they have no first-hand experience. The purpose of his book is to relate his knowledge of the theoretical premises of the orders to what he has observed about the application of principles in surviving classical buildings: 'that I might with so muche more perfection write of them as both the reading of the

thinge and seing it in dede is more than onely bare reding of it'.[4]

Who were the new group of English patrons for whom Shute was writing and why were they interested in Italian ideas? This is a question that has never been satisfactorily answered, particularly as the perspective of historical hindsight offers no clues as to why they should have been curious about the classical past. How did a group of men, committed to the Protestant cause, who engineered themselves into positions of power in 1547 by carefully manipulating Henry VIII during the last months of his life and by destroying the conservative and Catholic faction at Court led by the Howards, identify so closely with Italian ideas in architecture?[5] It is of course true that the break with Rome in the 1530s was not immediately followed by the wholesale rejection of the dominant Continental culture. Though some aspects of foreign travel became more difficult, it was some time before the educated, Protestant English withdrew into the peculiarly insular and priggish attitudes to Continental art that characterized the late sixteenth and seventeenth centuries. The reign of Edward VI saw the dissolution of the chantries and the height of post-Reformation iconoclasm, but the suspicious, xenophobic writings of the Elizabethan period had yet to emerge. These warned against the lure of Italy and the way that admiration for the recent achievements of Italian visual culture could be dangerously close to an acceptance of idolatry. The men in power at the court of Edward VI thought otherwise. They were keen on governmental and social reform and they saw the recent theoretical writing on architecture that had emerged from Italy as one of the means to those ends, as it stressed the importance of building works as initiatives for the public good.[6]

Two of the leading lights of this group were the Hobys, Philip and his much younger half-brother and heir Thomas (though they were outside the inner political circle and subsequently survived the coming of Queen Mary in 1553). Philip Hoby, whose Protestant sympathies had been sufficiently radical and therefore politically suspect for a brief spell of imprisonment under Henry VIII in 1543, was made Master of the Ordnance and a Privy Councillor in 1547, but spent much of Edward VI's reign abroad on diplomatic service. He was in contact with leading Venetian men of letters and knew the painter Titian. Thomas Hoby was 'very expert in knowledge of dyvers tongues' and is chiefly remembered for his translation of Castiglione's *Il Cortegiano* (*The Courtier*). This was the classic early sixteenth-century text on

Renaissance manners and the accomplishments of education, and Hoby's translation was published in 1561. The Hoby brothers were responsible for the refashioning of an old courtyard house of the medieval Knights Templar, adjacent to and part of their grant of Bisham Abbey on the Thames (Fig. 117). Classical ideas were partially introduced here and appear only in the pedimented windows with their thin mouldings, set into a stone wall which is built up by brick gables. The fourteenth-century porch was left standing and the Hoby brothers clearly felt no concern about mixing materials. Bisham lacks the consistency and rigour of other buildings of this group but it demonstrates, like Lacock Abbey, that even where much older buildings were adapted they could be influenced by new architectural ideas, and that these might lend a new purity and simplicity to certain details.[7]

Edward Seymour, Duke of Somerset and Lord Protector, was the chief architectural patron of this mid century period, both because of his position and because of the extent of his patronage. Although hardly anything of his work survives, he was responsible for at least five major building projects. He built Somerset House, in London, on the site of a house formerly belonging to the Bishop of Chester; at Syon, a few miles along the Thames out of London, he began the conversion of the former Bridgettine nunnery into a great court-yard house; he probably carried out minor changes to his family home of Wolfhall in Wiltshire; he initiated a major rebuilding at Berry Pomeroy Castle in Devon; and he planned a new Wiltshire house at Bedwyn Brail, for which only foundations were ever prepared.[8] All these projects were initiated in the years 1547 to 1549. The accounts kept by Somerset's cofferer, John Pickerell, which survive in the British Library, speak of the great expense to which the Duke was prepared to go. By the time of the Duke's attainder and execution in 1552, over £10,000 had been spent on Somerset House alone.[9] Quite apart from any considerations of style, this was a scale of expense that dwarfed what any previous courtier had spent on a single house, even allowing for the inflation of the years around mid century. Somerset was clearly prepared to spend to uphold his high, quasi-kingly office. Somerset House was the most important and influential

*117 Bisham Abbey, Berkshire. This had been a house of the Knights Templar in the Middle Ages and had long been secular property when the Hobys obtained it. The south front shown here illustrates the partial introduction of classical ideas.*

building of this group, thanks to its position in London, but other houses reflected and shared some of its innovative architectural features.

In the two brief years until his fall in 1549, Somerset's brother Thomas Seymour, who married Henry VIII's widow Katherine Parr, commissioned work at Sudeley Castle, Gloucestershire, newly granted by Edward VI. Whatever he completed here was swept away in subsequent work, but when Sir William Sharington was questioned about Thomas Seymour's expenses in 1549 he attested that Seymour owed him £1100 for building work at Sudeley.[10] Lacock, which Sharington was busily converting at this time, was one of three other building projects which appear to be linked by the work of the same mason (Fig. 118). The masonry details and the use of classical ornament at Lacock are very similar to the work undertaken for John Dudley, Duke of Northumberland, at his newly-acquired castle of Dudley in the West Midlands. This apparent connection is supported by a letter from Sharington to John Thynne, written in June 1553, in which Sharington apologizes for being unable to send Thynne the mason John Chapman from Lacock. The reason given is that he has been summoned to work at Dudley Castle and has already sent on his working tools and a 'chimney (fireplace) that so long he hath been working of'. Since this letter comes only weeks before the death of Edward VI and Northumberland's subsequent ill-fated stand against Queen Mary, Chapman may have had very little time at Dudley Castle. As a result, Thynne was subsequently able to secure his services for Longleat, where he worked for several years. Chapman therefore provides the crucial link between three great mid century houses — Dudley, Lacock and Longleat.[11] Visual evidence also suggests that the mid century transformation of Broughton Castle, near Banbury in Oxfordshire (Fig. 119), is closely linked with this circle of patrons, of which Sharington appears to have been the guiding hand, though it is only possible to establish tentative connections between the owner of Broughton, Richard Fiennes, and the Court.[12]

Sir John Gates, Vice-Chamberlain of Edward VI's household, who lived in some state at the royal house of Pyrgo Park in Essex, and Sir Thomas Palmer, who lived at Backenho in Bedfordshire, were two other figures who also suffered in the destruction of the Protestant faction in 1553. They too were building in these years but there is no telling what their houses looked like.[13] In contrast, the buildings of the courtier Sir Nicholas Poyntz do survive in part and are now being more closely

ABOVE 118 *Lacock Abbey, Wiltshire. Chimneystacks inserted by Sharington over the east range. Built of stone, with classical mouldings to the caps, these are a notable departure from the brick stacks that were still the height of fashion in the 1540s.*

ABOVE RIGHT 119 *Broughton Castle, Oxfordshire. The mid sixteenth-century attempt to put symmetry on an older building disguises the off-centre entrance to the hall; see the doorway into the side of the left-hand bay.*

BELOW RIGHT 120 *Newark Park, Gloucestershire, possibly built in the 1540s. The house stands on high ground and the huge windows on the upper floor were for surveying hunting land. The doorcase is a remarkably purist example of a classical order for its date.*

investigated after years of neglect. His house at Iron Acton and his hunting lodge of Newark, near Ozleworth (Fig. 120), both in Gloucestershire, are clearly indebted to the new architectural ideas. In Poyntz's will he left his 'new house of Osleworth . . . upon the hill' to his wife for the span of her lifetime. This suggests that the lodge at Newark must have been built before 1557, and possibly

*ABOVE 121    Lacock Abbey, Wiltshire. The Ionic column in the stable court, perhaps the beginning of an arcade that Sharington planned in his work of 1540 to 1553.*

even before 1550, because a long tradition records that it was constructed with stone taken from Kingswood Abbey, whose manorial lands Poyntz was granted as early as 1540.[14]

All these houses, with the exception of Acton Court, which was adapted from a medieval court-yard house, are principally of stone, or are ashlared to appear as if they were. What are the major features that give the group coherence and indicate their significance? Here we are hindered by lack of sufficient surviving evidence from making anything but tentative conclusions, but such evidence as there is suggests a quite different use of Continental sources from earlier buildings. There is a remarkably purist approach to the use of the classical orders, as in the Doric doorcase at Newark (see colour plates) and the single attached Ionic column found in the stable court at Lacock (Fig. 121). At Broughton (Fig. 122), Ionic and Corinthian orders appear on the window which was the centre-piece of

*LEFT 122 Broughton Castle, Oxfordshire. The upper-floor window of the north front, decorated with Ionic and Corinthian orders. A date of 1554 appears on the chimney above.*

*ABOVE 123 Lacock Abbey, Wiltshire. Consoles of the Sharington period removed for repair.*

Richard Fiennes' new facade. Somerset House, Newark, Bisham, Lacock and Dudley all have windows of a similarly upright format, commonly divided by a single mullion and transom into four lights which have straight heads to them (although the original windows of this type at Newark are now incorporated into inside walls, since the house was extended at a later date). Generally, there is no extraneous ornament of the kind that covered the earlier brick and terracotta houses. Ornament is confined to features of detail, like the small paterae, or circular shapes, found at the junction of mullion and transom in the windows at Lacock and as in the introduction of supporting brackets to window ledges and shelves, carved in the form of the classical console (Fig. 123). These are found in the

'Queen Anne Room' at Broughton and in the lower of Sharington's two tower rooms at Lacock.[15]

The only certain evidence for a newly-built, strictly proportioned and symmetrical facade among this group of houses is John Thorpe's drawing of the Strand front of Somerset House (Fig. 124). The basic placing of the main features of the architecture is not new; the gateway at the centre and the prominent bays at the ends echo the central gatehouse and corner turrets of many early Tudor country houses and collegiate establishments. But the style of the details, the relationship of one part of the facade to another, the relatively low height of the building and the use of stone throughout represent the new direction in architecture.

Though a key building for the development of country houses, it should be remembered that Somerset House was an urban palace; this facade could only have been seen at close range and possibly only by a raking view along the street. This would have detracted from its visual symmetry but emphasized the quality of its materials and the details of its classicism. It may be that this facade was the only part of the house to be completed by the time of Somerset's fall from power; whether much work had been carried out on the great courtyard behind can only be inferred from later accounts for repairs when the house was owned by the Crown. But the accounts of Somerset's cofferer also make it clear that provision for internal work included extraordinary items that seem to emphasize the classical identity of the house. The sum of £41 5s was spent, for example, on 'marble pyllers bought in Fflaunders'.[16]

There is no certainty that the new architectural ideas which were most consistently expressed in the Strand front of Somerset House would have maintained their momentum, even if the circle of patrons which sponsored them had remained in power after 1553. The stylistic break which these houses represent may have been more apparent than real. Where their influence did live on, for example in the building of Sir Thomas Smith's Hill Hall, it does seem that the exploration of this abortive, purist classicism was subsequently renewed but considerably widened in scope.

Sir Thomas Smith entered the Court circle as the Duke of Somerset's Master of Requests in

124  *The Strand front of Somerset House, built about 1550. It was rare for a completely new house such as this to be built in London at a time when most courtiers were adapting former bishops' and abbots' houses as their London residences. (London, Sir John Soane Museum)*

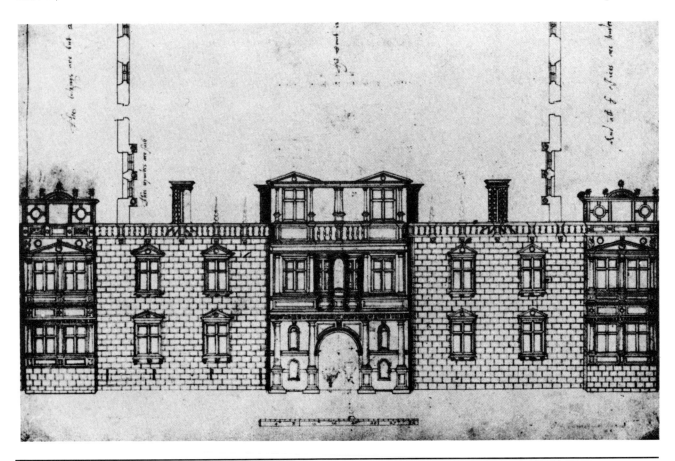

1547. He was appointed Secretary of State in 1548 and his close identity with Somerset himself was marked by a brief spell of imprisonment in 1549. In the reign of Queen Elizabeth he assumed some of the highest offices in government and he has confidently been identified as the author of the most important text concerned with political and social reform in the middle of the sixteenth century, *The Discourse of the Common Weal of this Realm of England*.[17] By the 1560s, he owned many of the leading foreign texts published to date on architectural theory. Smith not only studied in France and at the University of Padua in his early years, but was subsequently ambassador to France. It is usually assumed that his visits to France in the 1560s account for the second remodelling of Hill Hall, which extensive archaeological investigation has recently shown was gradually adapted in stages, each of which reflects an increasing use of Continental ideas. On the other hand, it is also true that Smith's architectural tastes were remarkably and increasingly eclectic, both in terms of the building materials he favoured and with regard to the books and buildings he consulted. He seems to have derived as much from purely visual sources, such as prints showing backgrounds of architectural fantasy on a classical theme, as from architectural theory. Smith's work at Hill Hall is fascinating and impressive, but not really coherent. Shute's plea for clarity and careful measurement got lost, in Smith's case, amid the conflicting attractions and possibilities presented by a wealth of source material.[18]

In contrast, Thynne's final house at Longleat displays the single-minded application of classical ornament. The exterior of the house exudes confidence in the handling of classical design and the floor levels are carefully delineated by stacking the orders one above the other. Yet this careful and ordered solution to the external appearance of a great house was not to be repeated; as has often been noted, Longleat is a unique moment in English architectural history. Its fine visual balance between horizontal and vertical accents gives way in later Elizabethan houses to the re-assertion of features that spring from a strong undertow of tradition in English domestic architecture. It is aspects of this deep-rooted tradition that link such distinct buildings as the castles of the later Middle Ages with the great houses of Vanbrugh in the early eighteenth century. The familiar features of this tradition include a concern that the point of entry should be accented in some way, usually by its height or wealth of decoration, as seen in the medieval and Tudor gatehouse or in the projecting entrance porch of later houses. Secondly, the skyline of these buildings is usually full of variety and interest, with a great number of chimneystacks and turrets providing contrasts of light and shade (Figs. 26 and 118).

Longleat is not only remarkable for its external architectural logic but also for the fact that it marks a decisive shift away from the inward-looking courtyard houses of the early part of the century. The house is still designed around a conglomeration of courtyards, but now they all have a common outer wrapping that disguises the complexities of the internal plan and gives all the major rooms a view on to the outer world. The courts are really light wells for the less important rooms that back on to the larger rooms around the outside of the house. As the architect Roger North wrote in the seventeenth century, as part of his categorization of house-plans according to their convenience for living, 'a court inclosed, where one or 2 sides are doubled, is tollerable, because the better rooms are layd to the best light, and the others postponed to the court'.[19] This double-pile design and the existence of a basement storey also meant new arrangements for the accommodation of servants and led to the formalization of the family/servant relationship and to the disappearance of most traces of the communal life of earlier households.

Apart from its internal arrangements, the siting of Longleat was also highly prophetic of things to come and in particular of the advent of profound social changes that feature so largely in the history of the country house. The visual coherence of Longleat can be appreciated because it can be seen from a great distance within the vast park in which it stands (Fig. 125). Like many (though by no means all) former monastic sites, it lies remote from other settlement. Whilst the majority of country houses were still close to, or on the edge of villages in the sixteenth century, as time progressed more and more country houses were built in the way with which perhaps we are most familiar, at the centre of a great walled park and at the end of a long drive.[20] This development has much to say about the place of the great landowner in society and about how the relationship between the powerful and their immediate local communities had changed over the centuries since the Middle Ages. This visual evidence for a change in what was represented by the outward aspect of the great house was mirrored in much polemical literature of the mid sixteenth century, which por-

OVERLEAF 125 *Longleat House, Wiltshire. The house set in its parkland.*

trayed the landowner as no longer in a patriarchal and therefore protective relationship with his servants and tenants, but rather as a distant, managerial and self-seeking figure. Later generations of country-house owners were to revitalize the practice of dining in the great hall with their staff as an occasional or annual event. This was a token revival of the medieval past, when the hall was the daily meeting place of the lord and those who served him. For some writers of the mid sixteenth century, however, this neglect of the welfare of their immediate dependents was symptomatic of the landowners' wider abnegation of their responsibilities towards society.

These writings have a strong flavour of the censoriousness of later Protestant literature, in that they are quick to condemn all visible signs of unnecessary outward show as vanity, a concern that applied to buildings as much as clothes and other material goods. The literature is also tinged with regret at the passing of what were conceived to be sound national customs and at the invasion of foreign habits, a cry of complaint that is common to all ages. But most of all, these writings identified a new kind of upper class that was not fulfilling the duties of the old; there is a perceived betrayal of the social ideals under discussion at this time. Splendour of building was no compensation for dereliction of social duty. William Harrison commended the general rise in the national standard of living, but at the same time lamented the passing of traditional English domestic architecture that was simple and plain on the outside, but well-provisioned within.[21] The anonymously published *Institucion of a Gentleman* of 1555 pointed specifically to the fact that lack of good provisioning meant that traditional duties of hospitality had diminished. Mixed with regret for the past and the inevitable attack on the trifling fashions of foreigners, the book makes much of the new concern for visual splendour which advertises the owner's wealth but betrays his lack of responsibility: 'In the auncient tyme when curious building fed not the eyes of the wayfaring man, then might he be fed and have good repast at a gentleman's place so called. Then stoode the buttery dore without a hatche, yeomen had then no cause to curse small dysshes, Flanders cookes had then no wages for their devises . . . This varietie and change from the olde English maner hath smally enriched gentlemen, but muche hath it empoverished their names.'[22]

The principal function of the great house as a place of hospitality is taken up by the writer Lawrence Humphrey, in his book on the duties of the nobility, published in 1563. The house 'be it large' is 'but to entertayne straungers. For, therein is not largenes discommended.' He also makes a very interesting point about the physical and social remoteness of the new country houses by comparing them to the villas of the ancient Roman nobles. They reserved their manors and farms for sport and refreshment, leading the life of the villa for a day as an escape from the urban environment, but they did not live in these places permanently: 'For flyeng cities . . . to build outleyes [outlying] farre from townes, to dwell scatteringe as the people Nomades [like Nomadic peoples], what it availeth . . . I can not yet reache by conjecture. For safe, it is not as already proved. And living solitary, they purchase envy . . . .'[23] Humphrey here puts his finger on the motivation behind the competitive drive to build country houses that first appeared in the early Tudor period and later put even the wealthiest Elizabethans into severe debt.

As far as domestic architecture is concerned, the early Tudor period was an age without architects in the sense that we use that word today. We know the names of many of the master masons and surveyors of the Royal Works and there is evidence that in some cases they worked in the 'private sector' of courtier houses. But at a time when England lacked any concept of architecture as a profession, it is impossible to trace the story told in this book in terms of the 'authorship' of buildings by men whose occupation was that of architectural design. The names we can identify find their way only into specialist dictionaries of architecture. It has been shown that the true makers of these buildings were their patrons, those who paid for them. Country houses were the vehicle for the increasingly comfortable lifestyle that the powerful of this age expected and were adorned with signs of social prestige, often emphasized by the addition of gold and vivid colour. Yet, despite their importance, it is clear that few builders had the time or inclination to supervise the construction and decoration of their houses very closely. In the early Tudor world of rapidly rising and often dramatically falling fortunes, houses were built with tremendous speed and alacrity. Modern archaeological exploration of the standing remains of these structures declares them badly-built, a patchwork of compromises in order to get things done as quickly as possible. It was a time of great enterprise, but also of great experiment.

During the reign of Queen Elizabeth, the general inflation which had begun to affect the country before mid century caught up with the building trade. Country houses were still built in great numbers, but they were now a far greater monetary investment and the signs are that more care was taken, that buildings were better planned and built to last. Whilst Thynne may not have intended it that way, the final Longleat, which is so seminal a point of reference for the history of the country house, was the result of many stages of rethinking, with increasingly radical and thoroughgoing reorganization. The building energy of the early Tudors had had the effect of equating the possession of a new country house with social status. But it was the Elizabethans who were to reap the benefits of experiment and who would match the needs of those who lived in these buildings to their design even more successfully.

# Gazetteer

*A Survey of Early Tudor Country Houses*

THIS IS INTENDED as a survey of important domestic buildings of the period *c.* 1490 to *c.* 1550; it is not a gazetteer of all early Tudor houses. The majority of the early sixteenth-century houses mentioned in the text are listed here, plus a number of other houses where size, documentation or the significance of the patron suggest they should be included. The dominant role of courtiers in building of the period is reflected in the preponderance of buildings in the south, Midlands and west. The major royal and episcopal houses and castles which underwent major modifications at this time are included as are the most important monastic conversions (usually initiated by courtiers). Certain major royal and courtier houses in London (most of them now vanished) that were built on a country-house scale and are well recorded are here, otherwise town houses are omitted. Some of the buildings listed below remain, often in a much-altered state, but far more have disappeared. Whether surviving or not, houses are listed according to present county divisions, as established in 1974. The grid reference is given in each case (save for sites in inner London), followed by details of the patron's chief posts in government or at Court, or social standing in the country. A brief discussion of the building then follows, giving dates of construction (in some cases certain, in others suggested by secondary evidence) and a description of appearance (in the case of altered or lost houses, from visual or other evidence). Only building work of the early Tudor period at each site is mentioned; the subsequent history is not discussed, save to put the present Tudor remains in context.

Buildings marked with an asterisk (*) are currently (1987) open to the public, some by appointment only.

For further references and bibliography on the houses that follow, see *The History of the King's Works*, Vol. IV (ed. H. Colvin, 1982) and M. Howard, *The Domestic Building Patronage of the Courtiers of Henry VIII* (unpublished Ph.D thesis, London 1985).

## AVON

\***Horton Court** ST 7684. William Knight (1476–1547) was Henry VIII's chaplain, later his secretary 1526–8 (when he travelled to Italy), then Bishop of Bath and Wells from 1541. This much-restored house of Knight's early years (*c.* 1521, with an inscription of this date) is attached to a mid 12c hall. The garden ambulatory or loggia, of six bays, has four 'anticke' heads in roundels on its rear wall.

**Thornbury Castle** ST 6590. Edward Stafford, Duke of Buckingham (1478–1521), cousin of Henry VIII, was the premier peer of the kingdom but never held high office and was executed for treason. Thornbury was begun on a huge scale in 1507/8 but unfinished at the Duke's death. It has a fortified entrance range but a luxurious private set of apartments for the Duke and Duchess, with canted bay windows jutting out on to the privy garden.

## BEDFORDSHIRE

**Ampthill** TL 0337. Henry VIII took over the 15c castle of Lord Fanhope in 1524. The fortified aspect of the house clearly disappeared in subsequent years as state apartments were created. A survey of 1567 suggests that the great court was entered from the E with hall on the N. In ruins by 1605, the late 17c Ampthill Park now stands on the site.

**Cardington Manor** TL 0945. Sir William Gascoigne (d. 1540), Treasurer and Comptroller of the Household to Wolsey, built a large manor house on the moated site, possibly after 1530. The remains have windows with round-headed lights, two stepped gables with elaborate cut brick and a great brick chimney.

**\*Warden Abbey** TL 1343. Robert Gostwick (d. 1561), related to the Gostwicks of Willington (see below), had the former Augustinian house from 1545. The surviving brick fragment, with chimney and stair turret, was part of a range he built in the angle between cloister and church, though the Bucks' 18c print shows a large, possibly courtyard house.

**Willington Manor** TL 1150. Sir John Gostwick (by 1493−1545) was Master of the Horse and subsequently Comptroller in Wolsey's household and after 1535 was Treasurer of the Court of First Fruits and Tenths. By the early 1540s he had made a 'sumptuus new building of brike and tymbre' here (Leland); only fragments now remain as part of a later house. \*Dovecot and stable buildings survive, probably built with re-used monastic stone.

## BERKSHIRE

**\*Bisham Abbey** SU 8585. Sir Philip Hoby (1500/5 −58) served on many missions abroad under Henry VIII and Edward VI and, though briefly imprisoned for Protestant sympathies in 1543, was one of the few Englishmen in contact with the arts of Catholic Europe; he knew Titian and Pietro Aretino. He was Master of the Ordnance from 1547. His brother, Sir Thomas (d. 1566), was a renowned scholar and translated Castiglione into English. After 1553, they transformed a medieval house of the Knights Templar into a compact courtyard house with brick and stone additions and windows in the mid century Renaissance style.

**Sonning Palace** SU 7575. The house of the Bishops of Salisbury has vanished, but was excavated in 1916. A new hall, with a porch, oriel and attached stair were built mid 15c and towards 1500 a new gatehouse of brick was added, with octagonal turrets at the angles, as mentioned by Leland. The site was surveyed after the Crown took possession in 1574.

**Sunninghill Park** SU 9367. The Royal Lodge here was rebuilt in 1511 and sums for maintenance appear in the accounts of the Constable of Windsor Castle in the 1520s and 1530s. The exact site is unknown.

**\*Windsor Castle** SU 9676. Henry VII carried the building of St George's Chapel to completion, rebuilt the adjoining Lady Chapel and added a (now removed) tower with canted bay windows to the royal lodgings in the upper ward. Henry VIII rebuilt the great gatehouse on the S side of the lower ward and created a terraced walk beneath the royal lodgings.

## BUCKINGHAMSHIRE

**\*Chenies** TQ 0198. Sir John Russell (c. 1485−1555) came from the West Country, rose through Henry VIII's Privy Chamber to be Lord Privy Seal from 1542 and was created Earl of Bedford in 1550. The original 15c house he acquired by marriage in 1526 and one of the lodging ranges he added to it, both of brick, survive, though much restored.

**Denham Court** TQ 0386. Sir Edmund Peckham (by 1495−1564), Cofferer of the Household to Henry VIII, built a new house here, recorded in a 17c map. After 1688, it was completely replaced by the present Denham Place.

**Ditton Manor** SU 9884. A royal house was built here 1511−16 on the same moated site as the present early 19c house, though details of payments and later repairs do not permit a reconstruction.

**Doddershall House** SP 7220. Two early 16c ranges of a house built by the Pigot family remain, originally in brick, now largely roughcast rendered. The hall (now subdivided) was in the range facing SE; it had entrance porches to both E and W. There are naïve 16c stone medallions with heraldry and profile heads reset into a brick chimneystack.

**\*Dorney Court** SU 9379. Owned by a succession of families in the early 16c (Kestwold, Lytton, Hill and Sir William Garrard, Lord Mayor of London), who built a brick and timber house with adjoining hall and parlour ranges, a solar lying above the parlour. There was originally an enclosing forecourt. The panelled great hall and other interiors remain.

**\*Nether Winchendon** SP 7311. Sir John Daunce (1484−1545), originally a goldsmith, whose expertise led to appointments on commissions for the coinage and as treasurer for war. His son married the daughter of Sir Thomas More. He considerably improved the dilapidated medieval house that he leased from 1527; some surviving evidence of his work includes brick chimneystacks and the frieze of the parlour.

## CAMBRIDGESHIRE

**Buckden Palace** TL 1967. Specific dating is not possible, but John Russell, Bishop of Lincoln 1480−94, probably added brick inner and outer gatehouses and enclosing walls to the great brick tower of his predecessor, Bishop Rotherham (1472−80). These additions all bear Russell's arms and still survive; hall and domestic buildings are gone.

**Childerley Hall** TL 3761. Sir John Cutte (d. 1520) was Under-Treasurer of England. Only certain features of the brick house for which Cutte was responsible, according to Leland, are visible today; some walling on the N side, the disposition of the dormer gables and renewed chimneys.

**Downham, Bishop's Palace** TL 5284. John Alcock, Bishop of Ely (1485–1500), Comptroller of the royal building works under Henry VII, built the manor house here, of brick with stone dressings. Two fragments, with some walling between, survive, incorporated into farm buildings.

*****Hinchingbrooke House** TL 2271. Sir Richard Williams (d.1545) was Thomas Cromwell's nephew. The Benedictine nunnery was suppressed in 1536 and granted to Williams in 1538. He retained the cloister buildings and the church, though he divided it into two floors (a rediscovered fireplace on the upper floor has his initials). More radical changes were made after c. 1550 by his son, Henry, making a new approach from the N.

*****Kimbolton Castle** TL 0967. Sir Richard Wingfield (1469–1525) went on many foreign embassies, was Joint-Deputy at Calais 1513–19 and died at Toledo, Spain. He obtained Kimbolton in 1522 and built 'new faire lodgyngs and galeries' (Leland). Only minor doorways and brick-vaulted cellars suggest Tudor work in the present house of c. 1690–1714.

**Kirtling Hall** TL 6857. Sir Edward North (c. 1496–1564), Treasurer, then Chancellor to the Court of Augmentations (1544), was later raised to the peerage by Queen Mary. Only the detached brick gatehouse with its oriel window, built just after 1533, now remains of North's building. The courtyard house that stood NW of it was possibly 1550s–60s.

**Madingley Hall** TL 3960. Sir John Hynde (c. 1480–1550), lawyer and judge, was a prominent local servant of the Crown. After acquiring Madingley in 1543, he built a brick house with a hall range (single-storey hall and great chamber above) and cross wings. Hynde's initials and royal heraldry are found on decorative stonework. Most of the chief range survives, along with additions of 1590s, all much restored.

## CHESHIRE

*****Little Moreton Hall** SJ 8358. William Moreton (d. 1563) employed the carpenter Richard Dale to add bay windows (dated 1559) to the hall and withdrawing room of a half-timbered house of the second half of the 15c. The S gatehouse range with a gallery on the top floor may also have been built at this time, or possibly later in the 1570s.

*****Norton Priory** SJ 5581. Sir Richard Brooke bought the former Augustinian monastery in 1545, ten years after its dissolution; he was still paying off the price of over £1000 in the 1550s. The Bucks' 18c view shows that Brooke largely used the W range of the cloister, constructing a stair to its upper floor. Nothing remains of the Tudor house, but the monastic fragments and site have been fully excavated in modern times.

**Ridley** SJ 5654. Leland mentions that the stone and timber house was built by Sir William Stanley, courtier to Henry VII, and that it now (i.e. the early 1540s) belonged to the Egertons. An early 16c stone gateway survives.

## CORNWALL

*****Cotehele** SX 4269. Sir Richard Edgcumbe (d. 1489), supporter of Henry Tudor in exile, ambassador to France and Scotland after 1485, and his son, Sir Piers Edgcumbe (d. 1539), who fought in France 1513–14, enlarged the old house into a courtyard, using granite ashlar. Most of their work, including the great hall and other interiors, survives.

*****Mount Edgcumbe** SX 4353. Sir Richard Edgcumbe (c. 1499–1562), son of Sir Piers (see above), held many local administrative posts in Cornwall and built the new family house here 1547–54 from a plan which, according to the contract with the Devon builder, he devised himself. Remarkably centrally-planned, with a tower at each corner and a two-storeyed hall at the centre, it prefigured the Elizabethan Wollaton. Burned in World War 2, the house is now rebuilt.

## CUMBRIA

**Rose Castle** NY 3452. The remaining N and W ranges of the house of the Bishops of Carlisle appear mainly 19c, but the new chapel built by Bishop Bell (1487–9) still carries his initials on the tower and the tower of Bishop Kyte (1521–37) carries his monogram.

*****Naworth Castle** NY 5662. Thomas, Lord Dacre (1467–1525), Lord Warden of the Marches who fought at Flodden, probably rebuilt the hall and other parts of the medieval castle around 1520, as indicated by his coat of arms.

**Wharton Hall** NY 7706. Sir Thomas Wharton (c. 1495–1568) fought against the Scots, served as Warden of the Western Marches under Henry VIII and was created Baron in 1544. He added to the 14/15c hall house around 1540, building a new hall, courtyard and defensible gatehouse. Much of his work remains.

## DERBYSHIRE

*****Haddon Hall** SK 2366. Sir George Vernon reached his majority in 1535 and it is likely that his stepfather, Sir William Coffin (by 1492–1538), Gentleman of the Privy Chamber and Master of the Horse to two of Henry VIII's wives, was equally responsible for the early Tudor work here.

# DEVON

**Berry Pomeroy Castle** SX 8261. The de Pomeroy family renewed the gatehouse and curtain walls of the 13c castle in the late 15c. After Edward Seymour, Protector Duke of Somerset, took possession in 1547 he began a new quadrangular house within the castle; work may have also begun on a loggia flanked by staircase towers. Later Seymours never completed the scheme. Ruinous but currently (1987) under investigation.

\***Cadhay** SY 0896. John Haydon (d. 1587), lawyer, legal adviser to the City of Exeter, built the house probably just after 1545, using rubble from the suppressed College of Secular Priests at Ottery St Mary and Salcombe sandstone with Beer limestone dressings for facing the house. The hall range faces N with the parlour range (this has original turret stair and flanking bays) at the E end. The S side of the court with long gallery was probably added in the late 16c and the courtyard dressed with its chequer-work and statuary c. 1617.

\***Compton Castle** SX 8644. John Gilbert (d. 1539) added the dry moat on the S, W and E sides of the early 15c castle. The five towers he built in the new curtain wall were habitable, designed with vaulted ceilings and fireplaces and with machicolations serving as windows and privies. He also built at the E end of the hall to provide better service areas.

**Holcombe Court** ST 0519. Sir Roger Bluet built the compact and impressive stone courtyard house c. 1520–30; big buttressed tower over the porch, with an attached stair turret.

# DORSET

\***Athelhampton** SY 7794. Sir William Martyn (d. 1504), who was Lord Mayor of London in 1493, built the battlemented hall range; his grandson Robert (d. 1550) probably added the parlour range with its larger windows, gables and octagonal buttresses. The dressings of the later range are in Ham Hill stone. A detached gatehouse has gone.

**Bingham's Melcombe** ST 7701. In the mid 16c the Binghams enlarged an earlier modest hall range house with detached gatehouse by the addition of a W range and a sophisticated oriel to the hall. Most of this survives. The oriel is in limestone ashlar while Ham Hill stone was used for other windows, plinth mouldings, string course, finials, shafts and the family coat of arms.

**Clifton Maybank** ST 5813. Sir John Horsey was one of the most powerful men in the Somerset and Dorset area as Sheriff, JP and a radical executor of royal policy. His house here, one of an important group in Ham Hill stone, was built shortly after 1546 but largely taken down in the 18c. The centre of the entrance front was removed to Montacute House, Somerset, where it remains.

\***Mapperton** SY 5099. Robert Morgan built the hall range (altered in the 17c) and one wing of a half H-shaped house in the mid 16c. The use of Ham Hill stone and the polygonal angle buttresses and finials make this house one of a group with Clifton Maybank and other Dorset houses. An upper room in the N range has important mid 16c plasterwork.

**Melbury House** ST 5706. Sir Giles Strangways (1486–1546) studied law, held minor posts at Court and fought in France in the 1520s, but was chiefly a man of local importance in Dorset. His house of Ham Hill stone was newly built when Leland saw it in the early 1540s; the basic courtyard plan, with external gable ends, and the prospect tower remain, though the house was altered in the 17c and enlarged in the 19c.

\***Milton Abbey** ST 7902. Sir John Tregonwell (by 1498–1565), lawyer and diplomat, became a chief Commissioner in the surrender of West Country monasteries in the late 1530s. He remained Catholic and was knighted by Queen Mary. He bought Milton, a dissolved Benedictine house, in 1540 for £1000. He retained much of the abbot's lodging, embellishing it with his own heraldry. The present house is largely 18c though the late 15c abbot's hall remains.

\***Parnham House** ST 4700. The merchant Robert Strode built the E-plan house about 1550, possibly earlier, in local stone with ashlar facing. The house was altered in the 17c, by John Nash c. 1810 and again early 20c. The Oak Room has linenfold panelling and a frieze of 'anticke' work, said to have come from West Horsley (see Surrey).

\***Sandford Orcas** ST 6221. Edward Knoyle inherited the house in 1533 and built (perhaps toward c. 1550) the small, largely unchanged house in Ham Hill stone. A gatehouse attached to the N side is entered from the W, with two right-angle turns required to reach the E-facing hall range. Two-storeyed bay windows light hall and great chamber above.

\***Wolfeton House** SY 6792. Sir Thomas Trenchard (d. 1550) built a compact stone courtyard house here early in the 16c (a date of 1534 remains), with internal and external changes about 1550. The gatehouse with round angle turrets (and an original wooden newel stair within), the hall and the impressive mid century dog-leg staircase are the main survivals of Trenchard's work, with some very interesting classicizing detail.

# DURHAM

**Bishop Auckland** NZ 2029. There are substantial 16c buildings in the complex palace still belonging to the see of Durham, mainly due to Thomas Ruthall (Bishop

1509–23) and Cuthbert Tunstall (1530–59), whose arms appear in the stonework.

**\*Durham Castle** NZ 2742. Tudor bishops of Durham modernized the 11–12c castle and much of this can be seen; Richard Fox (1494–1501) created new offices S of the hall and built new brick fireplaces in the W range. He also made new sets of chambers in the N range, where Cuthbert Tunstall (1530–59) later built a communicating gallery and chapel.

## EAST SUSSEX

**\*Battle Abbey** TQ 7516. Sir Anthony Browne (c. 1500–48) was Master of the Horse to Henry VIII from 1539 and one of the conservative faction at Court in the King's last years. He concentrated his conversion of the site of the former abbey (dissolved in 1538) in the outer court, making his house from the abbot's lodging. He added to the 13c gatehouse range and raised new lodgings on the undercroft of the guest range.

**Bolebrook House** TQ 4735. Sir Roger Lewknor (d. 1543), Sheriff of Sussex, built the house, of which a three-storeyed brick gatehouse and a gabled range beyond survive; the windows suggest later 16c alterations.

**Buckhurst** TQ 4935. Only the stone gatehouse remains of the house built by John Sackville (by 1484–1557), who held high local office in Surrey and Sussex and was brother-in-law to Thomas Boleyn (see Kent, Hever). Early evidence suggests that it formed part of an enclosing wall around a half-timbered house and heraldry suggests a date of c. 1510–25.

**\*Firle Place** TQ 4707. Sir John Gage (1479–1556) was Vice-Chamberlain (1528) and Comptroller of the Household (1540) to Henry VIII. His double-courtyard house at Firle was subsumed by the building of the 18c house, though the original roof timbers remain concealed by the present plastered ceiling of the hall and there are also Tudor gables, some fireplaces, doorways and a fragment of interior wall-painting.

**Isfield Place** TQ 4417. John Shurley (d. 1527) held minor Court posts and probably built a small, square house here, in brick with stone dressings, of which some early 16c windows remain on the E side.

**Laughton Place** TQ 4913. Sir William Pelham (c. 1486–1538) twice married into leading courtier families. He enlarged the medieval moated house here in brick, notably with a tower (altered in the 18c), which is all that survives. It served as private lodgings and also as watch tower and is decorated with terracottas and Pelham heraldry.

## ESSEX

**\*Audley End** TL 5238. Thomas Audley (1487/88–1544), lawyer, Speaker of the Commons in 1529 and Lord Chancellor in 1533, gained a peerage in 1538. The present house is largely 17c, on the site of Audley's post-1538 conversion of the Benedictine abbey of Walden. Audley's house preserved the monastic cloister, with the hall created in the W range.

**Beckingham Hall** TL 9011. Stephen Beckingham (d. 1558) began remodelling the house in the 1540s and built a low brick gatehouse with circular angle turrets and adjoining wall. Though he never achieved further changes to the modest brick and timber earlier house, panelling once here (now in the Victoria and Albert Museum) suggests that he added some expensively-fitted interiors.

**Belhus** TQ 5680. The irregularly-planned courtyard house of diapered red brick was described as 'newly builded' in 1526 in the will of its owner, the lawyer John Barrett, whose third wife was sister to the courtier Henry Norris. The hall was in the S range with its bay and porch on the exterior of the court. Altered mid 18c, the house was demolished in the 20c.

**\*Castle Hedingham** TL 7835. John de Vere, father (1490?–1540) and son (1512?–62), Earls of Oxford, were hereditary Lords High Chamberlain. The only remains of extensive late 15c work undertaken here in and around the 12c keep are the bases of octagonal gatehouse towers and a bridge across the moat, both in brick.

**\*Gosfield Hall** TL 7829. It is likely that Sir John Wentworth (1494–1567), possibly a member of Wolsey's household in the 1520s and later Sheriff of Essex and Herts, was the builder of the brick courtyard house after he inherited in 1539. His chapel at the local church is dated 1561. The symmetrical W range preserves the best Tudor work, with a long gallery on the first floor.

**Hallingbury Place** TL 5119. Henry Parker, Lord Morley (by 1486–1556), was a prominent courtier and literary figure (the translator of Petrarch) at Henry VIII's court. Only the 16c stable block remains; the house formerly here (largely 18c but with brickwork from the older, 16c structure) was demolished in 1924.

**Horham Hall** TL 6131. Sir John Cutte (see Cambs, Childerley) was building the house by 1505, but it was probably unfinished at his death in 1520. The hall range survives today, of brick with stone dressings. An adjoining wing to the NE (shown in a 17c painting) and an enclosing wall once gave the appearance of a courtyard house.

**Ingatestone Hall** TQ 6499. Sir William Petre (1505/6–72), Secretary of State in Henry VIII's last years, Chancellor of the Order of the Garter under Mary and Privy Councillor from 1566. Three sides of the inner court of his modest, well documented brick house, built after 1538, remain and also some early interior features, including the long gallery.

*Layer Marney TL 9217. Henry Marney (1456/7–1523) and his son John (by 1485–1525), Lords Marney, the father Lord Privy Seal in 1523, were both important military figures. Of the 1510s–20s plan for a huge courtyard house, only the spectacular brick gate-house (with polygonal turrets rising to eight storeys on the S side) and flanking wings, both with terracotta enrichment, were ever completed.

Leez Priory TL 7116. Sir Richard Rich (1496/7–1567) was Solicitor-General and Chancellor of the Court of Augmentations under Henry VIII, then became Lord Chancellor and created Baron Rich under Edward VI. He acquired the suppressed Augustinian priory of Leez in 1536 and clad the stone walls of church and monastic buildings in brick to form a fashionable Tudor house. The inner gatehouse is the most significant and least restored part of what remains today.

New Hall TL 7509. Henry VIII built a large house here from 1517–21, in brick, at a cost of £17,000. The gate was on the S side of the main court, the hall on the E, the chapel on the W. Some remains survive in the basement of the present, partly late 16c house (now a convent) and there is a fine carved, coloured and gilded coat of royal arms in the chapel.

Rochford Hall TQ 8790. Sir Richard Rich (see Essex, Leez). The house was formerly owned by Mary Boleyn and her husband Sir William Cary, a prominent courtier, but Rich, who bought it from their son, Henry, is likely to have been responsible for the large double courtyard house, built of brick partly rendered in plaster. The house largely remains, though much altered.

St Osyth's Priory TM 1215. Thomas Darcy (1511–58), courtier to Henry VIII, was created Lord Chamberlain and ennobled by Edward VI. He acquired the suppressed Augustinian house in 1553 and kept the late 15c stone gateway and brick abbot's house (both of which survive). The frater may have become his new great hall; all evidence of this has gone, but the new towers he added to flank the hall remain, as do the ruins of his new range at the E end of the site.

Weald Hall TQ 5793. Sir Brian Tuke (d. 1545) was French secretary to Henry VIII by 1522 and Treasurer of the Chamber from 1528. The Tudor appearance of this completely lost house (much altered in the 18c, demolished in 1950) is recorded in an early painting. Built of brick, it was a hall range with cross wings, incomplete at Tuke's death.

## GLOUCESTERSHIRE

Acton Court ST 6783. Sir Nicholas Poyntz (1510–57) was prominent at Court in both personal and military service to Henry VIII, marred only by a brief imprisonment in 1541. He adapted a large medieval courtyard house with new ranges in brick. Recent archaeological examination suggests the work was undertaken very rapidly.

*Newark Park ST 7993. Sir Nicholas Poyntz (see Acton Court, above) built this small house as a hunting lodge, mentioning it as 'new' in his will. Only the E front retains its mid 16c appearance; here large mullioned and transomed windows and the doorcase put the house firmly in the mid century fashion for classicism.

Southam Delabere SO 9725. Sir John Huddleston (c. 1489–1547), an important judge and King's man in Gloucestershire, married into the Clifford and Seymour families, rebuilt this house after 1512 (mentioned by Leland). There are considerable remains of the hall and adjacent ranges and, internally, some original glass and panelling.

*Sudeley Castle SP 0327. Sir Thomas Seymour (by 1509–49) was uncle, Privy Councillor and Lord Admiral to Edward VI. He was executed for treason. During the two years of his ownership of Sudeley (1547–9, whilst married to Henry VIII's widow, Katherine Parr), he built lavishly at the 15c castle, but all trace of his work disappeared in extensive further remodelling of the 1570s.

## GREATER MANCHESTER

*Smithills Hall SD 7012. The 15c half-timbered courtyard house was extended, partly rebuilt in stone and internally refitted by Andrew Barton after 1516. There was once a gatehouse to S; now N (hall), E (chapel and parlour) and W ranges remain, with 19c extensions further W. Panelling of c. 1530 in the E range.

*Wythenshawe Hall SJ 8489. Robert Tatton rebuilt the hall of the half-timbered house in the 1530s, creating remarkable symmetry with central porch and projecting wings. The house was later altered and refaced in the 19c, but now restored.

## HAMPSHIRE

*Basing House SU 6652. Sir William Paulet (by 1488–1572) held a series of important posts in Henry VIII's household, and was Lord Treasurer and Marquis of Winchester under Edward VI. He obtained licence to crenellate Basing in 1531 and began rebuilding the castle in brick. At a later date he built a second, adjacent house to the N. The remains of these buildings have been extensively excavated in recent years.

*Bishops Waltham Palace SU 5517. A house of the Bishops of Salisbury, altered by Bishop Langton (1493–1501). Leland says he built the base court in brick and timber but only flint walls of the main court remain, the W range being most intact. The great hall was clearly reconstructed, with a new, lower floor formed out of the medieval undercroft.

**Micheldever** SU 5138. Sir Thomas Wriothesley (1505–50) rose through his service to Thomas Cromwell and became Secretary of State in 1540. In 1547 he became Earl of Southampton, but was then largely out of favour under Edward VI. Micheldever was his first great house, under construction 1534–6. Nothing remains, but the site was excavated in 1973.

*****Mottisfont Abbey** SO 3227. Sir William (later Baron) Sandys (d. 1540) served at Calais from 1517 and was Lord Chamberlain from 1526. He acquired the former Augustinian house by exchanging his manor of Chelsea with the King in 1536. He then supervised the conversion of the property, creating a double-courtyard house. Only part of this survives, largely 18/19c in appearance, but the converted monastic nave has 16c windows on the N side and brick turrets on the S.

*****Netley Abbey** SU 4508. Sir William Paulet (see above, Basing) was granted the suppressed Cistercian Abbey in 1536. He formed his great hall from the church and extensively developed the E range for domestic use. The E end of the monastic church is now the best surviving part of the ruined monastic/country house complex.

*****The Vyne** SU 6356. Sir William Sandys (see above, Mottisfont) much enlarged his moated family home into a double-courtyard house which Henry VIII visited three times. Externally, save for the Tudor chapel, only certain areas of brickwork are 16c. Internally, more remains, including the upper-floor long gallery, with resited 1520s panelling.

**Tichborne Park** SU 5630. Richard (d. 1519) and Francis Tichborne (d. 1565) may have been the builders of the large (stone-faced) half H-shaped house once here, recorded in a painting of 1670, which had a Roman Catholic chapel attached. Its size and projecting bays suggest it was close in form to Wriothesley's nearby house at Micheldever (see above).

*****Titchfield Abbey** SU 5408. Sir Thomas Wriothesley (see above, Micheldever) acquired the former Premonstratensian monastery late in 1537. Letters reveal the process of conversion, resulting in the hall being made from the frater and a gatehouse opposite, in the former nave. Only the impressive ruins of the gatehouse range and minor walls and foundations now remain.

**Warblington** SU 7205. Margaret Pole, Countess of Salisbury, daughter of Edward IV's brother, the Duke of Clarence; she was executed in 1541. The moated brick courtyard house here was built after 1514. A description of 1632 says that it was about 200 feet square. Only one octagonal tower and part of the arch of the gatehouse and adjacent wall remain.

# HEREFORD and WORCESTER

**Alvechurch** SP 0272. Leland describes the house of the Bishops of Worcester NE of the town as repaired by Bishop Latimer as being all of timber and with 'no peace of old worke'. It was pulled down in 1780.

**Tickenhill Manor** SO 7875. A royal house, rebuilt when Prince Arthur used it in the late 1490s and repaired for Princess Mary and the Council of the Marches 1525–8. Stukeley's 1721 drawing of the remaining E wing shows a timber-framed building with brick chimneys. Nothing now remains.

# HERTFORDSHIRE

**Cassiobury** TQ 1196. Richard Morison (by 1514–56) was a protégé of Wolsey, later Gentleman of the King's Privy Chamber and a pamphleteer in support of royal policies. He died a Protestant exile. Early prints of his completely lost house show a 16c building, probably carried out after Morison acquired Cassiobury in 1545.

*****Hatfield Old Palace** TL 2309. The W hall range survives of the brick courtyard house built here for Bishop Morton of Ely in the 1480s. It passed to the Crown in 1538 and there were minor repairs in subsequent years before becoming Princess Elizabeth's main residence in 1555–8.

**Hunsdon House** TL 4114. Between 1525 and 1534 Henry VIII spent £2900 on building, adding to the 15c house. Most of the work was in brick; royal apartments and a great gallery were created. Hunsdon is gone, but its Tudor appearance is recorded in the background of the 1546 portrait of Prince Edward, now at Windsor.

**Markyate Cell** TL 0616. The priory of Benedictine nuns was dissolved in 1537. Humphrey Bourchier (d. 1540) of the Royal Household 'did much coste in translating of the priorie into a maner-place, but he left it nothing endid' (Leland). It stood to the NE of the priory church and some flint walling is all that remains, incorporated into a brick house of 1825–6.

**The More** TQ 0594. Thomas Wolsey, Archbishop of York 1514, Cardinal and Lord Chancellor 1515, rebuilt this house. It was Crown property from 1531, but ruinous by 1598 and nothing now remains. A survey of 1568 and excavation reveal a moated inner court, an outer court beyond the moat to the S and a great 250-foot timber long gallery leading N across the moat into the garden.

**Salisbury Hall** TL 1900. According to Leland, Sir John Cutte (see Cambs, Childerley) built a house on this moated site. The present, modest 17c house has some Tudor brickwork, including blocked arches beside the porch. A late 18c drawing shows a wing that may have been the remains of Cutte's work. The five stone and one plaster roundels in the hall with profile heads of Roman emperors may be mid 16c but are thought to have come from Sopwell (see below).

**Sopwell Priory** TL 1605. Sir Richard Lee (1501/2–75) was much employed by the Crown as an expert on coastal and other defences. The first house he built here following the grant of the former Benedictine nunnery in 1538 followed the cloister plan closely but a second house, probably begun 1560s, was built to the 'H' plan. Some walls of this later house survive, built of brick with stone dressings.

**Standon** TL 3922. Sir Ralph Sadler (1507–87) was a protégé of Cromwell, became one of the chief Secretaries of State in the 1540s and was prominent in diplomacy with Scotland until his death. Granted the site of Standon in 1540, he built a brick courtyard house of which part of the entrance range survives, with a date stone of 1546.

## HUMBERSIDE

**Hull Manor House** TA 0902. Henry VIII acquired the house in 1539. It is known largely through the four drawings or 'plats' (one a bird's-eye perspective view) made at this time by John Rogers, military engineer to the King. These show plans to form the usual sets of royal apartments and defend the property but it is not known what was carried out.

**Leconfield** TA 0143. Henry Percy, father and son (1478–1527 and c. 1502–37), Earls of Northumberland, were unusual among northern peers for their willingness to attend Court. Away from London, they lived largely on their Yorkshire estates. Only the moated site remains of the large house here, described by Leland as of timber but with a new brick and stone range. It decayed after passing to the Crown in 1535.

**Wressle** SE 7031. The Percys' (see Leconfield, above) second great Yorkshire house. Leland's long description confirms a major early 16c refurbishment of the 14c fortified house. The single surviving range has windows of Tudor date.

## ISLE OF WIGHT

*\*Appuldurcombe House* SZ 5579. Sir James Worsley (d. 1538) had minor posts at Court before assuming the key royal posts of Captain of Carisbrooke Castle and Steward, Surveyor and Receiver of Crown Lands on the Isle of Wight in 1520. Mention of his recent building here is made in a lease of 1527 and his house is recorded in a drawing of 1690 before demolition; three ranges of buildings are shown around a flagged court. The impressive ruins of the later 18/19c house now occupy the site.

## KENT

*\*Allington Castle* TQ 7557. Sir Henry Wyatt (c. 1460–1537), Privy Councillor to Henry VII, and his son Sir Thomas (1504–42), poet and courtier of the close circle around Anne Boleyn. Allington was purchased in 1492; some of the Wyatts' domestic improvements to the 13c moated castle can still be seen off the N end of the hall and in the (heavily restored) gallery range dividing the two courtyards.

**Birling** TQ 6860. George Neville, Lord Abergavenny (c. 1471–1535), Lord Warden of the Cinque Ports (from 1513), never quite regained favour after the execution of his father-in-law, the Duke of Buckingham, in 1521. Birling is described as Neville's house by Leland and he is buried in the local church. Some external evidence of the present c. 1800 house suggests early Tudor building work.

**Boughton Malherbe Place** TQ 8849. Sir Edward Wotton (1489–1551) served at Calais under Henry VIII and was Privy Councillor to Edward VI. One range survives of his ragstone house, extended in brick and stone c. 1553. A panelled room from the house of the 1520s is now in the USA.

**Canterbury, Archbishop's Palace** TR 1557. Leland mentions work here by John Morton, Archbishop from 1486 to 1500. The most important surviving late 15c building is the N part of the great N-S range built to connect the 11c hall (now gone) with the 13c hall (whose S wall survives as part of the present late 19c palace).

*\*Canterbury, St Augustine's Abbey* TR 1557. The Benedictine abbey was dissolved in 1538. The abbot's inner court to the NW of the church was converted into a royal palace in time for the arrival of Anne of Cleves in December, 1539. The King's apartments were made from the abbot's lodging in the E range, the Queen's in the W (gatehouse) range and S range (where a new brick and timber range was built).

**Charing Palace** TQ 9549. Some ruins remain of the Archbishop of Canterbury's house. The c. 1300 stone gatehouse, hall and other detached buildings were made into a more regular quadrangle by Archbishop Morton c. 1486–1500 with much use of brick. Henry VII and Henry VIII stayed here and the house became Crown property in 1545, but was subsequently neglected.

**Dartford Priory** TQ 5474. Henry VIII probably substantially demolished the former Benedictine nunnery here in creating a royal house in the 1540s, at a cost of about £6000. The brick SW gate and part of the outer court remain.

**Ford Manor** TR 2064. Leland says that Archbishop Morton of Canterbury 'made almost the hole house at Forde'. It was largely pulled down in 1650.

*Hever Castle TQ 4745. Sir Thomas Boleyn (1477–1538) was father of Anne Boleyn, became Earl of Wiltshire and was Treasurer of the Royal Household and Keeper of the Privy Seal. The Boleyn family moved here from Blickling, Norfolk, at this period and the 14c moated castle was modernized with new windows and internal refurbishment.

*Ightham Mote TQ 5956. Sir Richard Clement (c. 1478–1538), a member of Henry VII's Privy Chamber until 1509, with minor Court posts thereafter. He modernized the medieval stone and timber moated house, in which the chapel of 1521–9, with its wagon roof painted with royal arms and badges, still remains (though reconstructed in the 19c).

*Knole TQ 5354. Archbishop Thomas Bourchier of Canterbury built the inner court c. 1460. The outer, or Green Court, is early 16c, but whether built by later Archbishops (Morton or Warham) or after the Crown took possession in 1537 is uncertain. Both courts survive, with 17c alterations.

*Leeds Castle TQ 8453. Henry VIII spent £1300 to improve the 13–14c castle around 1518–22, directed by the constable Sir Henry Guildford (1478/89–1532), who was Master of the Horse until 1522, then Comptroller of the Household. Tudor work is still seen in the windows and some internal features of the 'Gloriette' (tower of privy lodgings). The castle was granted to Sir Anthony St Leger, Lord Deputy of Ireland, in 1552.

*Lullingstone Castle TQ 5763. Sir John Peche (d. 1522), courtier, Deputy of Calais in 1509, is the likely builder of the brick double-courtyard house ('castle' is a misnomer), probably continued by his daughter, Elizabeth, who married Sir Percyvall Hart (d. 1581). The W-facing inner court remains, but with external 16c work only on the N side, in brick and flint, otherwise mainly early 18c. However, the splendid early Tudor outer brick gatehouse remains close to its original state.

Maidstone Palace TQ 7656. The originally late 14c building now has an Elizabethan facade and it is difficult to tell what Archbishop Morton did in the late 15c for Leland to say that he 'made and translatid a great peace of the house'. The 15c stables may be his work.

*Otford Palace TQ 5359. Archbishop Warham of Canterbury pulled down all but the walls of hall and chapel of the moated manor house here and rebuilt in stone c. 1514–18, with a vast brick outer court of 270 by 238 feet. It became Crown property in 1537 and further building took place. Portions of the N entrance range to the outer court remain.

*Penshurst Place TQ 5243. Edward Stafford, Duke of Buckingham (see Avon, Thornbury), entertained Henry VIII here in 1519. About this time he may have built the upper parts of the 3-storey W range and the lobby tower, introducing brick additions to the medieval

stone house. These works could equally have been royal works after the Duke's fall in 1521.

Rochester Priory TQ 7467. The Benedictine priory attached to the Cathedral was dissolved in 1540 and Henry VIII then (1541–2) turned the S and E cloister ranges into a royal house. The custodian, George Brooke, Lord Cobham, was granted the property by Edward VI and began demolition before his death in 1558.

*Roydon Hall TQ 6649. Thomas Roydon (1484–1557), from Essex, became a Kentish gentleman by marriage. The house he built c. 1535 is still evident from brickwork and gables on the N and W sides of the square main block and from the fragment of a brick entrance range on the N side.

Shurland House TQ 9871. Sir Thomas Cheyney (1482/7–1558), cousin of Anne Boleyn, was Lord Warden of the Cinque Ports (1536) and Treasurer of the Household (1539). Henry VIII's visit here in 1532 gives a possible date for the completion of Cheyney's large brick courtyard house. Only the ruined entrance front remains, but the layout of the house is recorded in a drawing made for a survey of the 1570s.

*Sissinghurst TQ 7937. Sir John Baker (c. 1488–1558), lawyer, became Attorney-General in 1536, Chancellor of the Exchequer in 1540 and later Speaker of the Commons. He may have built and certainly embellished the existing 16c brick building which must always have served as the entrance range to a courtyard beyond, of which only a later 16c tower remains.

Westenhanger TR 1131. Sir Edward Poynings (1459–1521) returned from exile with Henry VII in 1485, served at Calais and in Ireland, was then Privy Councillor and Comptroller of the Household by 1509. Only a large six-light window and a fireplace remain among the ruins of this largely 14c house to show the important additions Poynings made.

## LANCASHIRE

Hornby Castle SD 5868. Acquired by Edward (d. 1523) and Thomas (d. 1560) Stanley, Lords Mounteagle, who rebuilt large parts of the old castle. Only the tower, first built in the 13c, now has 16c features (the remains of an oriel, carved stone panels) after 19c remodelling. An inventory of 1523 records the castle as having at least three courts, or 'wards'.

*Samelsbury Hall SD 5829. Sir Thomas Southworth (d. 1546) fought in Scotland in 1523 and was Sheriff of Lancashire in 1541–2. His new S range to the 15c hall house is half-timbered to the N and brick (early for Lancashire) to the S, where there is a re-used monastic window (probably from Whalley Abbey). The remains of the hall screen are dated 1532.

## LEICESTERSHIRE

*Belvoir Castle SK 8813. Thomas Manners, Baron Ros, later Earl of Rutland (d. 1543), began work at Belvoir after 1528. When Leland saw it in the 1540s, the medieval keep was 'tournid to pleasure' as a prospect tower and the bailey formed the irregular quadrangle of the Tudor building; this work is still reflected in the shape of the present castle following 19c remodelling.

*Bradgate House SK 5412. Thomas Grey, Marquis of Dorset (1451–1501), Privy Councillor, the first patron of Wolsey. He built a large brick house here c. 1490–1500. It faced N, with the hall at the centre, kitchens on W, chapel and apartments on E. Only ruins remain.

Groby House SK 5207. Thomas Grey (see Bradgate, above). Leland says he filled in the ditch of the old castle here and, alongside its ruins, began a brick gatehouse and brick towers of a new house, but left it unfinished. Some of this work remains, part of a later 16c house.

*Lyddington Bede House SP 8797. The late 15/ early 16c Bishops of Lincoln rebuilt the 14c moated house. Hall (with fine panelled ceiling) and great chamber (with arms of Bishop Russell (1480–94) over the fireplace and those of Bishop Smith (1496–1514) in the glass). The house passed to the Crown in 1547 and became a hospital in 1602.

Withcote SK 7905. Roger Ratcliff (d. 1538), Gentleman Usher of the Privy Chamber, built a new house here, noted by Leland but now completely gone. The glass of the nearby church, made under Ratcliff's patronage, is often attributed to the royal glazier Galyon Hone, suggesting the high quality of craftsmen that he commanded.

## LINCOLNSHIRE

*Grimsthorpe Castle TF 0423. Charles Brandon (c. 1485–1545), created Duke of Suffolk in 1514, was brother-in-law and lifelong intimate of Henry VIII. He was an important military commander and became Great Master of the Royal Household in 1540. He owned Grimsthorpe through his fourth marriage to the heiress Katherine Willoughby and transformed it in the late 1530s with former monastic stone. Some exterior walling and window openings of the Tudor period are visible in the present house.

Hainton TF 1784. Thomas Heneage (d. 1553) served Wolsey, then in the 1530s became Chief Gentleman of Henry VIII's Privy Chamber, though he left (or was dismissed) from Court in 1546. Leland says he built with 'much cost' at Hainton (where he was later buried) with brick and monastic stone; nothing survives of this house.

Irnham Hall TF 0226. Leland notes that Sir John Thimelby (d. 1550) 'hath build a fair place' here, though it was possibly begun by his father, Sir Richard (d. 1522). Two long stone wings remain with evidence of early 16c work; battlemented bays but otherwise largely unadorned. The interior is mainly 19c.

Sempringham Priory TF 1132. Edward Clinton (1512–85) became Lord High Admiral under Edward VI and was created Earl of Lincoln in 1572. Having obtained the dissolved Gilbertine priory in 1539, he may have used the prior's lodging until he built a new house in Elizabethan times. No buildings remain; priory and later house are known only through excavation.

Sleaford TF 0645. John, Baron Hussey (c. 1466–1537), courtier, Comptroller of the Household in 1509, was executed for inaction in the King's cause when faced by the northern rebels in 1536. Leland confirms that Hussey built a new house of stone and timber at Sleaford, the last fragment of which (then called 'Old Place') vanished in the 19c.

## LONDON

Baynard's Castle Henry VII rebuilt this royal house on the river between Blackfriars and Paul's Wharf c. 1496–1501. It was an irregular quadrangle and the river frontage was extended in 1551. It was largely destroyed in the Fire of 1666.

Bermondsey Abbey Sir Thomas Pope (1506/7–59), lawyer, Treasurer to the Court of Augmentations from 1536, later Privy Councillor. He founded Trinity College, Oxford. Nothing remains of Pope's post-1543 conversion of the former Cluniac house, though what survived in the early 19c was recorded in J.C. Buckler's water-colours, now in the British Library. The cloister became the main courtyard.

Bridewell Palace Henry VIII spent nearly £20,000 on this major London house on the S side of Fleet St, 1516–22. Excavation showed an outer court reached by a bridge over the Fleet river. The inner court had the usual sets of royal apartments and a long gallery led S towards a frontage on the Thames. It became a workhouse in 1556 and parts remained until the 19c.

*Bruce Castle at Tottenham. Sir William Compton (1482–1528), Groom of the Stool to Henry VIII 1509–26 and Head of the Privy Chamber. He entertained Queen Margaret of Scotland at a house here in 1516 which he had probably rebuilt; this is recorded in a 17c print and its basic shape remains, though much altered. The brick circular tower nearby appears 16c, but its function remains a puzzle.

*Charterhouse Sir Edward North (see Cambs, Kirtling) bought the former Carthusian monastery in 1545. The great cloister was not used (though the later owner, the Duke of Norfolk, made a gallery out of the W cloister range post-1564). North's main court was formed by expanding the domestic quarters (with hall on the N side) and retaining the service court to the W. Much of the 16c buildings survive, restored after World War 2.

**Chelsea** Sir Thomas More (1478–1535), Lord Chancellor 1529–32 and executed for denying the King's supremacy in 1535, had a house here, though its site is uncertain. Holbein's drawing for his (now lost) painting of the More family may record one of its interiors. A second house here belonged to William Sandys (see Hants, Mottisfont), which became royal property by exchange in 1536.

**\*Croydon, Old Palace** TQ 3365. Much of the late medieval inner court remains of this former house of the Archbishops of Canterbury. The brick ranges are principally pre-Tudor from the time of Thomas Bourchier (c. 1460–80), but John Morton extended the chapel in the 1490s.

**Elsings** TQ 3396. Sir Thomas Lovell 1450–1524. Treasurer of the Household and Chancellor of the Exchequer to both Henry VII and Henry VIII, he retired at the ascendancy of Wolsey in 1515. An inventory of 1524 records that he built a large two-courtyard house here with a gallery in the outer court. The house became royal property in 1539. It is now completely gone, but one range was excavated in the 1960s.

**\*Eltham Palace** TQ 4274. The surviving great hall was finished by Edward IV c. 1480. This remained a major Tudor palace but little remains of 16c work, such as Henry VII's royal apartments (only brick footings) and Henry VIII's new chapel of 1519–22 (foundations).

**Fulham Palace** TQ 2576. Bishop Fitzjames of London's new palace of c. 1510–20; only the elevations looking into the courtyard survive, built of brick with diaper work and moulded brick dressings, though many window openings are later. The vast moat that once surrounded this riverside palace has gone. Current excavations (1986) are revealing service buildings to the N.

**\*Greenwich Palace** TQ 4077. No detailed accounts survive for Henry VII's rebuilding of this major palace, much used by all the Tudors, in 1499–1501; excavation (and later visual evidence) shows it stood in the great court of the present Royal Hospital. The royal lodgings looked on to the river.

**\*Hall Place, Bexley** TQ 4973. The merchant Sir John Champneys (d. 1556), Lord Mayor of London in 1534, bought the house in 1537 and built, or completed, a hall range with cross wings, largely of ex-monastic stone. This was extended in the 16–17c into the large 2-courtyard house that remains today; some original interior features survive.

**\*Hampton Court Palace** TQ 1369. Wolsey (see Herts, The More) bought the site in 1514 and began the palace later enlarged by Henry VIII from the 1520s. Though 16c state apartments were demolished at the end of the 17c, there remain the most substantial brick Tudor buildings in the country, with base court, great hall, chapel, kitchens and service courts.

**Hanworth** TQ 1271. Only part of the moat and 2 terracotta roundels (built into later houses) remain of the royal house which Henry VII largely rebuilt 1507–9 and Henry VIII embellished in 1532 for Anne Boleyn.

**Holy Trinity** or **Christchurch, Aldgate** Thomas Audley (see Essex, Audley End) acquired much of the site in 1534 after the dissolution of the Augustinian monastery in 1532. From later 16c evidence it appears that his house was formed largely from the monastic cloister and part of the nave and choir; other parts of the monastic complex were divided into tenements. Nothing now remains.

**Lambeth Palace** The chief London residence of the Archbishops of Canterbury, the brick gatehouse was constructed by Archbishop Morton c. 1495, with square, 5-storeyed towers. One upstairs room retains linenfold panelling.

**Richmond Palace** TQ 1874. Only part of the NE-facing gatehouse on Richmond Green remains of Henry VII's great palace by the river, mainly complete by 1501. It was mostly of brick, but the great 'keep' of royal apartments was of stone. It was also famous for its timber galleries, built as walks around the gardens and between lodgings. The site has been fully excavated.

**St Bartholomew's Priory, Smithfield** The former Augustinian priory was the main London house of Sir Richard Rich (see Essex, Leez) after 1540. He used the prior's lodging E of the chapter house range, which had been newly built in the early 16c by Prior Bolton. Nothing remains of the domestic buildings, but the oriel window which Bolton constructed to look into the choir of the remaining church shows something of the quality of the building that Rich took over.

**St James's Palace** After acquiring the dissolved hospital in 1532, Henry VIII built a 4-courtyard brick house, which stood among fields in the 16c. The main Tudor parts of the present palace are the gatehouse, parts of the adjoining ranges facing N and the chapel, with its original ceiling.

**Somerset House** Begun by Edward Seymour (c. 1506–52), Protector to Edward VI and Duke of Somerset, in 1547–9. The Strand front is recorded in Thorpe's late 16c drawing. It was subsequently royal property. The 18c Somerset House, built by Sir William Chambers, is now on the site.

**Suffolk Place, Southwark** Charles Brandon (see Lincs, Grimsthorpe). This lost house was his London residence during the years of his marriage to Mary Tudor (1515–33). Wyngaerde's drawing of c. 1550 shows a large brick double-courtyard house, apparently with extensive terracotta decoration, fragments of which were discovered in the 19c.

**\*Syon House** TQ 1778. The Bridgettine nunnery was suppressed in 1539. After sporadic royal use it was granted to Edward Seymour, Protector and Duke of Somerset, in 1547. He spent £5000 adapting it into a brick quadrangle house, though the exact relationship of nunnery to house has never been clarified. The c. 1550 work is the core of the present house and some medieval brick undercrofts also remain. Robert Adam's 18c interiors may follow the 16c series of state rooms.

**Throckmorton Street** Thomas Cromwell (c. 1485–1540), Chief Minister to the King in the 1530s. Of his four London houses, this building near Austin Friars is best known, through letters of 1532–5 about building work and later records. Prominent features were the great gate on to the street and a winding stair to the hall with glazed bay windows. Much of the house was of brick, with windows of stone.

**Whitehall** Wolsey (see Herts, The More) transformed the London home of the Archbishops of York after 1514. After 1529 it was the chief London palace of Henry VIII. The apartments of state were on the E side of the present Whitehall (towards the river), the King's recreative buildings (tennis court, etc.) on the W. Contemporaries noted the internal splendour of the palace, especially the galleries. Destroyed by fire in 1697, the brick cellar called 'Henry VIII's winecellar' is all that remains.

**West Drayton** TQ 0679. Sir William Paget (1505/6–63) built a large house here at the time he was Secretary of State in the 1540s. It was inventoried in 1556. Only part of the brick gatehouse range survives.

# NORFOLK

**\*Baconsthorpe Castle** TG 1238. Sir Henry Heydon (d. 1503), Steward to Cicely, Duchess of York, completed his father's courtyard house in a mix of brick and knapped flint 'with exceeding cost' (Leland). Some ruins remain within the moat; outside it are the remains of the new house formed from the gate of the old about 1560 by Sir Christopher Heydon.

**East Barsham Manor** TF 9133. Probably built by Sir Henry Fermor (d. 1536), High Sheriff of Norfolk. The detached gatehouse and double-pile house survive, with an early single-storey hall. Decoration includes a wide range of cut and moulded brickwork on chimneys, buttresses and finials, and heraldry on the gatehouse. Terracotta was used for heads inset into the frieze. All was well restored in the 20c.

**East Harling** TL 9986. Sir Thomas Lovell (see London, Elsings) built a house here of which nothing remains. A tower survived until the 18c; the cast bronze

medallion from it with Lovell's portrait in profile is usually believed to be the one now in Westminster Abbey and attributed to Torrigiano, the maker of Henry VII's tomb.

**Great Cressingham Manor** TF 8501. A moated brick house built for Christopher Jenney c. 1509–14. After 1542 John Jenney built a new hall (now gone) and added his monogram to the gatehouse, in terracotta. A fragment survives of the gatehouse range, with elaborate external panels in terracotta.

**Great Snoring Rectory** TF 9434. Sir Ralph Shelton, son of the builder of Shelton Hall (see below), rebuilt the house around 1525. Two ranges survive, one rendered, the other in brick with terracotta friezes, similar to East Barsham, but with more 'anticke' ornament.

**Hunstanton Hall** TF 6741. Sir Roger le Strange (d. 1505), courtier to Henry VII, built the quadrangular house. Only the brick gatehouse (with broad square turrets like Lambeth Palace) survives, as part of a later building. The house was inherited by his nephew, Sir Thomas le Strange (d. 1545), courtier to Henry VIII.

**Kenninghall** TM 0386. Thomas Howard, Duke of Norfolk (1473–1554), Earl Marshal of England, held many high offices at Court and was leader of the Catholic faction in Henry VIII's last years. The King's death in 1547 saved him from execution following attainder. He built a new and large brick house here, probably in the 1520s. Later 16c inventories record its many rooms and contents, but only one small range survives.

**Mount Surrey** TG 2708. Henry Howard, Earl of Surrey (1516/8–47), poet and courtier, was executed for treason only days before Henry VIII's death. He began a costly new house here in 1544, incurring great debt. Nothing is known of its plan (though its contents are recorded) and it appears to have disappeared by the end of the 16c.

**\*Oxburgh Hall** TF 7401. Licence to crenellate at Oxburgh was obtained by Sir Edmund Bedingfield (a staunch Yorkist who later made his peace with Henry VII) in 1482, after which the moated brick courtyard house was begun. The 7-storeyed gatehouse facing N is largely original work; its flanking ranges and the E and W sides to the court are much restored. The S hall range was demolished in 1778.

**Saxlingham Old Hall** TG 0239. Sir John Heydon (d. 1550), four times Sheriff of Norfolk, abandoned the family home at Baconsthorpe (see above) and built a courtyard house here, now ruined. It was mainly of flint, with some brick, showing Heydon and Willoughby arms over the gatehouse.

**Shelton Hall** TM 2191. Sir Ralph Shelton (d. 1497/8), High Sheriff of Norfolk, built a large, moated, multi-courtyard brick house here at the time of his rebuilding of the church, c. 1487. It is recorded in an 18c drawing based on an older source, showing extensive battlements and ogee-capped round towers to the corners and the gatehouse.

**Thorpland Hall** TF 9130. Built by the Calthorpe family. One symmetrical range remains of this important brick house, with some original brick chimney-stacks and brick decoration similar to Great Snoring (see above) nearby.

## NORTHAMPTONSHIRE

**Apethorpe Hall** TL 0295. William Blount (*c.* 1478–1534) and his son Charles (1516–44), Lords Mountjoy, were prominent courtiers. William was Chamberlain to Katherine of Aragon. Apethorpe was owned by the Blounts from 1515 to 1543 when it was sold to the Crown. They are likely to have added to an earlier house and much of this early Tudor work can still be seen, though the house was further enlarged in Jacobean times.

*****Boughton House** SP 9081. Sir Edward Montagu (d. 1557), lawyer, Chief Justice of the King's Bench, was appointed to Edward VI's Privy Council in 1547. After 1528 he enlarged a pre-existing small house here of which the hall and adjacent ranges form the core of the present great house. Internal evidence of *c.* 1550 includes fireplaces and blocked doorways.

**Collyweston** SK 9903. A stone house largely built, according to Leland, by Margaret Beaufort, mother of Henry VII (d. 1509), and later used by the Duke of Richmond. Henry VIII visited in 1541 and it was repaired for Queen Elizabeth in 1566. Ruinous by the 18c, nothing now remains.

*****Deene Park** SP 9492. Sir Robert Brudenell (*c.* 1461–1531), King's Councillor, acquired the house in 1514, and his son Sir Thomas (*c.* 1497–1549) built the turretted and buttressed S range behind the great hall of an earlier house and also altered the E or solar range. Though altered in Elizabethan times and later, the house retains important early Tudor panelling and evidence of the arrangement of rooms at that time.

*****Delapre Abbey** SP 7659. The former Cluniac nunnery was taken over by Bartholomew Tate of London in 1545 (he died in 1572) and the cloister was retained. Mid 16c doors and a spiral stair, next to the former church, remain on the S side of the N range, showing that he made two floors of the nave. The courtyard formed from the cloister is still intact, with much 17c and later rebuilding.

**Fawsley Hall** SP 5556. Sir Edmund Knightley (d. 1542) is usually thought to have built the house. The E-facing great hall with its oriel window and part of the kitchen and brewhouse ranges of the court to the W survive. After much neglect, the house has recently been restored. A series of heraldic stained-glass

windows from here is now in the Burrell Collection, Glasgow.

**Grafton Manor** SP 7546. Henry VIII obtained the house in 1526 and building work went on here before each of his many subsequent visits. It stood near the church and one fragment, probably of the service quarters, remains to the S of the present manor house.

**Horton House** SP 8254. Sir William Parr (by 1484–1547), after long service at Court, was Chamberlain of the Household to his niece, Queen Katherine Parr 1543–7. He moved his landed interests from the north of England to Northants about 1536 and built Horton. The house has now gone; one remaining Tudor range appears in an 18c drawing and shows similarities to other early 16c Northants houses such as Deene (see above).

*****Rushton Hall** SP 8483. Sir Thomas Tresham (d. 1559), Sheriff of Northants and MP, remained a Catholic and became Prior of the Order of the Knights Hospitaller of St John of Jerusalem under Queen Mary. His half H-shaped house, the hall with its original bay to the court, has survived, though the height of the building was raised and it was made into a full courtyard by late 16/17c changes.

## NORTHUMBERLAND

*****Norham Castle** NT 9047. A border castle of the Bishops of Durham, strengthened by Fox after 1497 and again by Bishop Tunstall after the attack by the Scots in 1513. Wolsey (Bishop from 1523) leased it to the Dacre family. There are 16c remains of great hall and chamber, and defences.

## NORTH YORKSHIRE

**Bishopthorpe Palace** SE 5947. Thomas Rotherham, Archbishop of York 1480–1500 (formerly Bishop of Lincoln, see Cambs, Buckden), doubled the size of the house by adding the N range in brick. This essentially remains, though the only original details are several internal doorways and one window. He also built a new E window to the chapel (later removed).

**Cawood** SE 5737. A manor house of the Archbishops of York. The surviving stone gatehouse was built for John Kempe (1426–51), but the adjoining brick ranges could be later. The house was certainly kept in periodic repair. Archbishop Thomas Rotherham died here in 1500, Archbishop Savage (1500–07) spent money on building and Wolsey was arrested here in 1530.

**Hornby Castle** NZ 2394. Leland noted that William, Lord Conyers (1468–1524), who fought at Flodden and was Constable of the royal castles of Middleham and Richmond, much improved the 14c castle of Hornby. The remaining keep and S range have some early

Tudor windows and doorways. Other features have been removed, including the great entrance portal with Conyers' name on the arch and his arms above, now installed in the Burrell Collection, Glasgow.

**\*Newburgh Priory** SE 5476. Anthony Bellasis (d. 1552) of Co. Durham, an ordained lawyer, commissioner for the visitation of the monasteries, acquired the former Augustinian house in 1540. It is uncertain how much work he carried out, for the surviving remains are of a large, gabled Jacobean house. The main block has some medieval and Tudor stonework and appears to be adapted from the frater range; if so, the church would have stood in the space between the present projecting wings.

**\*Skipton Castle** SD 9851. Much of the modernizing work to the 14c castle by Henry, Lord Clifford (1493–1542), who became Earl of Cumberland in 1525, can still be seen, including the large windows in Conduit Court and the long gallery range added in 1535, with two symmetrically placed bay windows and a polygonal tower at its end.

## NOTTINGHAMSHIRE

**Haughton House** SK 6772. The courtier Sir Michael Stanhope (by 1508–52), later Chief Gentleman of the Privy Chamber to Edward VI and executed after the fall of the Duke of Somerset, his brother-in-law. In 1537 he sold the house here to Sir William Holles (d. 1590). Kip's view shows its significance, though it has now gone. Old sources noted Stanhope arms on the gatehouse, but Holles rebuilt the hall in 1545.

**Hodsock 'Priory'** SK 6185. Sir Gervase Clifton (d. 1569), or his predecessor Robert Clifton, built a house here. Only the gatehouse remains; significantly, for Nottinghamshire, it is of brick. Some original plasterwork in the room over the arch.

**\*Holme Pierrepont Hall** SK 6239. Sir William Pierrepont (d. 1534) probably built the surviving S range c. 1510–20 of locally-made bricks. This was the entrance range to the court and it contains sets of lodgings, recently restored. Part of the E range is also early 16c.

**Kneesall** SK 7064. John, Baron Hussey (see Lincs, Sleaford), was responsible for the small brick house here, with terracotta (a unique occurrence in this part of England) around the windows and forming part of the internal staircase. It was probably used as a hunting lodge and built in the 1520s.

**\*Newstead Abbey** SK 5354. Sir John Byron (1487/8–1567) was at Court from 1519, but he chiefly served the King in local government in Nottinghamshire, his home county, and in war. He bought the dissolved Augustinian priory in 1540 for £810 and converted the entire cloister complex into a house, leaving only the

W front of the church standing. There is now little external evidence of 16c work but much of the fabric of the first conversion remains in the structure of the present 16–19c house.

**Scrooby** SK 6590. Leland described a great moated house of the Archbishops of York here. It was of two courts and built of timber, though the hall was of brick. Thirty-nine rooms appear in an inventory of the 1530s.

## OXFORDSHIRE

**Beckley Park** SP 5711. Sir John Williams (c. 1500–59) was Master of the King's Jewels and Treasurer of the Court of Augmentations to Henry VIII. In 1554 he was Chamberlain to Philip of Spain and given a peerage. Beckley is an important survival of a mid-16c brick hunting lodge, standing between the outer and inner moats of an older site.

**\*Broughton Castle** SP 4138. In the 1550s, Sir Richard Fiennes (d. 1573) altered the present moated, stone house by changing the N front and moving the entrance to the hall. He also gave the house a symmetrical appearance by building two bays to the hall, with a first-floor oriel between. Internally he created a new great parlour, bedchamber and gallery. His work is in the 'Sharington' style of mid century. All the important features of his work remain.

**Ewelme Manor** SU 6491. Leland describes a house of two courts, built in the late 1480s for the Duke of Suffolk. It was constructed of brick and timber, with stone also used in the inner court. Royal property after 1513, the usual royal suites of rooms are mentioned during repairs in 1518. One complete range survived until the 18c; fragments of this are part of the present house.

**\*Greys Court** SU 7283. Robert Knollys (d. 1521), Usher of the Privy Chamber to Henry VII, received the manor of Rotherfield Greys from Henry VIII. He erected new brick and timber buildings amid the remains of a medieval stone house. The present house and some outbuildings show considerable evidence of 16c brickwork.

**Hanwell Castle** SP 4343. Sir William Cope (d. 1513) was Cofferer to Henry VII, his son Sir Anthony (1488/92–1551) a writer of religious works and classical history and Chamberlain to Queen Katherine Parr in the 1540s. The Copes' brick quadrangular house was begun by 1513, finished by the 1540s. The SW tower and part of the S range remain.

**Langley Manor** SP 3017. A royal house from 1478 to 1550, it was much used by Henry VII and occasionally by Henry VIII. Building went on 1496–9; some original walling incorporated into the present 19c house has the initials HE and a Tudor rose.

**Rycote** SP 6604. Documentary evidence now suggests that Sir John Williams (see above, Beckley) owned this property from the 1530s and built the large brick courtyard house recorded in 17–18c views. A fragment of a corner turret and part of the stable wing remain, and can be seen from the adjacent *Rycote Chapel.

***Stonor House** SU 7388. Sir Walter Stonor (1477–1550), soldier, courtier, High Sheriff and MP for Oxon, Constable of the Tower, recovered Stonor from Sir Adrian Fortescue in 1535 and turned the 15c brick and timber house into a courtyard. Leland noted Stonor's work and the impressive setting of the house half-way up a hill. Further changes *c.* 1600 made the house more symmetrical.

**Woodstock Manor** Henry VII spent over £4000 on building (1494–1503) a 2-courtyard house of stone, with much heraldry and an inscription to himself over the gate. It was sometimes used by later sovereigns and its site is in the park of Blenheim Palace, during the creation of which the last remains were demolished *c.* 1710.

**Wytham Abbey** SP 4708. Traditionally said to have been the site of an 8c nunnery, this was newly-built in stone for the Harcourt family in the early 16c. After 1538 it was owned by John Williams (see above, Beckley and Rycote). Though much restored in the 19c, the main courtyard remains, with original windows on E (gatehouse) and W sides.

## SHROPSHIRE

**Plaish Hall** SO 5396. Sir William Leighton rebuilt an older stone house in brick (the earliest known use in Shropshire) to an H-shaped plan, with entrance facing SE. One room retains a (restored?) early 16c ceiling with painted decoration and emblems.

**Tong Castle** SJ 7907. Leland mentions Sir Henry Vernon's (d. 1515) 'olde castle of stone new al of brike' and this lost house is recorded only in the Bucks' 18c view and its copies. These show the hall with forward projecting wings for domestic apartments and offices. This was replaced by Capability Brown's house of 1765, in turn pulled down in 1954.

## SOMERSET

**Bruton Abbey** ST 6834. Sir Maurice Berkeley (by 1514–81) was Gentleman of the Privy Chamber to Henry VIII and Edward VI. 18c plans and drawings show that he adapted the cloister ranges of the former Augustinian abbey, for which he paid £500 in 1539. The church probably served both parish and abbey pre-1539. An adjacent field marks the site of the lost house.

***Brympton d'Evercy** ST 5414. John Sydenham (d. 1542) built the W-facing hall and parlour range about 1520. The parlour and staircase turret have friezes of quatrefoils and lozenges, carrying the royal arms. Larger windows were inserted in the hall when it was made 2-storeyed in the later 16c.

***Lytes Cary** ST 5326. The mid 15c hall was given new windows, porch and bay about 1515–20. A 2-storeyed bay at the centre of the S wing lights the parlour and great chamber above and is dated 1533; this is the work of John Lyte, who married Edith Horsey (see Dorset, Clifton Maybank). The plaster ceiling of the great chamber may be original.

***Poundisford Park** ST 2220. The merchant William Hill built this important H-plan house after 1546, partly with stone from Taunton Priory. All component parts are buttressed and gabled in the distinctive West Country manner of this period. The interior has many original and Elizabethan features. Roger Hill, brother of William, also built the Lodge at this time, which is similar in plan.

## SOUTH YORKSHIRE

***Sheffield Manor** SK 3785. George Talbot, Earl of Shrewsbury (1468–1538), was a military commander and Lord Steward of the Household to Henry VIII. His new stone house here is mainly ruinous today but the later 16c turret house remains and the site has been fully excavated. Galleries are mentioned in documents concerned with Wolsey lodging here after his arrest in 1530 and the imprisonment of Mary, Queen of Scots, in 1582.

## SUFFOLK

***Christchurch Mansion** TM 1744. Edmund Withipoll (d. 1582), from a Bristol family of merchants, man of letters (he was a pupil of Lupset, chaplain to Wolsey), built the E-shaped brick house just outside the old town walls of Ipswich in 1548–50. The site was that of an Augustinian priory. The house is now a museum and includes a panelled room from the Ipswich house of the courtier Sir Anthony Wingfield (1485–1552).

**Crows Hall** TM 1962. There are remains of the W (gatehouse) and N ranges of this brick, moated house, with arms of the Framlingham family; it was noted by Leland. The usual date given is 1508, though terracottas in the outbuildings suggest it may be 1520s.

***Framlingham Castle** TM 2863. Thomas Howard, Duke of Norfolk (see Norfolk, Kenninghall), continued the improvements of his predecessors in the construction of a new brick mansion within the curtain wall of the early 13c castle. The early Tudor bridge and gatehouse, some fireplaces in the NW corner and great brick chimneystacks survive amid the present ruined structure.

**Gifford's Hall, Stoke-by-Nayland** TM 0137. The courtyard house of the Mannock family, where building may have begun in 1459 (contract for bricks), but brick gatehouse with cusped tracery similar to Layer Marney (see Essex) appears *c.* 1500. Brick porch to hall also early 16c, but the other ranges altered.

**\*Hengrave Hall** TL 8268. Sir Thomas Kytson (1485–1540) of the Merchant Adventurers Company, Sheriff of London 1533, had extensive financial dealings with the Crown. Building work at this important surviving house is documented from 1525 to 1540. Major features are the use of a mixture of stone and yellow brick, the corridor around three sides of the court and the oriel over the gate, paid for in 1538.

**Henham Hall** TM 4578. A brick courtyard house of Charles Brandon (see Westhorpe), called 'newly built' in 1538 when exchanged with the King. A drawing made before the house was burnt in 1773 records its entrance front.

**Little Saxham Hall** TL 7963. Sir Thomas Lucas, Solicitor-General to Henry VII. Building accounts of 1505–14 survive for this house which was demolished in 1773. Little is known of its appearance save that it was moated, with two courtyards, and with battlements on hall and parlour bays.

**\*Melford Hall** TL 8646. Sir William Cordell (d. 1581), Solicitor-General and Master of the Rolls to Mary and Elizabeth, bought a former manor of the Abbots of Bury and built the present house of three ranges around an open court in 1545–54. Brick construction, with stone entrance porch displaying the classical orders. Only a second-floor long gallery, now refitted, survives of Cordell's interior.

**Redgrave Hall** TM 0478. Sir Nicholas Bacon (1509/10–79) was Solicitor to the Court of Augmentations when he built the now lost house from 1545–54. Contemporary with Christchurch and Melford, also in Suffolk, it was brick and half H-shaped. Documents record a cost of £1253.

**Shrubland Old Hall** TM 1252. Built for Sir Philip Booth, High Sheriff of Suffolk in 1507 and husband of Alice Bedingfield of Oxburgh (see Norfolk). Only a fragment remains, with terracotta windows displaying the family arms. Other windows were at some stage moved to local churches.

**Westhorpe** TM 0496. Charles Brandon, Duke of Suffolk (see Lincs, Grimsthorpe) built the now completely lost house here (except for the moat with its Tudor bridge). From 18c descriptions, it was clearly a substantial building of brick and figurative terracotta of the period *c.* 1515–30, comparable with Brandon's contemporary London house (see London, Suffolk Place).

**West Stow Hall** TL 8170. Sir John Crofts, Master of the Horse to Henry VIII's sister Mary, built the surviving brick gatehouse in the 1520s. The turrets display Mary's arms and terracotta figures. The gatehouse was originally detached; later in the 16c a covered way was built to the main house. This also survives, but the house is largely renewed.

**\*Wingfield Castle** TM 2276. Moated castle of the de la Poles, medieval Dukes of Suffolk. The late 14c gatehouse and entrance range (flint with brick battlements) survive, as does the brick and half-timbered house at right angles to it, built possibly in the 1540s by Sir Henry Jerningham, courtier to Queen Mary.

## SURREY

**Beddington Place** TQ 3165. Sir Nicholas Carew (by 1496–1539), Gentleman of Henry VIII's Privy Chamber in 1518, Master of the Horse from 1522, was frequently at the French Court and also travelled to Italy. He was executed after the Exeter conspiracy. He may have further enlarged his father, Sir Richard's, new house after 1520. The great hall with its hammer-beam roof and some cellars are the only substantial remains of their house.

**Bletchingley** TQ 3250. Edward Stafford, Duke of Buckingham (see Avon, Thornbury), had a house here described as 'newly and properly built' at his fall in 1521. It was later granted to Anne of Cleves after her divorce from Henry VIII. A 17c map shows a double-courtyard house of which only the upper part of a brick arch (perhaps once a gatehouse entry) remains, incorporated in a farmhouse.

**Byfleet** TQ 0641. A modest lodge on royal property was rebuilt by the keeper, Sir Anthony Browne (see East Sussex, Battle), in 1529–30, and here he died in 1548.

**Chobham Park** SU 9761. Henry VIII acquired this manor from Chertsey Abbey in 1537 and 11,000 bricks were brought here for enlarging the buildings. Royal apartments were created. The site was moated, but otherwise no visual impression is possible and there are no remains.

**Esher Palace** TQ 1464. Bishop Waynflete of Winchester built in brick here in the 15c (the great gatehouse still survives). Wolsey added a gallery which Henry VIII later removed to Whitehall. Crown property in 1537, Queen Mary later returned it to the see of Winchester.

**Guildford Friary** TQ 0049. Henry VIII paid for new royal lodgings within the precincts in the early 1530s, then assumed the property at the dissolution in 1538. The usual royal apartments are recorded. Neglected by Elizabeth, the buildings were demolished in the 17c. Friary Street marks the site.

**Nonsuch Palace** TQ 2363. Henry VIII's most famous lost palace was begun in 1538 and almost complete by 1547 at a cost of £23,000. Excavated in 1959–60. Built round two principal courts, the outer was conventional and fortified, the walls of the inner covered with a sculptural programme in stucco and slate.

**Oatlands Palace** TQ 0764. Excavation, plus a copy of a late 16c drawing, permit a reconstruction of the lost palace, built mainly in brick, on which Henry VIII spent £16,500 from 1537 to 1545. It was built around three courts, the innermost originally an older house and moated, the outermost a great walled yard with service buildings. The second court had the distinctive feature of a series of gable ends facing in to the court, unlike other royal palaces (such as Hampton Court) with their continuous brick battlements.

**\*Reigate Priory** TQ 2550. Sir William Howard (c. 1510–73), ambassador under Henry VIII, imprisoned briefly in 1541 but pardoned, was later Lord Admiral (1553), Chamberlain to Mary and Elizabeth and given a peerage. He gained the former Augustinian house in 1541 and turned the church into his hall range. The present, largely 18–19c house retains the splendid hall fireplace and a large five-light window of the 16c.

**\*Sutton Place** TQ 0153. Sir Richard Weston (1465/6–1542) was a member of Henry VIII's Privy Chamber, ambassador to France, Treasurer at Calais (1525) and Under-Treasurer of England (1528). Three ranges of his brick and terracotta courtyard house, built in the 1520s, remain, though the interior is much altered.

**Woking Old Hall** TQ 0257. Henry VII came into possession in 1503 and spent £1400 on building here, 1503–9. There were repairs and alterations under Henry VIII. The moated site remains, with some brick foundations and the stone and brick basement of a building range.

## WARWICKSHIRE

**Compton Wynyates** SP 3341. Sir William Compton (see London, Bruce Castle) was probably responsible for both phases of early Tudor building at this still intact courtyard house, apparently complete by 1523. According to Leland, he brought materials from the demolished Fulbrooke Castle and these include the present bay window and roof to the hall.

**\*Coughton Court** SP 0806. Sir Robert Throckmorton (d. 1519, on pilgrimage to the Holy Land) and his son, Sir George (d. 1553), a courtier, built the stone and timber-framed house here in the period c. 1510–50. The hall was demolished in the 18c, but three ranges remain, all much altered save for the imposing stone gatehouse.

**\*Kenilworth Castle** SP 2872. A royal castle kept in good repair by Henry VII, who carried out work here in 1492–3 and 1503–4, and Henry VIII, who erected the 'pleasance', a building of timber in the base court. Nothing remains of this early Tudor work and the castle ceased to be Crown property in 1553.

**Pooley Hall** SK 2602. The house is said by most sources to be of 1509, but it could be later, judging by the windows. Three brick ranges survive; the S was the chapel, but the role of the other ranges is uncertain.

**Wormleighton** SP 4453. Sir John Spencer (d. 1522) built the brick courtyard house on land first acquired in 1506. An earlier lease specified the building of a house comparable to the nearby Cope house at Hanwell (see Oxon). One range remains, with large 3– and 4–light windows of a scale comparable with Sutton Place (see Surrey).

## WEST MIDLANDS

**Moor Hall** SP 1296. John Vesey, Bishop of Exeter 1519–51, built extensively at his home town of Sutton Coldfield (the Moot Hall and 51 houses for weavers), but little is known of his own house, where he died in 1554. It stood half a mile N from the church and was described by Leland as 'a praty pile of brike'.

## WEST SUSSEX

**Cakeham Manor House** SZ 7999. Roger Sherborn, Bishop of Chichester 1508–36, implemented a 15c licence to crenellate and added the surviving brick tower to the 13c house. It is an irregular pentagon, with brick mouldings but no ornament, and has an attached stair turret giving access to the roof.

**Chesworth** TQ 1730. Owned by the Dukes of Norfolk by 1506 who clearly added the now-fragmentary brick range and probably more to a medieval open hall, which also survives in part. The similarity to Kenninghall (see Norfolk) suggests work of the 1520s. The house was inventoried in 1549.

**Chichester, Bishop's Palace** SU 8605. The main block was rebuilt after a fire, in the late 12c. In the W wing adjoining this, built in the 15c, Bishop Sherborn (1508–36) added new windows and a downstairs parlour. Original heraldic ceiling paintings by Lambert Barnard of pre-1528 survive in the parlour.

**\*Cowdray House** SU 8821. Sir William Fitzwilliam (1490–1542) was Treasurer of the Household by 1529, later Lord High Admiral and Lord Privy Seal. He was created Earl of Southampton in 1542. He was chiefly responsible for the large brick and stone courtyard house begun here by Sir David Owen. After 1542 his half-brother, Sir Anthony Browne, and his heirs completed the work. Extensive ruins remain after the fire of 1793.

**Halnaker House** SU 9008. Thomas West, Lord de la Warr (*c.* 1472—1554), held minor posts at Court and supported the conservative, Catholic faction in Henry VIII's last years. Later he was Privy Councillor to Queen Mary. He acquired Halnaker by marriage in 1494 and substantially rebuilt the house. He surrendered it to the Crown in 1539 and the Tudor work is recorded only by early prints and descriptions.

**Michelgrove** TQ 0906. Sir William Shelley (by 1479—1549), lawyer and judge, held high local office in Warwickshire and Sussex and was recorder of London. The lost brick courtyard house, where Henry VIII was entertained in 1534, had a central hall lit by a clerestory, close in plan to Mount Edgcumbe (see Cornwall), but it is unclear whether this was a Tudor feature or introduced in the 1769 alterations.

**Offington** TQ 1504. Thomas West (see Halnaker, above) moved to his older property of Offington in 1539 when he surrendered Halnaker. By the time of his will in 1554 the house had 70 rooms and 'newe work' is mentioned. The house has completely disappeared but West's tomb survives in the nearby church of Broadwater.

*****Stansted Park** SU 1276. Either Thomas Fitzalan (d. 1524) or his son William (d. 1544), Earls of Arundel, built a courtyard house here in brick; two ranges appear in Kip's view of *c.* 1700, which shows a square, turretted gatehouse flanked by symmetrical gables (with terracotta decoration?). A fragment of this Tudor range remains, made into a chapel for the later house nearby (originally late 17c, rebuilt after 1900).

## WEST YORKSHIRE

*****Temple Newsam** SE 3532. Thomas, Lord Darcy (1467—1537), courtier, became an opponent of royal policy by the 1530s and was executed after the Pilgrimage of Grace. He built a large brick courtyard house here, probably in the period 1520—35. The present 3-sided, early 17c building only partially replaced it. The extensive brickwork on the W front and some internal features survive from the Tudor house.

## WILTSHIRE

**Bromham** ST 9665. Sir Edward Baynton (d. 1544) was Vice-Chamberlain of the Household to Queen Anne Boleyn and all of Henry VIII's subsequent wives. The stone gatehouse, moved to the entrance to Spye Park and altered in the 18c, is all that survives of Baynton's great house built, according to Leland, in the 1530s.

**Lacock Abbey** ST 9168. Sir William Sharington (*c.* 1495—1553), Groom of the Privy Chamber from 1542, was arrested for fraud as vice-treasurer of the Bristol mint under Edward VI. After 1540, he transformed the Augustinian nunnery here into a double-courtyard house, demolishing the church, adding a tower and stable court and using new 'Renaissance' detail in windows and doorways. Lacock is an important monastic conversion, though with 18–19c modifications.

*****Littlecote House** SU 3070. Sir Edward Darrell (1465/6—1530), Sheriff and JP in Wiltshire and minor courtier, inherited a small 14c house (the present 17c chapel was the hall). He began a new courtyard of flint with brick rubble to the E, completing the N range, with its first floor long gallery (though this range was later raised in height). The S side, with the present great hall and stair, is of brick and dates from the later 16c.

*****Longleat House** ST 8043. Sir John Thynne (d. 1580) was secretary to Protector Somerset in the late 1540s, when he bought the former Augustinian house. The first phase of his work at Longleat (1546–9) saw the modest adaptation of the priory buildings. This was replaced by more ambitious houses of 1553—67 (partly destroyed by fire) and 1568—72, resulting in the building which remains.

*****Wilton House** SU 0932. Sir William Herbert (1506/7—70) was Chief Gentleman of the Privy Chamber by 1546, later held many high offices and was made Earl of Pembroke. He was granted the dissolved nunnery in 1544 after three years' lease. A survey of 1566 shows a complete quadrangular house, the only surviving feature of which is the porch to the hall (now moved). Further investigation of the great 17c house that replaced Herbert's may show whether he built exactly on the site of the nunnery.

**Wolf Hall** SU 2362. Edward Seymour, Duke of Somerset (see London, Somerset House), entertained Henry VIII at his old family home here, though he probably spent little on it compared to his other works. 16c work in the present house may be Elizabethan. In his last years (1546—53) Seymour planned a huge new house nearby at Bedwyn Brail.

# Footnotes

*The use of 'op. cit.' refers to a previous footnote in the same chapter. References to footnotes in previous chapters are cited by chapter and footnote number. The place of publication is London unless otherwise stated. The following abbreviations are used for frequently cited sources.*

Airs (1975)   M. Airs, *The Making of the English Country House.*

Anglo (1969)   S. Anglo, *Spectacle. Pageantry and Early Tudor Policy.*

*AJ Archaeological Journal.*

Blunt (1973)   A. Blunt, *Art and Architecture in France 1500–1700* (2nd revised paperback edn., Harmondsworth).

*BAAJ British Archaeological Association Journal.*

*CL Country Life.*

Croft-Murray (1962)   E. Croft-Murray, *Decorative Painting in England,* vol. I, *Early Tudor to Sir James Thornhill.*

*DNB Dictionary of National Biography.*

Elton (1977)   G. R. Elton, *Reform and Reformation. England 1509–58.*

Garner & Stratton (1929)   T. Garner & A. Stratton, *The Domestic Architecture of England during the Tudor period,* 2 vols, 2nd edn.

Girouard (1978)   *Life in the English Country House* (New Haven & London).

Girouard (1983)   *Robert Smythson and the Elizabethan Country House* (New Haven & London).

Goldthwaite (1980)   *The Building of Renaissance Florence* (Baltimore & London).

Harrison   W. Harrison, *The Description of England,* ed. G. Edelen (Ithaca, 1968).

Hoskins (1976)   W. G. Hoskins, *The Age of Plunder. The England of Henry VIII 1500–47.*

Howard (1985)   M. Howard, *The Domestic Building Patronage of the Courtiers of Henry VIII* (Ph.D University of London, 1985).

*King's Works*   H. Colvin ed., *The History of the King's Works,* I & II The Middle Ages (1963); III & IV 1485–1660 (1975, 1982).

Leland   J. Leland, *Itinerary,* ed. L. Toulmin Smith, 5 vols. (1906–08).

*L & P Letters and Papers Foreign and Domestic of the Reign of Henry VIII 1509–47,* ed. J. S. Brewer, J. Gairdner, R. H. Brodie (1862 et seq.).

*Lisle Letters The Lisle Letters,* ed. M. St Clare Byrne, 6 vols. (Chicago, 1981).

Mercer (1962)   E. Mercer, *English Art 1553–1625* (Oxford).

Pevsner   N. Pevsner, *The Buildings of England* (with various co-authors) vols., dates as cited (Harmondsworth).

PCC   Wills proved in the Prerogative Court of Canterbury.

PRO   Public Record Office, London.

RCHM   Royal Commission on Historical Monuments.

Russell (1969)   J. G. Russell, *The Field of Cloth of Gold.*

Salzman (1967)   L. F. Salzman, *Building in England down to 1540* (2nd corrected printing, Oxford).

Summerson (1970)   *Architecture in Britain 1530–1830* (paperback, based on 5th edn., Harmondsworth).

Tipping (1929 etc.)   H. A. Tipping, *English Homes,* 2nd edn., vols. as cited.

*VCH Victoria County History* vols., dates as cited.

## Introduction

1 A. T. Bolton's comment is quoted by H. Avray Tipping, *English Homes. Early Tudor* (1924), p. 121.

2 On the competition, see *The Houses of Parliament,* ed. M. H. Port (1976), chapter III.

3 See *King's Works* as cited in list of abbrevs.

4 See Girouard (1978) and Airs (1975) as cited in list of abbrevs.

## 1 'Simple and Plain to Sight': Building in Early Tudor England

1 *A Relation, or rather a true account, of the Island of England about the year 1500,* translated by C. A. Sneyd (Camden Society, 1847), p. 10. On the population of England and harvest fluctuations, W. G. Hoskins (1976), pp. 3–5, 85–8.

2 A useful summary of technological advances is found in Colin Platt, *Medieval England. A Social History and Archaeology from the Conquest to AD 1600* (1978), chapter on 'Reorientation under the Tudors'.

3 The agreement is printed in Salzman (1967), pp. 564–6.

4 Perhaps £5000 annually reached the papacy from England through Annates and other services; see C. S. L. Davies, *Peace, Print and Protestantism* (1977). On the importance of revenue from England, G. R. Elton, *The New Cambridge Modern History II: The Reformation 1520–59* (Cambridge, 1958), p. 443.

5 *A Relation . . . of the Island of England.* op. cit., p. 23.
6 The contract is printed in Salzman (1967), pp. 547–9.
7 On the importance of the patron's 'signature' as the expression of spending for personal renown and public good, see Goldthwaite (1980), pp. 83–90.
8 W.G. Hoskins, 'The Rebuilding of Rural England', *Past and Present* vol. 4 (1953), pp. 44–59.
9 L. Stone, *The Crisis of the Aristocracy 1558–1641* (Oxford, 1965), p. 551.
10 On the dominance of London, see P. Ramsay, *Tudor Economic Problems* (1963), pp. 109–12 and some qualification of this in Hoskins' discussion of the loan of 1522 (Hoskins, 1976, op. cit., pp. 19–25).
11 *A Relation . . . of the Island of England,* op. cit., p. 42.
12 Harrison, p. 199. The dating of this text is discussed by D.M. Palliser, *The Age of Elizabeth* (1983), appendix 3.
13 Harrison, pp. 200–01.
14 Platt (1978), op. cit., chapter 6, 'Conspicuous Waste'. On Rufford, see the comments of P. Fleetwood-Hesketh in the National Trust Guide (1985 edn.), pp. 7–9.
15 On Kenninghall, Leland IV, p. 120. John Marney's will is at PRO, PCC 25 Bodfelde.
16 For a useful introduction to the importance of architectural theory in Renaissance Italy, see the comments in A. Blunt, *Artistic Theory in Italy 1450–1600* (revised edn., Oxford, 1966). A recent study of architecture and public life, Goldthwaite (1980), chapter 2.
17 On later sixteenth-century understanding of the theoretical premises of architecture, M. Airs, 'The English Country House in the Sixteenth Century', *Oxford Art Journal,* no. 2 (1979), pp. 15–18, and on the developments in use of language and collecting of books and treatises, Lucy Gent, *Picture and Poetry* (Leamington Spa, 1981).
18 The document is printed in Salzman (1967), pp. 575–7.
19 K. Harrison, 'Vitruvius and Acoustic Jars in England', *Transactions of the Ancient Monuments Society,* new series XV (1968), pp. 49–57 and M. Howard, 'Health, medicine and the origins of architectural theory in England', *Les traités d'architecture de la Renaissance,* ed. J. Guillaume (forthcoming).
20 William Horman, *Vulgaria,* ed. M.R. James (London, Roxburghe Club, 1926), pp. 203, 210.
21 Andrew Boorde, *A Compendyous Regyment . . .* 1542 edn., p. 18. See M. Howard (note 19) for Boorde's life and Court connections.
22 On Leland, see T.D. Kendrick, *British Antiquity* (1950), pp. 45–64 and M. McKisack, *Medieval History in the Tudor Age* (Oxford, 1971), chapter 1. On the literature of travel, J. Hale, *The Travel Journal of Antonio de Beatis* (Hakluyt Society, 1979), introduction.
23 Leland I, p. 133.
24 Ibid I, p. 22; I, p. 73; I, pp. 53–4.
25 Ibid V, p. 72; II, p. 75; IV, p. 14; II, p. 40.
26 On the royal castles, H. Colvin, 'Castles and Government in Tudor England', *English Historical Review* 83 (1968), pp. 225–34.
27 Leland II, p. 51; II, p. 48.

**2 Power and the Courtier House**
1 *L & P* VI 927. On Audley's houses, Howard (1985), pp. 283–95 and on his political profile, S. Lehmberg, 'Sir Thomas Audley, A Soul as Black as Marble?', *Tudor Men and Institutions,* ed. A.J. Slavin (Baton Rouge, 1972), pp. 3–31.
2 *L & P* XXI (1) 1425.

3 The definition of 'courtier' is problematical; it has been suggested that the term 'king's servant' is perhaps more apt. The definition followed in this book is a broad one, largely following the words of G.R. Elton that 'the only definition of the Court which makes sense in the sixteenth century is that it comprised all those who at any given time were within "his grace's house"; and all those with a right to be there were courtiers to whom the fact, and the problems of the Court constituted a central preoccupation in their official lives and in the search for personal satisfaction'. (*Royal Historical Society Transactions,* 5th ser. 26 (1976), p. 217.) Since the 1950s, Elton has led the argument in favour of stressing the essentially new character of the bureaucracy of central government; see his most recent re-statement of this in *Reform and Reformation England 1509–58* (London, 1977). In this work, Elton acknowledges the important re-assessment of D.R. Starkey's unpublished thesis *The King's Privy Chamber 1485–1547* (Cambridge, 1973), part of which is embodied in Dr Starkey's book *The Reign of Henry VIII. Personalities and Politics* (London, 1985). Starkey argues for the continuation of the medieval tradition of the Royal Household playing a significant role in national affairs.
4 P. Hembry, 'Episcopal Palaces 1535–1660', in *Wealth and Power in Tudor England,* eds. E.W. Ives, J.J. Scarisbrick, R.J. Knecht (London, 1978), pp. 146–66.
5 J. Harvey, 'The Building Works and Architects of Cardinal Wolsey', *BAAJ* 3rd series, vol. VIII (1943), pp. 50–9, *King's Works* IV, pp. 126–9, 164–9, 300–05 on Wolsey's work at these buildings.
6 See A.D. Stoyel, 'The Lost Buildings of Otford Palace', *Archaeologia Cantiana,* vol. C, pp. 259–80.
7 P. Hembry, op. cit.
8 *King's Works* IV, pp. 222–8.
9 On royal buildings, ibid. Introduction to Part 1.
10 See the chapter on 'Expenditure and Conspicuous Consumption' in F. Heal, *Of Prelates and Princes. A Study of the Economic and Social Position of the Tudor Episcopate* (Cambridge, 1980).
11 On royal apartments, *King's Works* IV, pp. 11–13 and H. Murray Baillie, 'Etiquette and the Planning of State Apartments in Baroque Palaces', *Archaeologia* 101 (1967), pp. 169–99.
12 See the 1582/3 Survey of Thornbury in J. Leland, *Collectanea* I pt. ii, pp. 652–61.
13 On Milton and Tregonwell's tomb, Pevsner and J. Newman, *Dorset* (1972), pp. 286–93. On Tregonwell, J.H. Bettey in *Dorset Nat. Hist. (etc) Proc.* 90 (1969), pp. 295–302.
14 H. Miller, *The Early Tudor Peerage 1485–1547* (M.A. Thesis, London, 1950), p. 30; see further, the same writer's recent book *Henry VIII and the English Nobility* (Oxford, 1986), chapter 1. A recent and vigorous reminder, however, of the dominant social position of the peerage in this period is G.W. Bernard, *The Power of the Early Tudor Nobility. A Study of the Fourth and Fifth Earls of Shrewsbury* (Sussex and New Jersey, 1985).
15 See H. Leonard, *Knights and Knighthood in Tudor England* (Ph.D, London, 1970), chapter on 'The Royal Choice'. A list of important courtiers created knights is in Howard (1985), p. 58, note 19.
16 For the best account of the problem of Henry VIII's will, D.R. Starkey, op. cit. (note 3, above (1985)), chapter 8.
17 See Miller (M.A., op. cit.), pp. 139–43 and Bernard, op. cit., p. 174.

18 W.C. Richardson, *A History of the Court of Augmentations 1536–54* (Oxford, 1961), pp. 90–1.

19 See Howard (1985), pp. 349–50.

20 The inventory is at PRO, LR 2/119, fols. 51–62. See also Howard (1985), pp. 435–6.

21 Inventories of Guildford's goods are in his will (PRO, PCC 23 Thower) and in the State Papers (PRO, SP 1/70 fols. 86–95). See also *King's Works* III, pp. 261–2.

22 D. Knoop and G.P. Jones, 'The Impressment of Masons in the Middle Ages', *Economic History Review* VIII (1937–8), pp. 57–67. See *King's Works* IV for references to impressment for particular buildings.

23 The Stafford estates are surveyed at *L & P* III (1) 1286. Thomas Howard's house of Kenninghall is inventoried at PRO, LR 2/115 and 116; the properties of Dudley, Gates and Palmer at PRO, LR 2/119.

24 The letters to Cromwell are at PRO, SP 1/94, 95, and 96.

25 The grant of Sutton is at *L & P* III (1) 1324 (17). The grant of Kimbolton is at *L & P* III (2) 2682; Leland's comment is that 'Syr Richard Wingfield buildid new faire lodgyngs and galeries upon the olde foundations of the castelle', (Leland I, p. 2).

26 *L & P* XIII (2) 74; ibid., XIV (2) 113 (16); ibid., XV 282 (90).

27 The correspondence about Boxgrove was published in G.H. Cook, *Letters to Cromwell and others on the Suppression of the Monasteries* (London, 1965), pp. 90–1. The exchange is at *L & P* XV 436 (72). For West's comments on Offington, ibid., XIV (2) 547.

28 The exchange with the King is at *L & P* XIII (2) 1182 (18a). On Lincolnshire, see G.A. Hodgett, *Tudor Lincolnshire* (Lincoln, 1975). On Grimsthorpe, Pevsner and J. Harris, *Lincolnshire* (1964), pp. 553–8 and on Irnham, ibid., pp. 583–4.

29 H. Finberg, *Tavistock Abbey* (Cambridge, 1951), pp. 169–70; D. Willen, 'Lord Russell and the Western Counties', *Journal of British Studies*, XV (1975), pp. 26–45.

30 M.E. James, *Change and Continuity in the Tudor North. The Rise of Thomas, First Lord Wharton* (York, 1965), passim. On Wharton Hall, RCHM, *Westmoreland* (1936), pp. 240–2.

31 E. Hasted, *A History and Topographical Survey of the County of Kent* (2nd edn. Canterbury, 1797–1801), vol. VIII, pp. 64–73. For royal ownership, see *King's Works* IV, pp. 283–5.

32 Rev. J. Cave Brown, 'Shurland House', *Archaeologia Cantiana* XXII (1898), pp. 86–93 and J. Newman, *NE & E Kent* (2nd edn. 1976), p. 301. The royal sequestration is at PRO, SP 12/75 & 87.

33 C.L. Kingsford, 'Historical Notes on Mediaeval London Houses', *London Topographical Record* X (1916), pp. 56–8, 83–5, 87–8, 117–19; XII (1920), pp. 57–60.

34 *L & P* XII (2) 1338.

35 See further, Howard (1985), pp. 35–6.

36 *Lisle Letters*, III, no. 691.

37 Ibid., I, no. 64.

38 Rev. Canon E. Jackson, 'Wulfhall and the Seymours', *Wiltshire Archaeological Magazine* XV (1875), pp. 140–207.

39 Chaloner W. Chute, *A History of The Vyne in Hampshire* (Winchester 1888), pp. 139 ff. Chute's identifications of rooms inventoried in the sixteenth century with those in the present house are very dubious.

40 J.L. Whitehead, 'An Inventory of the Goods and Chattels of Sir Richard Worsley of Appuldurcombe, AD 1566', *Hampshire Field Club. Papers and Proceedings* V (1905), pp. 185–95; G.S. Thomson, *Two Centuries of Family History* (London, 1930), chapter 4.

41 On the Earl of Surrey, *L & P* XX (2) 658; XXI (2) 287. Polydore Vergil's comment on Brandon, *Anglia Historia*, ed. D. Hay (Camden Soc., 1950), p. 233.

42 For the note by Brandon, Historical Manuscripts Commission, *Ancaster MSS at Grimsthorpe* (London, 1907), p. 503. On Sadler, see A.J. Slavin, *Politics and Profit. A Study of Sir Ralph Sadler 1507–47* (Cambridge, 1966), p. 186; on Petre. F.G. Emmison, *Tudor Secretary. Sir William Petre at Court and Home* (1961), p. 273.

43 Airs (1975), p. 86. On Bacon, R. Tittler, *Nicholas Bacon. The Making of a Tudor Statesman* (1976), passim. As late as the 1560s, Loseley House in Surrey, built on a modest scale comparable with Redgrave, cost only £1600 (Airs, loc. cit.).

44 Airs, loc. cit.

45 Sharington's statement about his finances after his arrest in 1549 is found in S. Haynes, *A Collection of State Papers* (1740), p. 65.

46 The total cost of works at Nonsuch to 1545 was £24,536 (*King's Works* IV, p. 189). Even the cost of the conversion of the priory of Dartford (though with new brick ranges) was £6600 (ibid., p. 73). The royal costs were perhaps not only because of scale but also because of the demand for speed and the conveyance of huge numbers of artificers over long distances.

47 Howard (1985), pp. 288–95. The Audley account book is at PRO E101/674/24.

48 *L & P* XIII (1) 749.

49 W.R.D. Harrisson & Viscount Chandos, *Carvings, Oak Gallery, The Vyne, Hampshire* (Sherborne St John, 1979). On problems of the original arrangements at The Vyne, see Howard (1985), pp. 625–30 and R. Coope, 'The Long Gallery: Its origins, development, use and decoration' in *Architectural History*, vol. 29 (1986), p. 50. On Boughton Malherbe, see Tipping (1929) period II, vol. I, pp. 213–19.

50 A useful compilation of material on aspects of heraldry in this period is the catalogue of the 1978 exhibition at the British Museum, *British Heraldry*, ed. R. Marks, A. Payne. On East Barsham, see Garner & Stratton (1929) I, pp. 123–5 and Tipping period II, vol. I, pp. 149–60. On Madingley, RCHM, *West Cambridgeshire* (1968), pp. 179–86. Hynde's grant of the property is in *L & P* XVII (1) 66.

### 3 'Tournid to Pleasure': Architecture and the Sense of the Past

1 For chivalric culture in early Tudor England, A.B. Ferguson, *The Indian Summer of English Chivalry* (Durham, North Carolina, 1960). For a vigorous assertion of its importance in Court culture, see D.R. Starkey on Ightham Mote in *Archaeologia* vol. 107 (1982), pp. 153–63. On education, see K. Charlton, *Education in Renaissance England* (1965), J.H. Hexter, 'The Education of the Aristocracy in the Renaissance', *Journal of Modern History* 22 (1950), pp. 1–20 and Paul N. Siegel, 'English Humanism and the New Tudor Aristocracy' in *Journal of the History of Ideas* 13 (1952), pp. 450–68.

2 On the resistance to new learning, with evidence of the particular devotion to medieval romances through dedications, M.J.C. Dowling, *Scholarship, Politics and the Court of Henry VIII* (Ph.D, London, 1981), p. 2 and appendix.

3 On Vergil and Hall, M. McKisack, *Medieval History in the Tudor Age* (Oxford, 1971).

4 On Henry VIII and feudal dues, J.R. Hurstfield, 'The

Revival of Feudalism in Early Tudor England', *History* XXXVII (1952), pp. 131–45.

5 On moats, H.E.J. Le Patourel and B.K. Roberts, 'The significance of moated sites' in *Medieval Moated Sites*, ed. F.A. Aberg, C.B.A. Report no. 17 (1978), pp. 46–52 and F.V. Emery, 'Moated Settlements in England', *Geography* vol. 47 (1967), pp. 378–88.

6 Andrew Boorde, *A Compendyous Regyment* . . . 1542 edn., p. 20.

7 *King's Works* IV, p. 128.

8 On the complicated ownership of Rycote, M. Howard (1985), pp. 710–13.

9 Boorde, op. cit., p. 20; Leland I, p. 164 (on Stowey), p. 114 (on Little Haseley).

10 Thomas Coryate, *Crudities* (London, 1611), pp. 316, 329; John Evelyn, *Diary*, ed. E.S. de Beer (Oxford, 1959), pp. 7, 393.

11 On the continuing potential for violence among the upper classes, L. Stone, *The Crisis of the Aristocracy* (Oxford, 1965), chapter 5. On retaining, A. Cameron, 'The Giving of Livery and Retaining in Henry VII's reign', *Renaissance and Modern Studies* XVIII (1974), pp. 17–35.

12 A. Oswald, 'Tudor Outlook Towers', *Country Life Annual* 1957, pp. 84–8. On Laughton, see J. Warren and C. Haslam, *Transactions of the Ancient Monuments Society* new series XXVI (1982), pp. 146–56.

13 J. Stow, *A Survey of London* (first printed 1598), ed. C.L. Kingsford (Oxford, 1908), vol. I, p. 133. On similar surviving brick towers of this period in Antwerp, G. Peirs, *La terre cuite. L'Architecture en terre cuite de 1200 a 1940* (Liège, 1979), p. 43.

14 R. Haslam, 'Compton Castle', *CL* 170 (1981), pp. 1546–50.

15 On the problem of maintaining property, Penry Williams, *The Tudor Regime* (Oxford, 1979), p. 220. The Apethorpe documents are at *L & P* XII (2) 1236, 1255. On Hussey, Elton (1977), p. 260. On Kett and Mount Surrey, Stephen K. Land, *Kett's Rebellion* (Ipswich, 1977), p. 48.

16 For inventories, that of Sutton Place is in F. Harrison, *Annals of an Old Manor House* (1893), appendix IV; of Kenninghall, PRO, LR 2/115; of Markeaton, *Journal of the Derbyshire Archaeol. and Nat. Hist. Soc.* LI (1930), pp. 117–40; of Bingham's Melcombe, *AJ* XVII, pp. 151–7; of Hornby, PRO, SP 1/27, ff. 123-63.

17 PRO, LR 2/119, ff. 26–46.

18 For inventories, that of Michelgrove is in the *Sussex Arch. Colls.* LV, pp. 284–98; of Standon, *Burlington Magazine* LXXXII (1943), pp. 112–16; of Wollaton, *Hist. Mss. Commission Middleton* (1911), pp. 474–85.

19 On the need for caution about the apparent defensibility of medieval castles, R. Allen Brown, *English Castles* (4th edn. 1976) and C. Coulson, 'Structural Symbolism in Medieval Castle Architecture', *BAAJ* CXXXII (1979), pp. 73–90.

20 Of a total of 460 licences to fortify granted between 1200 and 1536, 135 were for religious buildings (largely precincts and buildings of religious houses, town inns and manor houses of churchmen); see C. Coulson, 'Hierarchism in Conventual Crenellation. An essay in the Sociology and Metaphysics of Medieval Fortification', *Medieval Archaeology* 26 (1982), pp. 69–100.

21 On the ceremonial of the Tudor court, S. Anglo (1969). On the influence of the Burgundian court, G. Kipling, *The Triumph of Honour* (Leiden, 1977).

22 On Ramon Lull, see M. Keen, *Chivalry* (1984), pp. 8–11 and on Caxton, J.P. Cooper, 'Ideas of Gentility in Early Modern England' in *Land, Men and Beliefs in Early-Modern History*

(1983), p. 49.

23 Leland I, pp. 102–3, II, pp. 55–6. On a specific fifteenth-century case of gains from war, K.B. McFarlane, 'The Investment of Sir John Fastolf's Profits of War', *Royal Hist. Soc. Trans* ser. V, vol. VII (1956–7), pp. 91–116.

24 Quoted by Keen (1984), op. cit., p. 154.

25 Anglo (1969), passim and J.G. Russell (1969), passim. On the problem of the Hampton Court painting, S. Anglo, 'The Hampton Court painting of the Field of Cloth of Gold considered as an historical document', *Antiquaries Journal* XLVI (1966), pp. 287–307.

26 Comments on the glass at the Guisnes palace are mentioned by Anglo (1969), p. 142.

27 On the canted bay and the Royal Works, see *King's Works* III, p. 308, where the invention is attributed to Robert Janyns.

28 For H.M. Colvin on the royal castles, see above, chapter 1, note 26.

29 Brandon certainly used Donnington as a residence during 1516 (*L & P* II, passim). For Symonds Diary, see edn. C.E. Long (1859), p. 143. On Donnington today, Pevsner, *Berkshire* (1966), p. 128.

30 On Castle Hedingham, Leland II, p. 25 and *CL* 48 (1920), pp. 336–43, 372–9; on Hornby, *VCH Lancashire* VIII (1914), pp. 194–9 and Pevsner, *N. Lancashire* (1969), pp. 146–7; on Framlingham, P.K. Baillie Reynolds, *Framlingham Castle* (HMSO, 1973); on Dudley, the articles of W. Douglas Simpson both in *AJ* XCVI (1939), pp. 142–58, *CL* (1944), pp. 119–25 and Pevsner, *Staffordshire* (1974), pp. 118–20.

31 Leland I, p. 98.

32 On Allington, J. Newman, *W. Kent and the Weald* (2nd edn. 1976), pp. 128–30; on Skipton, Pevsner, *Yorkshire, the West Riding* (1967), p. 486.

33 Most recently on Thornbury, A.D.K. Hawkyard in *Bristol and Glos. Arch. Soc. Trans.* XCV (1977), pp. 51–8. On the Duke of Buckingham, see K.B. McFarlane, *The Nobility of Later Medieval England* (Oxford, 1973), pp. 50–3, 207–12 and C. Rawcliffe, *The Staffords, Earls of Stafford and Dukes of Buckingham* (Cambridge, 1978).

34 On early excavation at Basing, C.R. Peers, *Archaeologia* LXI (2) (1909), pp. 553–64. The recent work has yet to appear in print, though some finds were discussed in *Post-Medieval Archaeology* 4 (1970), pp. 31–91 and 5 (1971), pp. 35–76. See also Pevsner and Lloyd, *Hampshire* (1967), pp. 88–9.

35 See Girouard (1983), p. 216 on the phases of chivalry.

36 R. Strong, *The Cult of Elizabeth* (1977).

37 Keen (1984), op. cit., pp. 238–43.

38 On the reception at Kenilworth, J. Nichols, *The Progresses and Public Processions of Queen Elizabeth* (1823, reprinted New York, n.d.), pp. 485–553.

## 4 The Courtyard and the Household

1 Courtyards did of course survive into the seventeenth century, but significantly where this happened they became little more than light wells, as the ratio of ground area of building ranges to court shifted in favour of the former. See, for example, courtyard plans from the important Smythson architectural workshop of the late sixteenth to early seventeenth century, discussed by M. Girouard in *Architectural History*, vol. 5 (1962), cat. nos. II/2 and II/3.

2 RCHM, *West Dorset* (1952), pp. 64–6; *King's Works* II, pp.

617–19, 872–82. On the development of lodgings along curtain walls, Girouard (1978), p. 67.

3 Coffin is recorded as 'of Haddon' in 1522 (L & P III (2), 2712). See P. Faulkner, 'Haddon Hall and Bolsover Castle, AJ CXVIII (1961), pp. 188–98 and N. Pevsner, Derbyshire (2nd edn., revised E. Williamson, 1978), pp. 221–9.

4 RCHM, Westmoreland (1936), pp. 240–2 and see the comments in M.E. James, Change and Continuity in the Tudor North. The Rise of Thomas, First Lord Wharton (York, 1965), passim.

5 VCH Oxfordshire, vol. VIII (1964), pp. 142–5.

6 On Bradgate, M. Forsyth, The History of Bradgate (Leicester, 1974) and Pevsner, Leicestershire (2nd edn., rev. E. Williamson 1984). On Tong, CL vol. 100 (1946), p. 578.

7 On Chenies, see Howard (1985), pp. 609–12. On Samelsbury, see VCH Lancashire, vol. VII (1911), pp. 307–10 and Pevsner, N. Lancashire (1969), pp. 216–17.

8 On Bodiam, see R. Allen Brown, English Castles (4th edn., 1976), pp. 144–6; Herstmonceux, Pevsner and I. Nairn, Sussex (1965), pp. 534–6; Oxburgh, Pevsner, N.W. & S. Norfolk (1962), pp. 282–3; on Shelton, Rev. J. Armstrong, Norfolk Archaeology XII (1895), pp. 234–42.

9 The documentary evidence for Wolsey's use of craftsmen and masons at both Oxford and his private residences is contained in J.G. Milne and John H. Harvey, 'The Building of Cardinal College, Oxford', Oxoniensia VIII/IX (1945), pp. 137–53.

10 G. Webb, Architecture in Britain. The Middle Ages (2nd edn., Harmondsworth, 1965), pp. 162–3.

11 Ibid., pp. 166–7. Plans of the Cambridge colleges are in RCHM, City of Cambridge (1959), parts I & II.

12 P. Faulkner, 'Some Medieval Archiepiscopal Palaces', AJ CXXVII (1970), pp. 130–46. On Croydon, A. Oswald, CL 137 (1965), pp. 806–10, 876–80. On Otford, see above, chapter 2, note 6.

13 King's Works IV, plan p. 130.

14 Ibid., pp. 225–6.

15 Ibid., pp. 179–205.

16 The contrast between the courts at Nonsuch is shown by a comparison of Hofnagel's view of the south front and the painting in the Fitzwilliam Museum, Cambridge, of the entrance side (ibid., plates 13 and 14). On the inner court, see J. Turquet, The Inner Court of Nonsuch Palace (Ph.D, University of London, 1983), passim.

17 On Charterhouse, in the light of post-war repairs, D. Knowles and W. Grimes, Charterhouse. The Medieval Foundation in the light of recent discoveries (1954) and A. Oswald, CL 126 (1959), pp. 418, 478, 538.

18 On Rycote, see chapter 3, note 8.

19 PRO, SP 12, f. 43.

20 Sir Thomas Smith, De Republica Anglorum. The maner of Governement or Policie of the Realme of England (London, 1583), p. 13. On the significance of the household, David Starkey, 'The age of the household: politics, society and the arts c. 1350–c. 1550'in S. Medcalf, ed., The Later Middle Ages (1981), pp. 225–90.

21 Lisle Letters vol. 2, no. 263a.

22 Ibid., vol. 5, no. 1253.

23 On the functioning of the Royal Household, see chapter 1, 'The Central Machine' in Penry Williams, The Tudor Regime (Oxford, 1979), especially pp. 24–7 and 49–52.

24 The predominantly male composition of households is discussed by Girouard (1978), pp. 27–8.

25 For the inventory of Sutton, see chapter 3, note 16. For Lacock, Wiltshire Archaeological Magazine LXIII (1968),

pp. 72–82 and that of Hornby is in the PRO, SP 1/27 ff. 123–63.

26 M. Binney, 'Holme Pierrepont', CL vol. 166 (1979), pp. 842–5 and Pevsner (2nd. edn., revised E. Williamson, 1979), pp. 147–8.

27 See note 25 above; Ingatestone Hall in 1600, Essex Record Office Publication no. 22 (1954); PRO, E36/150; W.B. Compton, Marquis of Northampton, History of the Comptons of Compton Wynyates (London, 1930), pp. 308–11; Yorkshire Arch. Jnl XXV (1920), pp. 91–103.

28 One interpretation of this arrangement, now much challenged, was put forward by W. Douglas Simpson, 'Bastard Feudalism and the Later Castles', Antiquaries Journal XXVI (1946), pp. 145–71. See also the more recent article by A.D.K. Hawkyard in Bristol and Glos. Archaeological Soc. Transactions XCV (1977), pp. 51–8.

29 Andrew Boorde, op. cit., p. 19.

30 Girouard (1978), chapters 3 and 4, passim.

31 On E. Barsham, see chapter 2, note 50.

32 The Kenninghall inventory is at PRO, LR 2/115. Halnaker appears in a drawing in the Bodleian, Oxford (see Garner and Stratton, vol. II, Fig. 247) and Appuldurcombe in a drawing of 1690 (see Sir Richard Worsley, The History of the Isle of Wight (London, 1781), p. 180).

33 On the stairs at Richmond and Nonsuch, King's Works IV, pp. 225, 199.

34 On the development of the turret stair, M. Wood, The English Mediaeval House (1965), pp. 333–5.

35 On Coughton, VCH Warwickshire III (1945), pp. 74–81.

36 See above, chapter 3, note 12.

37 On Littlecote, see C. Hussey, CL 138 (1965), pp. 1406–9, 1466–9, 1620–3, 1678–81. On Cadhay, P. Eden, AJ CXIV (1959), pp. 159, 163–5.

38 Pevsner and I. Nairn, Surrey (2nd edn. 1971), pp. 476–9; M. Howard, 'Sutton Place and Early Tudor Architecture', The Renaissance at Sutton Place (Sutton Place, 1983).

39 A recent and full discussion of the emergence of the long gallery is R. Coope, 'The "Long Gallery": its origins, development, use and decoration' in Architectural History, vol. 29 (1986).

40 Ibid., passim and Wood (1965), op. cit., p. 336. On the royal galleries, King's Works IV, pp. 17–21. The galleries at Poulteney's Inn, see chapter 1, note 18.

41 On collegiate plans, see notes 10 and 11. Horace Walpole described the Herstmonceux arrangement (see Correspondence, ed. W.S. Lewis (Yale 1937–74), vol. 35, p. 138) and it is shown in a drawing by James Lambert (see D. Calvert, The History of Herstmonceux Castle (n.d.), p. 25). On Knole, see the discussion by R. Coope, op. cit.

42 The original arrangements at Hengrave are described in J. Gage, The History and Antiquities of Hengrave (London, 1822).

43 On Melbury, RCHM, W Dorset (1952), pp. 164–7 and J. Newman and Pevsner, Dorset (1972), pp. 273–7.

44 For a discussion of Titchfield, see chapter 7.

45 On the complex problems of the original interior at Cowdray, see Howard (1985), pp. 426–30.

46 See M. Howard, in The Renaissance at Sutton Place, op. cit.

### 5 'A Fayre New Parlor': The Evidence of Inventories

1 L & P XIV (2) 547.

2 British Library, Add MS. 5702, ff. 61v–68r (a later transcript of the original).

3 On the decline of ceremonial, see Girouard (1978), p. 85.

4 Dickens' *Barnaby Rudge* was published in 1841; the quotation is from the 1973 Penguin edn., p. 44. The flavour of revival is best expressed in the prints in J. Nash, *Mansions of England in the Olden Time*, published in 1849, which were highly influential on country house redecoration.

5 Horace Walpole, 'Journals of Visits to Country Seats', *Walpole Society* XVI (1927–8), pp. 61–2 and his *Correspondence*, ed. W.S. Lewis, vol. 35 (Yale, 1973), p. 64.

6 Harrison, p. 197.

7 Barbara Wichester, *Tudor Family Portrait* (1955), pp. 112–13.

8 See Mercer (1962), pp. 102–08; he stresses that even in the seventeenth century 'architectural' panelling was still a rarity and still often heavily coloured and gilded.

9 The conclusions in this chapter are based on a study of 55 inventories, some of them unpublished. References to published and archival material are cited below in each case.

10 The Beddington inventory is in the *Surrey Arch. Colls.* XXXII (1919), pp. 158–61.

11 For the inventory of Dudley's house, *Archaeologia* LXXI (1921), pp. 39–42; of Easton Neston, *L & P* XV 650; of Lamphey, ibid. X 431.

12 On the history of Smithills, *VCH Lancashire* V (1911), pp. 11–14 and Pevsner, *S. Lancashire* (1969), pp. 89–90. See also the comments in J.T. Smith, 'Lancashire and Cheshire houses: Some problems of architectural and social history', *AJ* 127 (1970), pp. 156–81.

13 On Haddon, P.A. Faulkner, *AJ* 118 (1961), pp. 188–205 and Pevsner, *Derbyshire* (rev. Williamson, 1978), pp. 221–9.

14 For the Bramall inventory, *Lancashire and Cheshire Wills*, Chetham Soc. 33 (1855), pp. 79–81. For Markeaton, see chapter 3, note 16.

15 For Easton Neston and Lamphey inventories, note 11 above; for that of Compton Wynyates, W.B. Compton, Marquis of Northampton, *History of the Comptons of Compton Wynyates* (1930), pp. 308–11; for Firle, see R.G. Rice in *Sussex Arch. Colls.* XLV (1902), pp. 114–27.

16 The inventory of Lisle's house at Calais is in *Lisle Letters* vol. 6, pp. 189–210. For Kenninghall, see PRO, LR 2/115 and for Chesworth, *Sussex Arch. Colls.* XIII (1861), pp. 120–4. For West Drayton, see S.A.J. McVeigh, *Drayton of the Pagets* (1970). On withdrawing rooms, see Girouard (1978), pp. 94 and 99.

17 On the great chamber, Girouard (1978), pp. 40–54, 88–94. For the Dudley inventory, see note 11 above.

18 PRO, LR 2/115.

19 Susan Bourne, *An Introduction to the Architectural History of Towneley Hall* (Burnley, 1979).

20 J.L. Whitehead, *Hampshire Field Club Papers and Proc.* V (1905), pp. 277–98.

21 Pevsner and Hubbard, *Cheshire* (1971), pp. 112–13.

22 On the possible origin of the Ightham roof in the Royal Works, see D.R. Starkey, *Archaeologia* CVII (1982), pp. 153–63.

23 On The Vyne, Chaloner W. Chute, see chapter 2, note 39, and Pevsner and Lloyd, *Hampshire* (1967), pp. 634–8. On the tiles, J. Lees-Milne, *The Vyne* (rev. edn. 1981), p. 20. For most recent ideas on the glass, with earlier bibliography, two articles by H. Wayment, 'The Stained Glass in the Chapel of the Vyne' in *National Trust Studies 1980* (1980), pp. 35–48 and 'The Stained Glass of the Chapel of the Vyne and the Chapel of the Holy Ghost, Basingstoke' in *Archaeologia* CVII (1982), pp. 141–52.

24 On hangings and painted decoration, Croft-Murray (1962), chapters I and II. The Darcy inventory is at PRO, SP 1/121, ff. 65–71; that of Mottisfont is summarized at *Hist. MSS Commission Rutland* (1889), p. 331; for Kenninghall, see note 18 above; for Sutton Place, chapter 3, note 16.

25 Most important on evidence for paintings in sixteenth-century houses, S. Foister, 'Paintings and other works of art in sixteenth-century English inventories', *Burlington Magazine* CXXIII (1981), pp. 273–82.

26 Kenninghall, see note 18 above.

27 On the long gallery and, inter alia, the point about galleries leading to chapels, Rosalys Coope, see chapter 4, note 39.

28 On Haddon, see note 13 above. There are differing opinions on the date of the gatehouse and gallery at Little Moreton; see Pevsner and Hubbard, *Cheshire* (1971), pp. 255–7 and C. Rowell, Rev. J. Lake, *Little Moreton Hall* (National Trust, 1984).

29 Cavendish, *Life of Wolsey*, introd. by R.S. Sylvester (Oxford, 1959), pp. 32, 50 and 57 for an impression of the use of galleries.

30 *L & P* XVI 276. On royal galleries in England, *King's Works* IV, pp. 17–21. The most significant contribution to recent work on the French royal galleries is S. Beguin, J. Guillaume, A. Roy, *La galerie d'Ulysse à Fontainebleau* (Paris, 1985).

31 For Dudley's house, see note 11, and for Kenninghall, note 18.

32 The inventory of The Vyne was discussed by Chute (see chapter 2, note 39) and the gallery most fully by Rosalys Coope (see chapter 4, note 39).

33 Lacock was inventoried in 1575; see Thelma E. Vernon, *Wiltshire Archaeological Society Magazine* LXIII (1968), pp. 72–82. One of the more useful articles of many on the history of Lacock, C.H. Talbot in *BAAJ* new series XI (1905), pp. 175–210; see also Pevsner, *Wiltshire* (rev. Cherry, 1975), pp. 284–9. The Northumberland advice is quoted and discussed by P.v.B. Jones, *The Household of a Tudor Nobleman* (Urbana, 1917).

34 For Dudley's inventory, see note 11 and for Lord Lisle, note 16.

35 The Loseley inventory is in *Archaeologia* vol. 36 (part 2) (1855), pp. 288–93.

36 For Markeaton, see chapter 3, note 16.

37 Harrison, p. 200. For the Offington inventory, see note 2.

## 6 'The Anticke All Gilt': England and the Renaissance

1 On Beckingham Hall and the panelling, RCHM, *Essex* III (1922), pp. 223–24 and H. Clifford Smith, *Catalogue of English Furniture and Woodwork in the Victoria and Albert Museum. Vol. I. Gothic and Early Tudor* (1923), no. 272. On the relation of heraldry to its surrounding ornament, E.H. Gombrich, *The Sense of Order* (Oxford, 1979), pp. 272–4.

2 On Tudor attitudes to the classical remains of England, see Stuart Piggott, 'Antiquarian Thought in the Sixteenth and Seventeenth Centuries' in *Ruins in a Landscape* (Edinburgh, 1976), pp. 1–24.

3 Leland I, p. 105; John Johnson to Robert Tempest, *L & P* XX (2) app. 43, no. 67.

4 Quoted by Croft-Murray (1962), pp. 26–7.

5 Anglo (1969), p. 213.

6 On the triumphal columns and arches of the ancient world, Richard Brilliant, *Roman Art* (1974), pp. 111–28.

7 This view is most clearly articulated in the magisterial works of R. Blomefield, *History of Renaissance Architecture in England* (London, 1897) and J.A. Gotch, *Early Renaissance Architecture in England* (London, 1901), passim.

8 For the clearest discussion of these three phases, see Summerson (1970), chapters 1–3.

9 Goldthwaite (1980), p. 171.

10 The Palazzo Canacci is discussed in the Open University course A353, *Art in Fifteenth-Century Italy*, programme no. 3.

11 On European developments in the personnel of government, see J. Hale, *Renaissance Europe 1480–1520* (1971), section II. On the secretary, G.R. Elton on 'Constitutional development and thought in Europe' in *The New Cambridge Modern History II: The Reformation 1520–1559* (Cambridge, 1958), pp. 446–8.

12 J. Guillaume, 'La première Renaissance 1495–1525' in *Le Château en France*, ed. J-P. Babelon (Paris, 1986), pp. 179–90. On the point of the documentation of Italian artists in France, Blunt (1973), p. 18.

13 On Georges d'Amboise and Gaillon, Blunt (1973), pp. 23–5, 41–2; E. Chiriol, *Le château de Gaillon* (Paris, 1952), passim; and on a contemporary description R. Weiss, 'The château of Gaillon in 1509–10' in *Journal of the Warburg and Courtauld Institutes* 16 (1953), pp. 1–12.

14 On the programme at Nonsuch, see M. Biddle, 'The Stuccoes of Nonsuch', *Burlington Magazine* 1984, pp. 411–17, and idem, 'Nicholas Bellin da Modena: an Italian Artificer at the Courts of Francis I and Henry VIII', *BAAJ* 3rd ser. XXIX (1966), pp. 106–21. On French royal building, see Blunt (1973), pp. 27–30; F. Lesueur *Le Château de Blois* (Paris, 1970), Guillaume, op. cit. (note 12) and M. Châtenet, F-C. James, 'Les expériences de la région parisienne 1525–1540' in ibid., pp. 191–202.

15 Generally on these patrons, Blunt (1973), pp. 25–7. On Robertet's political career, N.M. Sutherland, *The French Secretaries of State in the Age of Catherine de Medici* (1962), pp. 11–12, 105. On Berthelot's and Bohier's buildings, see the work of J. Guillaume, 'Azay-le-Rideau et l'Architecture Française de la Renaissance', *Monuments Historiques de la France* 1976, no. 5, pp. 65–80 and his article on the first stage of the building of Chenonceaux in the *Gazette des Beaux Arts* vol. 73 (1969).

16 In 1537, Lord Hussey reported that 'the Kynges household shall be brought to the same order and state that the ffrenshe Kynges court is at' (*L & P* XII (1) 86). On the French model for the Royal Household, Elton (1977), p. 219.

17 On foreign craftsmen in the service of Henry VIII and Wolsey, A. Higgins, 'On the work of Florentine sculptors in England . . .' *AJ* 51 (1894), pp. 129–220. E. Auerbach, *Tudor Artists* (1954), pp. 144–90 lists payments. See also Croft-Murray (1962), pp. 17–19 and *King's Works* IV, pp. 22–6.

18 On the Italian contribution to fortifications, *King's Works* IV, pp. 367–401.

19 Croft-Murray (1962), p. 18.

20 On foreign travel, and a list of courtiers who are known to have gone to Italy, Howard (1985), p. 132, note 5.

21 See chapter 1, note 22.

22 On Weston, see the *DNB*. Sutton Place was built on land that fell to the Crown at the attainder of the Duke of Buckingham and granted to Weston in 1521; see *L & P* III, 1324 (1) 17.

23 On Chaumont, see L. Hautecoeur, *Histoire de l'Architecture Classique en France* (new edn., Paris, 1963), vol. I, part 1, p. 94.

24 Blunt (1973), pp. 25–6.

25 The use of the low entrance screen (a different dimension in architecture from the containing wall discussed as part of the development of courtyards in chapter 4) is associated with the early seventeenth century and houses like Castle Ashby and the Jacobean Audley End.

26 M. Whinney, *Sculpture in Britain 1530–1830* (Harmondsworth, 1964), p. 5 and A. Blunt 'L'influence française sur l'architecture et la sculpture decorative en Angleterre pendant la première moitié du XVIe. siècle' in *Révue de l'Art* no. 4 (1969), pp. 20–1.

27 On the Boxgrove source, see note by C.J.P. Cave in *Archaeologia* LXXXV (1936), pp. 127–8. See also J.S. Purvis, 'The use of Continental woodcuts by the Ripon school of wood-carvers in the early 16th century' in *Archaeologia* LXXXV (1936), pp. 107–28.

28 On the coastal trade, see Hoskins (1976), pp. 191–3.

29 See Whinney, op. cit., pp. 5–6 and A.P. Baggs, 'Sixteenth Century terracotta tombs in East Anglia', *AJ* CXXV (1968), pp. 296–301.

30 On terracotta, Baggs, op. cit.; J. Wight, *Brick Building in England from the Middle Ages to 1550* (1972), chapter 6; W.A. McIntyre, *Investigations into the Durability of Architectural Terracotta and Faience* (1929).

31 On West Stow, Tipping, period II, vol. 1, pp. 201–12 and Pevsner, *Suffolk* (rev. Radcliffe, 1974), p. 482.

32 J. Wodderspoon, *The Historic Sites of Suffolk* (Ipswich, 1839), pp. 59–64.

33 The letter about Brandon is at *L & P* III (1) 750. There is need for caution in assuming that terracotta is the medium referred to in using Brandon's moulds. For the Greenwich revels of 1527, royal beasts were made of papier-maché; see Anglo (1969), p. 217. The appearance of the palace at Guisnes and Hall's comments are discussed by Anglo in his article on the Hampton Court painting in the *Antiquaries Journal* XLVI (1966), pp. 287–307 and by J.G. Russell (1969), pp. 31–47.

34 The Layer Marney workshop is held responsible for these by Pevsner in *Suffolk*, op. cit., pp. 83–4, 265, 418–19. See also E. Wood in the *Suffolk Institute of Archaeology and Natural History Proc.* XVIII, p. 123.

35 On these houses, see Garner and Stratton I, pp. 123–5, 130–1 and Tipping, periods I & II, vol. 11, pp. 313–20 and period II, vol. 1, pp. 149–60. For the dating of Great Cressingham, *Post-Medieval Archaeology* vol. 3 (1969), pp. 196–7.

36 On Suffolk Place, see Howard (1985), pp. 324–8. The possible dating of Wyngaerde's panorama is discussed by E. Haverkamp-Begemann in *Master Drawings* VII (1969), pp. 375–9.

37 On Laughton, see chapter 3, note 12. On the Kneesall terracotta, N. Summers, *Thoroton Soc. Trans.* LXXVI (1972), pp. 17–25 and A. Quiney, 'The lobby-entry house: its origins and distribution', *Architectural History* vol. 27 (1984), pp. 456–66.

38 The work of Giovanni da Maiano is most fully discussed by Higgins, op. cit.

39 On brick and terracotta in the Low Countries, see

J. Hollestelle, *De Steenbakkerij in de Nederlanden tot omstreeks 1560* (Assen, 1961) (English summary pp. 270–6), and Peirs (see chapter 3, note 13), passim.

## 7 The Conversion of the Monasteries

1 On the expectation that monasteries would be put to educational use, J.J. Scarisbrick, *The Reformation and the English People* (Oxford, 1984), pp. 77–9.
2 See K. Thomas, *Religion and the Decline of Magic* (1978 edn., Harmondsworth), pp. 112–21. On changing attitudes to the results of the Reformation more generally, R. O'Day, *The Debate on the English Reformation* (1986).
3 This view is forcefully expressed in Hoskins (1976), chapter 6.
4 On the general issue of monastic ruins and attitudes to the past, M. Aston, 'English Ruins and English History: The Dissolution and the Sense of the Past', *Journal of the Warburg and Courtauld Institutes* 36 (1973), pp. 231–55. On Neath, see L.A.S Butler, *Neath Abbey* (1976) and RCHM, *Glamorgan* IV, part 1, *The Greater Houses* (1981), pp. 78–89.
5 This was the conclusion of the influential article by H.J. Habbakuk, 'The Market for Monastic Property 1539–1603' in the *Economic History Review* series 2, vol. X (1958), pp. 362–80, and has been largely substantiated since; see the local studies of Somerset by K.S.H. Wyndham in the *Proc. of the Somerset Arch. and Nat. Hist. Soc.* 123 (1979), pp. 65–73 and of Nottinghamshire by A. Cameron in *Thoroton Soc. Proc.* LXXIX (1975), pp. 50–9.
6 *Three Chapters of Letters relating to the Suppression of the Monasteries*, ed. T. Wright (1843), pp. 114–15.
7 *L & P* XIII (1) 102; ibid., XIV (1), 402. On the general question of the government's ambivalence, J. Youings, *The Dissolution of the Monasteries* (1971), pp. 56–61.
8 An example of this is the surrender by collusion of Titchfield; see David Knowles, *The Religious Orders in England. III The Tudor Age* (2nd edn., Cambridge, 1979), p. 350.
9 Sharington acquired Lacock for £783 (*L & P* XV 942 (110)) and Byron bought Newstead for £810 (ibid., XV 733 (66)), both in 1540. For Darcy's purchase of St Osyth's, *Calendar Patent Rolls of Edward VI* vol. 5, p. 98.
10 On the varying amount of destruction, Aston, op. cit., pp. 238–45. London's letter is printed in Cook (see chapter 2, note 27), p. 209. On the destruction of Lewes, see ibid., pp. 138–40. For John Freeman's letter on the Lincolnshire houses, see *L & P* XI 242.
11 Ibid., XII (1) 642.
12 Wright, ed., op. cit., pp. 110–11.
13 *Lisle Letters* vol. 5, no. 1098.
14 Wright, ed., op. cit., p. 223.
15 F. Emmison, *Tudor Secretary* (London, 1961), pp. 185–6.
16 Cook, ed. (see chapter 2, note 27), p. 90.
17 *L & P* XIII (1), 19.
18 The Lady Cockayne episode is discussed by Scarisbrick (1984), op. cit., pp. 99–100. Stewardship is discussed by Knowles, *The Religious Orders*, op. cit., vol. II, pp. 283–5.
19 On Coggeshall, G.F. Beaumont in *Transactions of the Essex Arch. Soc.* new series, XV (1921), pp. 60–76. On Tilty, W.C. Waller in ibid., VIII (1905), pp. 353–62, IX (1906), pp. 118–21 and F.W. Steer in *Essex Review* LVIII (1949), pp. 169–79, LIX (1950), pp. 39–50.

20 Dom. F. Hockey, *Beaulieu. King John's Abbey* (1976), pp. 199–200.
21 W.R. Rudd, *Norfolk Archaeology* XXII (1926), pp. 251–6 and Pevsner, *N.E. Norfolk and Norwich* (1962), p. 172.
22 *King's Works* IV on York (pp. 355–64), Newcastle (pp. 170–1) and St Augustine's, Canterbury (pp. 59–63).
23 G.W. Copeland, 'Some Problems of Buckland Abbey', *Trans. of the Devonshire Assoc.* 85 (1953), pp. 41–52.
24 On St Osyth's, Tipping, period II, vol. I, pp. 271–93 and Pevsner (rev. E. Radcliffe), *Essex* (1974), pp. 338–41. On Thame, W. Godfrey, 'The Abbot's Parlour, Thame Park', *AJ* LXXXVI (1929), pp. 59–68.
25 W. de G. Birch, *A History of Margam Abbey* (1897) and P. & D. Moore, 'Two topographical paintings of the Old House at Margam, Glamorgan', *Archaeologia Cambrensis* 123 (1974), pp. 155–69. On Whalley, Pevsner, *N. Lancashire* (1969), pp. 259–61.
26 Tregonwell's house was described by the Dorset historian John Hutchins from his childhood memories in his *History and Antiquities of the County of Dorset* (1774), vol. II, p. 438. See also A. Oswald, *CL* 139 (1966), pp. 1586–9.
27 The grant to Browne is at *L & P* XIII (2) 249 (8). On the building history, H. Brakspear, 'The Abbot's House of Battle', *Archaeologia* LXXXIII (1933), pp. 139–66; C. Hussey, *CL* 140 (1966), pp. 802–6, 900–04; J.N. Hare in *Proceedings of the Battle Conference on Anglo-Norman Studies 1980* (Bury, 1981), pp. 78–95.
28 Rich was granted the property in 1536 (*L & P* X, 1015 (33)). See A.W. Clapham, *Trans. of the Essex Arch. Soc.* new series XIII (1915), pp. 200–21; RCHM, *Essex*, vol. II (1921), pp. 158–61; Pevsner (rev. E. Radcliffe), *Essex* (1974), pp. 265–7. The survival of stone at the core of exposed brick walls has been confirmed by the recent researches of P.J. Drury.
29 A. Hamilton-Thompson, *Netley Abbey* (amended edn., 1973); Pevsner & D. Lloyd, *Hampshire* (1967), pp. 345–8.
30 The correspondence was published by W. St John Hope in *AJ* LXIII (1906), pp. 231–43. There are crucial omissions in this otherwise important article; for the original letters, see PRO, SP 1/116, 127, 128, 130, 131 and SP 7/1.
31 Leland I, p. 281.
32 For Hinchingbrooke, see RCHM, *Huntingdonshire* (1926) pp. 152–6 and *VCH Huntingdon* vol. II (1932), pp. 135–9. The change of orientation was suggested by P.G.M. Dickinson, *Hinchingbrooke House* (Huntingdon, 1970). On the problems of reconversion, M. Howard, 'Adaption and Re-adaption: The Fate of some early country house conversions' in *Dissolution and Resurrection*, Papers of the 1985 Oxford Conference (Gloucester, 1987).
33 On upper cloister walks at Audley End, see P.J. Drury, 'No other palace in the kingdom will compare with it: the evolution of Audley End, 1605–1745', *Architectural History* 23 (1980), pp. 1–39. Buckler's MSS of Bermondsey are British Library, Add. MSS 24432–3.
34 *L & P* XIII (2), 176; Leland II, p. 8; the estate map is in the Hampshire Record Office, 13M 63/420.
35 Pevsner (rev. E. Williamson, 1979), pp. 201–9; Howard (1985), pp. 351–6. The archaeological work to investigate the cloister walls was carried out by Mr Stanley Revill and I am grateful to Dr R. Coope for this information.
36 Sharington's conversion of Lacock was discussed in the cumulative work of H. Brakspear in *Archaeologia* LVII (1890), pp. 125–58 and in *Wilts. Arch. Magazine* XXXI (1901), pp. 196–240 and of C.H. Talbot in ibid., XXIX

(1896), pp. 11–19 and *BAAJ* new series XI (1905), pp. 175–210. See too the more recent comments of Pevsner (rev. B. Cherry, 1975), *Wiltshire*, pp. 284–9 and Howard (1985), pp. 645–51.

37 Howard (1985), pp. 351–6.

38 Ibid.

39 C.H. Talbot, 'On a letter of Sir William Sharington to Sir John Thynne, June 15th, 1553', *Wilts Arch. Magazine* XXVI (1892), pp. 50–1.

40. Summerson (1970), pp. 62–6.

## 8 'Withe Timbar, Brike and Flynte': Building Materials and their Regional Pattern

1 See the distinctions between 'vernacular' and 'polite' in E. Mercer, *English Vernacular Houses* (1975), pp. 1–3, and R.W. Brunskill in *Traditional Buildings of Britain* (1981), pp. 21–4.

2 Leland I, p. 23.

3 On the geological occurrence of building stone, see the maps in A. Clifton-Taylor, *The Pattern of English Building* (new edn. 1972), pp. 29–31 and his subsequent discussion. On the use of stone and the costs of carriage, see Salzman (1967), chapter 7 and Airs (1975), chapters 10 and 16.

4 See the comments in chapter 1.

5 Russell (1968), p. 37. On the rendering of brick, see Airs (1975), p. 96. The disguising of brick at Ingatestone probably post-dates the building of the house in the 1540s. On Eastbury, Pevsner (rev. Radcliffe, 1965), *Essex*, pp. 69–70 and RCHM, *Essex* II (1921), pp. 9–10.

6 Harrison, pp. 195, 199.

7 W.G. Hoskins, *Provincial England* (1963), p. 81.

8 Airs (1975), pp. 109–10. On the need for recently-felled trees, Clifton-Taylor, op. cit., p. 297.

9 Leland IV, p. 7.

10 Pevsner, *S. Lancashire* (1969), pp. 240–2, *Cheshire* (1971), pp. 112–13, 223. See also the important consideration of houses of this region by J.T. Smith, 'Lancashire and Cheshire Houses: Some Problems of architectural and social history' in *AJ* CXXVII (1970), pp. 156–81.

11 On Little Moreton, see chapter 5, note 28. On Pitchford, Pevsner, *Shropshire* (1958), pp. 227–8.

12 Leland IV, p. 3; E.W. Ives, 'Patronage at the Court of Henry VIII: The Case of Sir Ralph Egerton of Ridley', *Bulletin John Rylands Library* vol. 52 (1969–70), pp. 346–74.

13 Pevsner, *Shropshire* (1958), pp. 228–9; H.A. Tipping, *CL* 41 (1917), p. 41.

14 On the evidence for early brick, see Salzman (1967), chapter 8. The classic study (with many illustrations) is N. Lloyd, *A History of English Brickwork* (1925). More recently, J.A. Wight, *Brick Building in England from the Middle Ages to 1550* (1972) and R. Brunskill and A. Clifton-Taylor, *English Brickwork* (1977). On the discovery of brick at East Anglian churches I am indebted to a paper given by Dr Francis Woodman for the *BAA* in March, 1983.

15 The figures are from R.J. & P.E. Firman, 'A Geological Approach to the study of Medieval Bricks', *Mercian Geologist* vol. 2 (1967), pp. 299–318.

16 Leland I, pp. 45–6 mentions the use of brick at Leconfield; also on this house, see the recent *VCH Yorks. E. Riding* IV (1979), pp. 123–31. On Kneesall, see chapter 6, note 37. Leland V, p. 37 is also the chief source for the use of brick at Hainton. On the matrix of the bricks at Compton Wynyates, R.J. and P.E.

17 Firman, op. cit., p. 316.

18 The local character of English brick-making is stressed by Airs (1975), p. 104 and on England in the European context, with some comments on urban markets for brick, by Goldthwaite (1980), pp. 171–212. On the Royal Works, see *King's Works* IV, pp. 68, 127–8, 185, 207–08.

18 Leland I, pp. 102–03, 137–9; II, pp. 9, 72.

19 William of Worcester, *Itineraries*, ed. J.H. Harvey (Oxford, 1969), p. 48.

20 Salzman (1967), p. 142 on Stonor and Tattershall; M.W. Thompson, 'The Date of Foxe's Tower, Farnham, Surrey', *Surrey Arch. Colls.* 57 (1960), pp. 85–92.

21 T.P. Smith, 'Rye House and some early aspects of brickwork in England', *AJ* 132 (1976), pp. 111–50.

22 On brick chimneystacks and their development, Wight, op. cit., pp. 87–102.

23 On Nether Winchendon, see A. Oswald, *CL* 127 (1960), pp. 924–7, 986–9, 1062–9. For Framlingham, see chapter 3, note 30.

24 On the brick turret stair, see T.P. Smith, op. cit., pp. 146–7. The Laughton stair is illustrated by Wight, op. cit., plates 66, 68.

25 On Croydon, A. Oswald, *CL* 137 (1965), pp. 806–10, 876–80.

26 *King's Works* IV, p. 72. The brick at Farnham was also coloured; see M.W. Thompson (1960), op. cit., p. 88.

27 W. Thomas, *The Historie of Italie*, ed. G. Parks (Cornell, 1963), p. 24.

28 Mercer (1962), p. 91.

29 On ragstone, see A. Clifton-Taylor, op. cit., pp. 65–6.

30 A full account of Wolfeton is in RCHM, *Dorset*, vol. 3, part 1 (1970), pp. 63–7; but see useful additions to this in J. Newman & N. Pevsner, *Dorset* (1972), pp. 142–6 and, for further illustration, A. Oswald, *CL* 114 (1953), pp. 414–17, 484–7. On Fontaine-Henry, see H. Soulage-Bodin, *Les Châteaux de Normandie* I (Paris and Brussels 1928), pp. 39–46.

31 See Newman & Pevsner, *Dorset,* op. cit., pp. 80–3, 157–8, 207–08, 267–8, 273–7, 359–60.

32 Strangways' biography is in *The History of Parliament. The House of Commons 1485–1558*, vol. 3. On the Horseys, see P. Webb, 'John and Jasper Horsey — Two Tudor Opportunists' in *Dorset Proc.* 99 (1977), pp. 28–31 and 100, (1978), pp. 22–30.

33 On the point about the more widespread use of ashlar, see the chapter in A. Clifton-Taylor, *English Stone Building* (London, 1983).

34 Blunt (1973), pp. 26–7.

35 An important article on the different developments of courtier and gentry houses, mainly focused on the later sixteenth and seventeenth centuries, is E. Mercer, 'The Houses of the Gentry', *Past and Present* 5 (1954), pp. 11–32.

36 On Parnham, Newman and Pevsner, op. cit., pp. 87–8 and RCHM, *West Dorset* (1952), pp. 164–7. The revised dating for Barrington (it used to be thought a much earlier house), *VCH Somerset* IV (1978), p. 115.

## 9 'A Farther and More Ample Discourse': The Somerset Group and a Change of Direction

1 See Girouard (1983), chapter 1 and idem, 'The Development of Longleat House between 1546 and 1572', *AJ* 116 (1959), pp. 200–22.

2 On the mid century, see Summerson (1970), chapter 2, and Adam White, 'Tudor Classicism', *Architectural Review* 171 (1982), pp. 52–6.

3 On the first Renaissance style in France, Guillaume, chapter 6, note 12. For close studies of particular buildings, see idem on Azay-le-Rideau (see chapter 6, note 15) and his 'Oiron: Fontainebleau poitevin' in *Monuments Historiques* 101 (1979), pp. 76–96. On Philibert de l'Orme's return to France, A. Blunt, *Philibert de l'Orme* (London, 1958), pp. 19–28.

4 J. Shute, *The First and Chief Grounds* (facsimile of 1563 edition published by Gregg Press, London), fol. Aiii b. William Thomas (see chapter 8, note 27) may be one of the authors whom Shute is particularly attacking as derivative of the descriptions of others; see M. Howard (1985), p. 136, note 66. I am grateful to Dr Nigel Llewellyn for suggesting this.

5 On politics by faction at the death of Henry VIII see D.R. Starkey, *The Reign of Henry VIII. Personalities and Politics* (1985), chapter 8.

6 See J. Phillips, *The Reformation of Images: Destruction of Art in England 1535–1660* (California U.P. 1973). On the mixed English attitudes to Italy, see also the comments of J. Hale, *England and the Italian Renaissance* (rev. edn. 1963), chapter 1. On the mid century idea of Commonwealth, Elton (1977), pp. 319–25 and see W.R.D. Jones, *The Tudor Commonwealth 1529–1559* (1970).

7 On the Hobys, see the entries in the *DNB*. On Bisham, see documentary evidence in *The Travels and Life of Sir Thomas Hoby* (Camden Soc., 1902); *VCH Berkshire* III (1923), pp. 139–48; E.T. Long, *CL* 89 (1941), pp. 320–4, 342–6, 364–8.

8 Somerset's building activities at Somerset House, Syon and Wolf Hall are documented in M. Howard (1985), pp. 631–41. His work at Berry Pomeroy has been researched by H. Gordon Slade and is yet to be published. On the work at Bedwyn Brail, see the documents gathered by Rev. J.E. Jackson in *Wiltshire Arch. Magazine* XV (1875), pp. 178–86.

9 British Library Egerton MS 2815.

10 W.G. Clark-Maxwell, 'Sir William Sharington's work at Lacock, Sudeley and Dudley', *AJ* LXX (1913), pp. 175–82; W. Gilchrist-Clark, 'Unpublished documents relating to the arrest of Sir William Sharington, January, 1549', *Wiltshire Arch. Magazine* XXVII (1894), pp. 162–3. See also M. Howard (1985), pp. 642–4.

11 The letter from Sharington to Thynne was published in full by C.H. Talbot in *Wiltshire Arch. Magazine* XXVI (1891–2), pp. 50–1. See also the discussion in Girouard, *AJ* (1959), op. cit. Chapman also seems to have worked for the Royal Works; see the entry on him in J.H. Harvey, *English Medieval Architects* (2nd edn. Gloucester, 1984), p. 51, under William Chapman.

12 On Broughton, see Pevsner and Sherwood, *Oxfordshire* (1974), pp. 492–8 and H. Gordon Slade in *AJ* 135 (1978), pp. 138–94.

13 The inventories of their houses are at PRO, LR 2/119.

14 Poyntz's will is at PRO, PCC 22 Wrastley. Poyntz was certainly granted Kingswood Abbey (*L & P* XV 282 (57)) and the tradition of his using the stone from there dates back at least as far as R. Atkyns's *The Ancient and Present State of Gloucestershire* (1712), p. 597. The most recent work on Newark is R. Haslam, *CL* 178 (1985), pp. 943–7.

15 On the suggestion that the fireplace for Dudley may have ended up at Broughton, see H. Gordon Slade, op. cit. (note 12 above), p. 164.

16 On Somerset House, see Summerson (1970), pp. 45–6, and N. Pevsner, 'Old Somerset House', *Architectural Review* 116 (1954), pp. 163–7. Expenditure is recorded in the cofferer's account cited above (see note 9).

17 See M. Dewar, *Sir Thomas Smith: a Tudor Intellectual in Office* (1964) and the same author's edition of the *Discourse* (Washington, 1969).

18 This follows the conclusions of P.J. Drury, 'A Fayre House Buylt by Sir Thomas Smith: the Development of Hill Hall, Essex, 1557–81', *BAAJ* CXXXVI (1983), pp. 98–123.

19 H.M. Colvin and J. Newman eds., *Of Building, Roger North's Writings on Architecture* (Oxford, 1981), pp. 64–5.

20 See for example the conclusions on one county in L. & J.C. Stone, 'Country Houses and their Owners in Hertfordshire 1540–1789' in *The Dimensions of Quantitative Research in History*, ed. W.O. Aydelotte et al. (Oxford, 1972), pp. 56–123.

21 Harrison, p. 197.

22 Anon, *The Institucion of a Gentleman* (1555), p. 115 (author's pagination).

23 Lawrence Humphrey, *The Nobles, or of Nobilitye. The original nature, dutyes, right and Christian Institucion thereof* (1563).

# Index